Designing Experimental Research in Archaeology

Designing
EXPERIMENTAL RESEARCH
in Archaeology

Examining

Technology

Through

Production

and Use

EDITED BY

Jeffrey R. Ferguson

UNIVERSITY PRESS OF COLORADO

© 2010 by the University Press of Colorado

Published by the University Press of Colorado
5589 Arapahoe Avenue, Suite 206C
Boulder, Colorado 80303

 The University Press of Colorado is a proud member of
the Association of American University Presses.

The University Press of Colorado is a cooperative publishing enterprise supported, in part, by Adams
State College, Colorado State University, Fort Lewis College, Mesa State College, Metropolitan State
College of Denver, University of Colorado, University of Northern Colorado, and Western State
College of Colorado.

∞ The paper used in this publication meets the minimum requirements of the American National
Standard for Information Sciences—Permanence of Paper for Printed Library Materials. ANSI
Z39.48-1992

Library of Congress Cataloging-in-Publication Data

Designing experimental research in archaeology : examining technology through production and
use / Jeffrey R. Ferguson, editor.
    p. cm.
Includes bibliographical references and index.
ISBN 978-1-60732-038-8 (cloth : alk. paper) — ISBN 978-1-60732-022-7 (pbk. : alk. paper) 1.
Archaeology—Research. 2. Archaeology—Experiments. 3. Archaeology—Methodology. 4. Material
culture—History. 5. Technology—History. I. Ferguson, Jeffrey R., 1976–
  CC83.D47 2010
  930.1072—dc22

                                                                        2010005618

Design by Daniel Pratt

Contents

○ ○ ○
○ ○ ○
○ ○ ○

Contributors

○ ○ ○
○ ○ ○
○ ○ ○

JENNY L. ADAMS

Desert Archaeology, Inc.
3975 N. Tucson Boulevard
Tucson, Ariz. 85716
jadams@desert.com

DOUGLAS B. BAMFORTH

Department of Anthropology, University of Colorado–Boulder
UCB233
Boulder, Colo. 80309
douglas.bamforth@colorado.edu

MARGARET E. BECK

Department of Anthropology, University of Iowa
114 MacBride Hall
Iowa City, Iowa 52242
margaret-beck@uiowa.edu

LELAND C. BEMENT

Oklahoma Archeological Survey, University of Oklahoma
111 E. Chesapeake
Norman, Okla. 73019
lbement@ou.edu

DUSTIN BLODGETT

Anthropology Department, University of Wisconsin–Milwaukee
290 Sabine Hall
3413 N. Downer Avenue
Milwaukee, Wis. 53201

ANDREW P. BRADBURY

Cultural Resource Analysts, Inc.
151 Walton Avenue
Lexington, Ky. 40508
apbradbury@crai-ky.com

PHILIP J. CARR

Department of Sociology, Anthropology and Social Work, University of South Alabama
HUMB 34
Mobile, Ala. 36688
pcarr@jaguar1.usouthal.edu

JEFFREY R. FERGUSON

University of Missouri Research Reactor Center
1513 Research Park Drive
Columbia, Mo. 65211
fergusonje@missouri.edu

KAREN G. HARRY

Department of Anthropology and Ethnic Studies, University of Nevada–Las Vegas
4505 Maryland Parkway
Box 455003
Las Vegas, Nev. 89154
karen.harry@unlv.edu

ROBERT J. JESKE

Anthropology Department, University of Wisconsin–Milwaukee
290 Sabine Hall
3413 N. Downer Avenue
Milwaukee, Wis. 53201
jeske@uwm.edu

EDWARD A. JOLIE

Department of Anthropology, University of New Mexico
MSC01 1040
1 University of New Mexico
Albuquerque, N.M. 87131
edjolie@unm.edu

PATRICK M. LUBINSKI

Department of Anthropology, Central Washington University
400 E. University Way
Ellensburg, Wash. 98926
lubinski@cwu.edu

ERIK J. MARSH

Department of Anthropology, University of California–Santa Barbara
Santa Barbara, Calif. 93106
emarsh@umail.ucsb.edu

MAXINE E. MCBRINN

PaleoCultural Research Group
555 Burbank Street, Unit A
Broomfield, CO 80020
arch81c@yahoo.com

BRIAN S. SHAFFER

3804 Montecito Road
Denton, Tex. 76205
bsshaffer@charter.net

JOHN WHITTAKER

Department of Anthropology, Grinnell College
Grinnell, Iowa 50112
whittake@grinnell.edu

DANIEL M. WINKLER

Anthropology Department, University of Wisconsin–Milwaukee
290 Sabine Hall
3413 N. Downer Avenue
Milwaukee, Wis. 53201
dwinkler@uwm.edu

Figures

○ ○ ○
○ ○ ○
○ ○ ○

Tables

○ ○ ○
○ ○ ○
○ ○ ○

Preface

○ ○ ○
○ ○ ○
○ ○ ○

This volume developed as a result of a research project I began in 1999. I was inter-ested in interpreting the microwear patterns on an assemblage of large obsidian bifaces from the Malheur Basin in eastern Oregon. Microwear studies constitute an area of archaeological inquiry almost entirely dependent on experimental archaeol-ogy. Until wear patterns are developed under known and controlled conditions and then observed under magnification, it is not possible to confidently link unknown microwear traces with known uses for stone tools. In fact, even distinguishing between true microwear and pre- and post-depositional damage requires some knowledge of wear patterns developed through experimental means.

Microwear studies of flint tools have been commonplace for decades (Burroni, Donahue, and Pollard 2002; Keeley 1980; Kimball 1994; Nance 1971); however, obsidian has received relatively little attention (Lewenstein 1987), in part because of the lack of polish development in comparison to coarser-grained materials such as cherts. To try to interpret the patterns observed on the Malheur bifaces, I began an experimental program aimed at developing a variety of different wear patterns resulting from a broad spectrum of potential past tool uses. I read many reports on microwear analysis; most referred to some "experimentally derived reference collec-tion," but little was written about the process of developing a microwear reference collection. For example, I was interested in how to determine an appropriate set of wear-inducing behaviors, how to actually generate the wear patterns, and how to document the experiment.

In addition to microwear, other areas of experimental archaeology lack background on the development of experiments. Even when researchers describe experiments in detail, they rarely explain the reasons they chose a specific experimental design. For example, when replicating a bifacial edge for microwear experimentation, is it problematic to use a modern copper pressure flaker to prepare the edge, or will this create a microscopically poor replica of an archaeological edge flaked by antler or bone?

This volume was developed to coalesce a series of foundational papers that not only provide a literature review of specific areas of experimental archaeology but also detail some of the issues that must be considered in the development of an experimental archaeology project and some of the potential pitfalls seasoned experimental archaeologists hope to help others avoid. Using the information presented in this volume, researchers can more confidently begin an experimental research project without having to completely reinvent the wheel.

Following a theoretically oriented introduction, each of the remaining chapters addresses a particular classification of material culture. The authors were loosely guided by four main goals: (1) to provide a literature review; (2) to describe the potential for and limitations of experimental research; (3) to describe the development of an experiment, from raw material selection to methods of recording data; and 4) to suggest common mistakes to avoid, based on the authors' experience.

Chapters 2 and 3 cover ceramics. Karen Harry (Chapter 2) examines the experimental archaeology of ceramic manufacture, and Margaret Beck (Chapter 3) discusses ceramic vessel function and use. As with the larger body of experimental archaeological literature, studies of stone tool manufacture and use comprise the largest section of the book. In Chapter 4, Philip Carr and Andrew Bradbury discuss lithic debitage experiments. Douglas Bamforth discusses microwear research in Chapter 5. In Chapter 6, Robert Jeske, Daniel Winkler, and Dustin Blodgett describe heat alteration of lithic raw material. In the final lithic chapter, Jenny Adams writes about the experimental archaeology of grinding technology.

The remaining four chapters deal with materials not always preserved in archaeological sites. Edward Jolie and Maxine McBrinn (Chapter 8) discuss perishable studies, in particular basketry, fiber, and cordage. As an example of composite hunting technology, John Whittaker (Chapter 9) describes experimentation with atlatl technology. The final two chapters discuss faunal material. Leland Bement covers butchering practices and bone tools in Chapter 10, and Patrick Lubinski and Brian Shaffer address experimental zooarchaeology in Chapter 11.

A volume such as this cannot be completed without the generous gift of time and experience from all the authors, and this volume is no exception. The contributors have endured more than their fair share of delays, and I cannot sufficiently express my appreciation for their patience and understanding. I also owe a great deal of thanks to all those (including my wife) who have graciously listened to my descriptions of the volume. Michael Schiffer and an anonymous reviewer deserve credit for greatly improving this work. A final thank you to a number of former teachers and colleagues, too numerous to name individually, who have encouraged the book's development.

J.R.F.

REFERENCES CITED

Burroni, D., R. E. Donahue, and A. M. Pollard
  2002   The Surface Alteration Features of Flint Artefacts as a Record of Environmental Processes. *Journal of Archaeological Science* 29:1277–1287.

Keeley, L. H.
  1980   *Experimental Determination of Stone Tool Uses.* Prehistoric Archaeology and Ecology Series. University of Chicago Press, Chicago.

Kimball, L.
  1994   An Introduction to Methodological and Substantive Contributions of Microwear Analysis. *Lithic Technology* 19(2):81–82.

Lewenstein, S.
  1987   *Stone Tool Use at Cerros: The Ethnoarchaeological and Use-Wear Evidence.* University of Texas Press, Austin.

Nance, J. D.
  1971   Functional Interpretations from Microscopic Analysis. *American Antiquity* 36(3): 361–366.

Designing Experimental Research in Archaeology

CHAPTER ONE

Introduction

Erik J. Marsh and Jeffrey R. Ferguson

○ ○ ○
○ ○ ○
○ ○ ○

SOURCES OF ANALOGIES

Much of what archaeologists understand about variation in material culture and its behavioral correlates is derived from studies that create analogies with past behavior using modern material procurement, manufacture, use, reuse, and discard (Mathieu 2002; Stone and Planel 1999). These analogies generally describe two divergent methodologies that share a theoretical base: ethnoarchaeology and experimental archaeology. This volume focuses on experimental archaeology, "the fabrication of materials, behaviors, or both in order to observe one or more processes involved in the production, use, discard, deterioration, or recovery of material culture" (Skibo 1992a:18). This methodology offers a high degree of control of variables and explores specific research questions not usually accessible in ethnoarchaeological studies.

While ethnoarchaeological research can observe the production of material culture in a wider context, it can also be prone to the erroneous assumption that "all technological knowledge is explicit and can be elicited from any practitioner of the technology" (Schiffer and Skibo 1987:596). Informants in ethnoarchaeological projects may not want or be able to clarify the production and use of their own materials, whereas experimental archaeology can directly address questions such as how different tempers affect thermal performance characteristics of ceramic vessels (Beck, Harry, this volume; Schiffer and Skibo 1987). Ethnoarchaeological research has great utility for examining material culture in its social context, but experimental archaeology is preferred for isolating the effects and relationships of small sets of related variables (such as how stone flake length relates to platform thickness and angle).

The common theoretical foundation of ethnoarchaeology and experimental archaeology allows researchers to tack between complementary analogies generated by the distinct methodologies (Skibo 1992a). While this volume focuses on experimental archaeology, its authors relate their projects to inferences from ethnoarchaeology; their results provide hypotheses to be tested in less controlled ethnoarchaeological settings, where the effects of unanticipated or untested variables and factors can be observed. Future research stands to profit from continued close integration of these two methodologies in comprehensive research programs.

EXPERIMENTAL ARCHAEOLOGY

Izumi Shimada (2005:608) has lamented that little has changed in the decades since Ruth Tringham (1978:171) argued that "experiments in archaeology have for the most part been justifiably ignored because of (1) their lack of a strong theoretical base and a resulting lack of general applicability in testing archaeological hypotheses . . . and (2) their lack of rigor and attention to scientific experimental procedure in design, execution, recording, and analysis." While experimental archaeology may not always "furnish a foundation for explaining technological variation and change" (Schiffer et al. 1994:198), it is having increasingly greater influence on archaeological inference, as is its close cousin, ethnoarchaeology (Skibo 1992b; Stark 2003). This trend has developed largely through the efforts of Michael Schiffer, James Skibo, and colleagues (1994), who have implemented integrated experimental programs based soundly in scientific methods and directed expressly at archaeological issues.

The chapters in this volume build on the foundation established by Schiffer and colleagues (1994) to contribute more directly to archaeological inference through controlled experimentation. To accomplish this, experiments are theoretically contextualized and conducted with rigorous attention to research design and procedure. These foundational principles allow the modern analogies generated by experimental archaeology to clarify past behaviors and practices. The projects presented here are "nested within families of related principles" (Schiffer et al. 1994:198) as well as within suites of related experiments, as part of long-term, multifaceted experimental research programs. Such programs explore diverse behavioral patterns and their relationships in the complex, long-term processes of site formation, moving research well beyond Tringham's (1978) criticism.

Future research in experimental archaeology may be able to take cues from recent developments in ceramic ethnoarchaeology. While the chapters in this volume generally follow the "behavioral archaeology" approach developed in the 1980s by Schiffer and colleagues (1994), recent research in ceramic ethnoarchaeology shows a much broader range of theoretical approaches (Stark 2003:199) that may foreshadow new avenues for experimental archaeology. Another similarity may lie in the regional focus of many Americanist ceramic ethnoarchaeologists, who often overlook research from other areas of the world or research not published in English, leading to the fragmentation of ceramic ethnoarchaeology (Stark 2003:215). Within experimental archaeology, it may be prudent to engage current theoretical tensions emerging in ceramic ethnoarchaeology and better integrate research from around the world.

RESEARCH DESIGN

The chapters in this volume follow coherent and consistent research designs and procedures, focused on the goal of contributing to inference, such as developing material expectations for archaeological data (Lubinski and Shaffer, this volume). The authors place their experiments in a theoretical context, making comparisons either to similar experiments conducted by the same research program or to other well-documented experiments. Experiments establish themselves as relevant to archaeological inference through research designs that explicitly address existing theories based on previous research.

Philip Carr and Andrew Bradbury (this volume) suggest that research design can be improved by heeding lessons from other sciences, such as A. Franklin's (1981) characterization of "good" experiments. For Franklin, three types of good experiments—crucial, corroborative, and new phenomena—relate data to theory. Crucial experiments support an existing explanation or theory over an alternate explanation. Corroborative experiments furnish support for the basic idea of a single theory. New phenomena experiments produce results not expected based on existing explanations or theories, which may lead to the development of new theories. Karen Harry (this volume) follows a similar theoretical approach, arguing that experiments begin with a hypothesis or question that can be made more or less plausible by examining its consequences. Hence, effective research design makes explicit relationships with existing theories, and well-documented results can be directly integrated into subsequent experiments (Kingery 1982).

While archaeologists routinely work with small sample sizes from non-repeatable excavations, experimental archaeology provides a unique opportunity to corroborate conclusions through multiple trials of repeatable experiments. This methodology is fundamental to any scientific experiment relevant to theory (Carr and Bradbury, Harry, Lubinski and Shaffer, this volume) and can provide data otherwise unavailable to archaeologists. In the excavation of archaeological sites, "[n]o matter how much we dig, we work with impossibly small, unrepresentative samples of data" (Lekson 2008:13). However, data from controlled experiments can be completely recovered and resampled to better assess how well small samples represent a larger population (e.g., Lubinski and Shaffer, this volume). Experiments can test for equifinity, where multiple causes lead to the same effect—a persistent issue in interpretations of archaeological data (Carr and Bradbury, Lubinski and Shaffer, this volume). For example, the damaged edge of a lithic artifact may be the result of diverse combinations of human and non-human influences, which can be sorted out through experimentation (Bamforth, this volume). Multiple trials of controlled experiments that explore alternate causes with a common result can directly contribute to reducing ambiguity in the interpretation of archaeological data.

These advantages of experimental archaeology result from adherence to the scientific method and, as the authors in this volume emphasize, from multiple repetitions of the same experiment that explore alternate possibilities. To address this strategy, the authors outline step-by-step methods specific to their materials that will guide future experiments. This degree of standardization is uncommon in traditional archaeological research, but it is essential to experimental archaeology.

DIVERSE RESEARCH SETTINGS:
GREATER AND LESSER CONTROL OF VARIABLES

Experimental archaeology offers the choice to control some of the manifold variables involved in the use of materials in the past. To clarify the complex interactions of these variables, experimental archaeology has developed sophisticated modern analogies (Mathieu 2002; Stone and Planel 1999). Experimenters can decide how carefully to control variables and tack among highly controlled lab settings, more "natural" field settings (Lubinski and Shaffer, this volume), and, in some cases, ethnoarchaeological observations. These complementary methodologies share a common theoretical base (Schiffer 1987; Skibo 1992a, 1992b; Stark 2003; Tringham 1978), although with different research foci and potential. Many effective research programs integrate lab, "natural," and ethnoarchaeological observations, an approach that has the most potential to provide data that directly impact archaeological inference (e.g., Skibo 1992b).

The research presented in this volume focuses primarily on controlled laboratory experiments, but it also relies on related experiments and research from field and ethnoarchaeological settings. Controlled laboratory experiments are characterized by their replicability and tight control of very few variables, usually in a laboratory setting. Field experiments relax control of variables to more closely replicate possible prehistoric situations, thereby becoming less repeatable and more subject to equifinity (Lubinski and Shaffer, this volume). Different settings are appropriate for different research questions, and the most effective projects use a variety of approaches (Harry, Jolie and McBrinn, this volume).

Greater Control of Variables

Highly controlled experiments examine a narrow range of variables in laboratory settings under replicable conditions and suggest relatively "low-level" principles that may seem far removed from archaeological inference (Skibo 1992a, 1992b). Such experiments often focus on the physical and mechanical properties of materials humans use to make tools, most commonly flaked stone (e.g., Dibble and Pelcin 1995; Pelcin 1997; Speth 1975). These low-level experiments often describe universal properties of common materials and apply to the same archaeological material regardless of cultural setting. Greater control of variables also allows for double-blind tests, which have direct bearing on the interpretation of use-wear on archaeological artifacts (Bamforth, this volume). These experiments isolate few variables, so they must be related to other experiments and archaeological observations to have wider relevance.

While highly controlled experiments can be conducted in laboratory settings, projects aimed at learning how real people used real tools to accomplish real tasks in the past should "replicate realistic use contexts to the extent possible" (Bamforth, this volume; see also Harry, this volume), taking into consideration the necessary control of variables appropriate for the specific research question. In use-wear analysis, Douglas Bamforth (this volume) recommends incorporating both field settings for making and using tools and laboratory settings for analyzing use-wear, similar to Harry's (this volume) approach in selecting and gathering clays to make and test clay tiles in a laboratory.

In another example described by Harry (this volume), controlled laboratory experiments suggested that ceramic vessels with interior surface treatments boiled water more efficiently than those without untreated interiors (Schiffer 1990; Skibo 1992b). However, the same experiment repeated in more "natural" field settings showed that cooking food in vessels without interior surface treatments quickly clogged their pores. After food had been cooked in the vessels, they became as efficient at boiling water as vessels with interior surface treatments (Pierce 1999). Hence, multiple related experiments in different settings have the best potential for understanding past and present cooking practices.

In almost all experiments, the most difficult variable for which to control is the human user. If archaeologists conduct an experiment, they can more closely control the process to fit their ends. However, experimenters are often a poor proxy for those they seek to understand—people who were likely from a different time and culture, who were more skilled at making and using their material culture than are those conducting the experiment, and who have very different goals (Adams, this volume). To address this issue, Raymond Mauldin's (1993) experiment with ground stone was conducted by a Bolivian woman who was more familiar with, and more expert in, the use of the tools (Adams, this volume). Flintknapping experiments have consistently documented significant differences between amateur and expert knappers (Bamforth and Finlay 2008), and similar differences are evident in atlatl throwers' distance and accuracy. John Whittaker (this volume) uses data from recreational atlatl competitions as a general guide to the distance and accuracy prehistoric experts may have achieved with the weapon. These examples show how understanding the range of variation in selected human-related variables may help produce a stronger analogy with past behavior, especially when combined with more controlled laboratory analysis.

Lesser Control of Variables

Some ambitious experimental research programs have relaxed control of variables to observe large-scale aggregate effects. Such programs are difficult to repeat but are well suited for generating hypotheses and conducting related controlled experiments. Research conducted since 1972 at Butser Farm, England, has developed a setting analogous to an Iron Age farm. Within this setting, individual controlled experiments have been conducted using agriculture techniques and technology, such as crop rotation, types of manuring, use of livestock to work the fields, soil types, and arable weeds; other experiments have focused on grain storage, construction of buildings, earthworks, metallurgy, and kiln technology (Reynolds 1999a). A similar project at Lejre, Denmark, founded in 1967, builds on earlier Dutch experiments (see Steensberg 1979) and includes experiments focused on tools and construction techniques (Rasmussen and Grønnow 1999). Axel Steensberg's experiments in swidden agriculture using imitations of Neolithic tools, conducted in the 1950s, also incorporated large numbers of variables. As in other projects with many uncontrolled variables, these experiments reached few conclusions but did generate hypotheses and ideas to be tested in more controlled settings (Steensberg 1979).

Complex experiments with minimal control over variables are prone to an array of complications. In a long-term project similar to Butser Farm, the Pamunkey Project developed a rough analogy to a Middle Woodland period (ca. AD 1000) settlement in the southeastern United States. This scientifically conceived project produced and analyzed over 700 tools made of various materials, but it ended prematurely as a result of logistical problems, including disputes with the landowner (Callahan 1976). In a much smaller project, Nick Barton and C. Bergman (1982) attempted to compare the spatial dispersal of ancient and experimental lithic scatters in a sand matrix. However, unexpected bioturbation quickly "destroyed" the lithic scatters.

COMPREHENSIVE RESEARCH PROGRAMS

The authors in this volume unanimously call for comprehensive research programs, in contrast to isolated experiments—referred to variously as archaeological, exploratory, orientational, or imaginative experiments (Amick, Mauldin, and Binford 1989; Ascher 1961; Malina 1983; Schiffer et al. 1994). The relatively low cost and ease of conducting "weekend" experiments (Schiffer et al. 1994) make it common for such experiments to exist in isolation, lacking archaeologically relevant research questions, coherent research designs, and appropriate methods. In many cases the results of such experiments are not fully reported and cannot be integrated into the body of knowledge generated by experimental archaeology. The authors here reiterate the need for consistent and appropriate research methods, fundamental to the goal of contributing to archaeological inference.

In an effort to gain a more thorough understanding of ancient tools, their users, and their makers, effective research programs may include more perishable materials, such as the wood and fibrous hafting of projectile point weapons (Bamforth, Whittaker, this volume). While most experiments focus on materials recovered in archaeological sites, perishable items were both meaningful and functional in the lives of those who produced and used them. Compared with less perishable items such as stone tools, perishable artifacts constitute the vast majority of items in artifact inventories—especially those of hunter-gatherers—but they have received relatively little attention (Jolie and McBrinn, this volume). Given the generally poor preservation of such items, the cohesive program advocated by Edward Jolie and Maxine McBrinn (this volume) is especially necessary for a clearer understanding of these materials. The development of research programs that include perishable materials may be one of the few ways to approximate relationships between durable and perishable items. Such relationships may otherwise remain obscure given a research and preservation bias toward stone, as in the case of the Lignic period in Southeast Asia, when crude stone tools were used to make sophisticated wood tools (Ingersoll, Yellen, and MacDonald 1977). The atlatl is a synthesis of perishable and nonperishable materials, but archaeologists usually recover only a portion of this composite tool. Through trial and error and controlled tests, Whittaker (this volume) makes a step toward understanding how people made and used atlatls in the past.

In addition, comprehensive experimental research programs must address taphonomy, especially studies that aim to replicate artifacts as found by archaeologists (Carr and Bradbury, this volume). Further, taphonomy is a crucial aspect of comparative use-wear studies (Bamforth, this volume). More than other material classes, animal bones are especially affected by taphonomic processes (Lyman 1994); hence, they constitute a critical aspect of zooarchaeological experiments (Lubinski and Shaffer, this volume). In the case of bone tools or faunal technology, taphonomic processes may remove many details such as use-wear and cut marks (Bement, this volume), also an issue with stone tools (Bamforth, this volume). An advantage of experimental archaeology is that taphonomic variables can be controlled. While taphonomy is not the focus of this volume, it is indispensable to a full understanding of site formation processes (Schiffer 1987).

Experimental archaeology is especially appropriate for testing noncultural variables that do not vary by region, such as the physics of stone fracture, the chemical and mechanical processes of seed crushing (Adams, this volume), or the ways bones fracture (Bement, this volume). However, most factors in the formation of archaeological assemblages vary spatially, temporally, and culturally. Repeating experiments in other regions using alternate materials can help define the extent to which results are locally specific and suggest possible sources of variability (Jolie and McBrinn, this volume). For example, field-setting experiments may be limited to include only materials that were likely available in the time period and region under study. Repeating experiments in different regions using regionally specific materials is a simple way of increasing an experiment's relevance to regionally focused archaeologists (Carr and Bradbury, this volume).

Repetitions of regional experiments can suggest the degree to which results can be generalized to other regions. Larger experimental programs are well suited to careful documentation of long-term site formation processes, a particularly difficult variable to replicate or observe. For example, Anna Behrensmeyer's (1978) case study of bone weathering in Africa was based on data from a "natural" setting and showed how physical and chemical agents break down bone. While this study has been applied worldwide, regional taphonomic studies in Argentina emphasize differences with the patterns seen in Behrensmeyer's African study, based on bones from local animals exposed to local soils and weathering patterns (Belardi and Rindel 2008; Gutiérrez 2001). To clarify human decomposition in northern European bogs, Heather Gill-Robinson (2002) used fetal pigs to derive archaeological expectations for decaying human tissue in bog environments. At Overton Down, farm objects were placed in depositional contexts to be excavated after 2, 4, 8, 16, and 32 years, and so on (Bell et al. 1996). After placing leather, bone, pottery, and standardized plastic, experimenters were able to track the movement and degradation of different artifacts in an actively cultivated field. At Butser Farm, over 90 percent of plastic pieces remained within 2 m of their starting point, discrediting the notion that agriculture and cultivation widely disperse material culture (Reynolds 1999b; Schiffer 1987:129–131).

Experimental programs that integrate different materials, regions, experimental settings, and alternative hypotheses have the greatest potential to contribute to an understanding of archaeological data and argue for their larger role in archaeology (e.g., Skibo 1992a; see examples in Shimada 2005). For example, controlled experiments have shown that taphonomic processes vary greatly for different parts of a bone (Todd 1987), results that have contributed directly to the interpretation of human-animal relationships during the Formative period in central Argentina (Izeta 2007). Another Argentine project combined data from controlled bone fracturing experiments with ethnohistorical reports of local butchering preferences to describe the influences of butchering practices and taphonomic history on archaeological bone assemblages (Miotti 1998). In the United States, Schiffer and Skibo's

(1987) experimental studies examine the role of ceramic temper in the shift from Archaic to Woodland ceramic technologies in the eastern United States. In the Near East, trial and error suggested the best tool shape for harvesting different types of locally available grains. Laboratory microwear analysis of these tools developed clear material expectations for the analysis of lithic tools from archaeological sites (Anderson 1999).

CONCLUDING THOUGHTS

Compared with the logistical challenges and difficulties posed by excavation and ethnography, experimental archaeology is often more accessible to professional, student, and avocational researchers. This allows for research at low cost, with minimal or no travel, that does not disturb or destroy archaeological materials. However, projects that are easily carried out often exist in isolation, lack proper relevance to questions of interest to archaeologists, employ research designs and methods that undermine the results, and fail to fully report methods, if the results are reported at all. This book offers examples of experiments carried out in the context of relevant theory, with the goal of achieving broader archaeological or anthropological relevance.

Researchers typically turn to experimental research to help them understand or test hypotheses developed during the study of archaeological materials. For example, to explain a temporal shift from side to corner notching in an archaeological assemblage of projectile points, a researcher might hypothesize a specific functional difference related to breakage. The researcher in this case already has the question in hand and may then develop an experiment to quantify the fracture resistance of the two notching forms. The chapters here are designed to help researchers at this stage of the investigation. How does one design a proper experiment? What variables need to be controlled and tested? To what extent can modern materials substitute for those used in the past? What common mistakes can be avoided? The answers are found in the chapters that follow.

REFERENCES CITED

Amick, D. S., R. P. Mauldin, and L. R. Binford
1989   The Potential of Experiments in Lithic Technology. In *Experiments in Lithic Technology*, ed. D. S. Amick and R. P. Mauldin, 1–14. BAR International Series, vol. 528. Archeopress, Oxford.

Anderson, P. C.
1999   Experimental Cultivation, Harvest, and Threshing of Wild Cereals. In *Prehistory of Agriculture: New Experimental and Ethnographic Approaches*, ed. P. C. Anderson, 118–144. Costen Institute of Archaeology at UCLA Monograph, vol. 40. Costen Institute of Archaeology, University of California at Los Angeles, Los Angeles.

Ascher, R.
  1961   Experimental Archaeology. *American Anthropologist* 63:793–816.

Bamforth, D. B., and N. Finlay
  2008   Introduction: Archaeological Approaches to Lithic Production Skill and Craft
              Production. *Journal of Archaeological Method and Theory* 15:1–27.

Barton, N., and C. Bergman
  1982   Hunters at Hengistbury: Some Evidence from Experimental Archaeology. *World
              Archaeology* 14(2):237–248.

Behrensmeyer, A. K.
  1978   Taphonomic and Ecological Information from Bone Weathering. *Paleobiology*
              4:150–162.

Belardi, J. B., and D. Rindel
  2008   Taphonomic and Archeological Aspects of Massive Mortality Processes in
              Guanaco (*Lama guanicoe*) Caused by Winter Stress in Southern Patagonia.
              Quaternary International 180:38–51.

Bell, M., P. J. Fowler, and S. Hillson
  1996   *The Experimental Earthwork Project, 1960–1992.* Council for British Archae-
              ology, Research Report no. 100. Council for British Archaeology, York.

Callahan, E.
  1976   *The Pamunkey Project Phases I and II.* Experimental Archaeology Papers.
              Department of Sociology and Anthropology, Virginia Commonwealth Uni-
              versity, Richmond.

Dibble, H. L., and A. Pelcin
  1995   The Effect of Hammer Mass and Velocity on Flake Mass. *Journal of Archaeologi-
              cal Science* 22:429–439.

Franklin, A.
  1981   What Makes a Good Experiment? *British Journal of Philosophical Science* 32:
              367–379.

Gill-Robinson, H.
  2002   This Little Piggy Went to Cambria, This Little Piggy Went to Wales: The Tales
              of 12 Piglets in Peat. In *Experimental Archaeology: Replicating Past Objects,
              Behaviors and Processes*, ed. J. R. Mathieu, 111–126. BAR International Series,
              vol. 1035. Archaeopress, Oxford.

Gutiérrez, M. A.
  2001   Bone Diagenesis and Taphonomic History of the Paso Otero 1 Bone Bed, Pam-
              pas of Argentina. *Journal of Archaeological Science* 28:1277–1290.

Ingersoll, D. W., J. E. Yellen, and W. MacDonald (editors)
  1977   *Experimental Archaeology.* Columbia University Press, New York.

Izeta, A. D.
  2007   *Zooarqueología del Sur de los Valles Calchaquíes (Provincias de Catamarca y
              Tucumán, República Argentina): Análisis de Conjuntos Faunísticos del Primer
              Milenio A.D.* BAR International Series, vol. 1612. Archaeopress, Oxford.

Kingery, W. D.

1982   Plausible Inferences from Ceramic Artifacts. In *Archaeological Ceramics*, ed. J. S. Olin and A. D. Franklin, 37–45. Smithsonian Institution Press, Washington, D.C.

Lekson, S. H.

2008   *A History of the Ancient Southwest*. School for Advanced Research Press, Santa Fe.

Lyman, R. L.

1994   *Vertebrate Taphonomy*. Cambridge University Press, Cambridge.

Malina, J.

1983   Archaeology and Experiment. *Norwegian Archaeological Review* 16(2):13–22.

Mathieu, J. R. (editor)

2002   *Experimental Archaeology: Replicating Past Objects, Behaviors and Processes*. BAR International Series, vol. 1035. Archaeopress, Oxford.

Mauldin, R. P.

1993   The Relationship between Ground Stone and Agricultural Intensification in Western New Mexico. *Kiva* 58:317–330.

Miotti, L. L.

1998   *Zooarqueología de la Meseta Central y Costa de la Provincia de Santa Cruz: Un Enfoque de las Estrategias Adaptivas Aborígenes y los Paleoambientes*. Mueso Municipal de Historia Natural, San Rafael, Mendoza, Argentina.

Pelcin, A. W.

1997   The Formation of Flakes: The Role of Platform Thickness and Exterior Platform Angle in the Production of Flake Initiations and Terminations. *Journal of Archaeological Science* 24:1107–1113.

Pierce, C. D.

1999   Explaining Corrugated Pottery in the American Southwest: An Evolutionary Approach. PhD dissertation, Department of Anthropology, University of Washington, Seattle.

Rasmussen, M., and B. Grønnow

1999   The Historical-Archaeological Experimental Centre at Lejre, Denmark: 30 Years of Experimenting with the Past. In *The Constructed Past: Experimental Archaeology, Education and the Public*, ed. P. Stone and P. Planel, 136–145. Routledge, New York.

Reynolds, P. J.

1999a   Butser Ancient Farm, Hampshire, UK. In *The Constructed Past: Experimental Archaeology, Education and the Public*, ed. P. Stone and P. Planel, 124–135. Routledge, New York.

1999b   The Nature of Experiment in Archaeology. In *Experiment and Design: Archaeological Studies in Honour of John Coles*, ed. A. F. Harding, 156–162. Oxbow Books, Oxford.

Schiffer, M. B.
   1987   *Formation Processes of the Archaeological Record.* University of New Mexico
           Press, Albuquerque.
   1990   The Influence of Surface Treatment on Heating Effectiveness of Ceramic Ves-
           sels. *Journal of Archaeological Science* 17(4):373–381.

Schiffer, M. B., and J. M. Skibo
   1987   Theory and Experiment in the Study of Technological Change. *Current Anthro-
           pology* 28:595–622.

Schiffer, M. B., J. M. Skibo, T. C. Boelke, M. A. Neupert, and M. Aronson
   1994   New Perspectives on Experimental Archaeology: Surface Treatments and Ther-
           mal Response of the Clay Cooking Pot. *American Antiquity* 59(2):197–217.

Shimada, I.
   2005   Experimental Archaeology. In *Handbook of Archaeological Methods,* ed. H.D.G.
           Maschner and C. Chippindale, vol. 1, 603–642. AltaMira, Lanham, Md.

Skibo, J. M.
   1992a   Ethnoarchaeology, Experimental Archaeology and Inference Building in
           Ceramic Research. *Archaeologia Polona* 30:27–38.
   1992b   *Pottery Function: A Use-Alteration Perspective.* Plenum, New York.

Speth, J. D.
   1975   Miscellaneous Studies in Hard-Hammer Percussion Flaking: The Effects of
           Oblique Impact. *American Antiquity* 40(2):203–207.

Stark, M. T.
   2003   Current Issues in Ceramic Ethnoarchaeology. *Journal of Archaeological Research*
           11(3):193–242.

Steensberg, A.
   1979   *Draved: An Experiment in Stone Age Agriculture: Burning, Sowing and Harvest-
           ing.* National Museum of Denmark, Copenhagen.

Stone, P., and P. Planel
   1999   Introduction. In *The Constructed Past: Experimental Archaeology, Education
           and the Public,* ed. P. Stone and P. Planel, 1–14. Routledge, New York.

Todd, L. C.
   1987   Taphonomy of the Horner II Bone Bed. In *The Horner Site: The Type Site of the
           Cody Cultural Complex,* ed. G. C. Frison and L. C. Todd, 107–198. Academic
           Press, Orlando.

Tringham, R.
   1978   Experimentation, Ethnoarchaeology, and the Leapfrogs in Archaeological
           Methodology. In *Explorations in Ethnoarchaeology,* ed. R. A. Gould, 169–199.
           University of New Mexico Press, Albuquerque.

CHAPTER TWO

Understanding Ceramic Manufacturing Technology: The Role of Experimental Archaeology

Karen G. Harry

○ ○ ○
○ ○ ○
○ ○ ○

Since around 1980, archaeological interest in ceramic technology has intensified. Accompanying this increased attention has been a corresponding growth in the use of experimental methods to understand why prehistoric potters made the technological choices they did. In this chapter I review how experimental archaeology can improve our understanding of ceramic technology.

THE GROWTH OF CERAMIC EXPERIMENTAL STUDIES

Experimental archaeology has been defined as "the fabrication of materials, behaviors, or both in order to observe one or more processes involved in the production, use, discard, deterioration, or recovery of material culture" (Skibo 1992:18). Prior to the advent of the New Archaeology, most archaeological ceramic experiments were attempts to replicate manufacturing techniques used by earlier cultures (e.g., Bjørn 1969; Holstein 1973a, 1973b; MacIver 1921; O'Brien 1980). With few exceptions (e.g., Shepard 1956), these experiments made no attempt to develop universal principles that could be used to develop a general body of archaeological knowledge, nor did they address the question of why certain manufacturing technologies were selected. This emphasis began to change in the mid-1980s with the publication of David Braun's (1983) seminal article entitled "Pots as Tools." With this article, attention began to shift away from the then traditional areas of ceramic style and typology and toward functional issues regarding how ceramics were manufactured to meet particular needs. To explore these and other issues through experimental studies, in 1984 Michael Schiffer founded the Laboratory of Traditional Technology at the University of Arizona. Since that time, interest in ceramic experimentation has amplified, with Schiffer and his colleagues largely leading the effort.

Schiffer and colleagues (1994) distinguish between what they call "archaeo-logical experiments" and "experimental archaeology." The former are experiments conducted as "one-shot affairs" in isolation from other experiments. While such studies may be helpful in structuring future research, Schiffer and his colleagues argue that they are generally insufficient to allow robust behavioral conclusions to be drawn. Experimental archaeology, in contrast, entails the creation of an ongoing program of studies:

> In experimental archaeology, individual experiments do not exist in isolation, but draw expertise and technology from the program's tradition and, in turn, contribute to its elaboration. More importantly, the findings of one experiment are nested within families of related principles (correlates) that, together, furnish a foundation for explaining technological variation and change. (Schiffer et al. 1994:198)

According to this view, the goal of an experimental archaeology program is not so much the replication of a particular manufacturing sequence but rather the creation of a general body of knowledge (or correlates) that archaeologists can draw upon as appropriate to interpret prehistoric and historic ceramics (see Schiffer 2003; Schiffer et al. 1994). This body of knowledge, of course, is developed through cumulative individual experiments, and it matters little whether these experiments are conducted by one or multiple researchers. The difference between studies con-ducted as "archaeological experiments" and those conducted as part of an "experi-mental archaeology" program lies not in the number of individual experiments con-ducted but instead on how the results are interpreted. Under the approach followed here, the results obtained from any one experiment are understood to be proven true only for the conditions under which the experiment was conducted. Before the results are applied to archaeological data, the researcher should consider how closely the prehistoric or historic conditions matched those of the experiment, how relevant the differences between the two contexts are, and how likely it is that the results will hold true for other situations. Typically, experiments are undertaken to address questions arising from a specific database (e.g., why do the pots in my study region display a particular attribute?), and the results from one experiment may or may not be sufficient to answer the question posed. However, to develop a body of knowledge that can be drawn upon by archaeologists working in other cultural contexts, a body of principles must be established. Such principles can best be obtained from the cumulative knowledge generated from ongoing experiments.

WHY DO WE NEED CERAMIC EXPERIMENTS?

Archaeologists have several tools available to aid in the interpretation of ceramic artifacts, including principles obtained from the fields of ethnoarchaeology and ceramic engineering. Although ceramic analysts rely heavily on information from each of these fields, the body of available knowledge is often insufficient for the types of questions and issues archaeologists face. In these cases, data obtained from experimental archaeology can supplement these other sources of information.

Archaeologists are increasingly turning to the field of ceramic ethnoarchaeology as an information source, as evidenced by the number of recent overview articles on the topic (e.g., Arnold 2000; Costin 2000; Hegmon 2000; Stark 2003). Although ethnoarchaeological data have contributed substantially to the development of middle-range ceramic theory, they do not replace the need for experimental studies. Instead, experimental archaeology and ethnoarchaeology are best considered complementary strategies.

There are at least two situations in which experimental archaeology can be used to overcome limitations of ethnoarchaeological data. First, some prehistoric technologies may lack appropriate ethnographic analogs. For example, Eric Blinman and Clint Swink (1993) report that when trench kiln features were first identified in the American Southwest, archaeologists were unable to find any ethnographic, historic, or modern accounts of similar features. Because the trench kilns differed in structure and scale from other known Native American firing features, archaeologists turned to experimental work to determine how these features had been constructed and used. Second, there may be cases for which ethnographic analogs exist, but informants cannot provide the type of information archaeologists seek. As an example, an archaeologist may wish to examine whether a certain temper type enhances the use-life of cooking vessels. While ethnoarchaeological data can indicate whether this temper type is found in the cooking vessels of a particular social group, the potters may or may not be aware of the effects of the temper on the vessels' performance. Furthermore, even if the informants are aware of the temper's effect, experimental data may be needed to quantify the effect and to isolate how much of this effect is a result specifically of the temper as opposed to other attributes of the vessels.

Ceramic engineering principles (see Chiang, Birnie, and Kingery 1997; Grimshaw 1971; Kingery 1960) are another source of information. Modern material science studies provide information on a wide range of ceramic topics, including how firing conditions can affect ceramic attributes, how various aplastic inclusions behave under different firing and use conditions, and how different types of clays perform in various situations. Despite the abundance of data and literature on these subjects, however, information may be lacking for the types of issues archaeologists study. Because ceramic engineers generally focus on the high-fired, fine-grained, and homogeneous ceramics used in modern industry, principles derived from these studies are not always applicable to archaeological situations (Sillar 2003:178–179). Even when they are applicable, experimentation may be needed to determine if the magnitude of the effect is substantial enough to have been behaviorally significant (Schiffer and Skibo 1987:602). That is, was the effect great enough to have been recognized and appreciated by ancient potters, and, if so, was it significant enough to have caused them to have modified their production techniques as a result?

In some experiments, archaeological sherds rather than replicates have been used (e.g., Hensler 1999; Neupert 1993; Plog 1986; Steponaitis 1984). Although the use of sherds is appropriate for some types of questions, for others it is not. One problem is that it can be difficult to interpret data obtained from sherds. As discussed earlier, an ongoing area of current research deals with the ways different technical choices affect the performance of ceramic vessels. To understand the effect of any one attribute, all other variables must be held constant—something that is possible only under carefully controlled manufacturing conditions. Because of the enormous variability among archaeological specimens (for example, in thickness, curvature, temper and clay type, and original firing temperature), it is rarely possible to determine from sherd data alone which variables contributed to the test results. Results can also be influenced by how the vessel was used prior to being discarded and by post-depositional processes. Even when sherds are suitable for the research question being asked, there may be other reasons to use manufactured specimens. Many tests are destructive, and archaeologists may be reluctant to destroy or damage archaeological ceramics. Additionally, it may be difficult to locate enough archaeological samples with the required attributes to obtain statistically significant results (Kilikoglou et al. 1998:263).

REVIEW OF PAST STUDIES

The number of ceramic experimental studies conducted is substantial. Although a detailed review of these studies is beyond the scope of this chapter, in this section I summarize the major trends in ceramic experimental research to provide an idea of the kinds of issues that can be studied through this approach. Not surprisingly, the majority of experiments have focused on understanding the technological aspects of pottery manufacture, from the perspective of exploring what manufacturing techniques ancient potters used and what outcomes, in terms of the resulting performance characteristics, may have led to the selection of those techniques. Although experimental studies are generally less well suited to exploring social and ideological questions than technological ones, some researchers have recently begun to explore the use of experimental data for addressing social issues as well.

Identifying Manufacturing Techniques

Early experiments were generally undertaken with the goal of replicating specific archaeological ceramic wares or types (e.g., Bjørn 1969; Holstein 1973a, 1973b; MacIver 1921; O'Brien 1980). Although these "archaeological experiments" made no explicit attempt to develop a body of ceramic theory, they did lay the foundation for future studies. In particular, these studies contributed to our understanding of how to design experiments and how to interpret archaeological ceramics and firing features.

Recent studies have focused more explicitly on specific research questions. For example, M. A. Courty and V. Roux (1995) have examined experimentally produced specimens to identify attributes that could be used to distinguish wheel-thrown vessels from those that were coil-built and then shaped on the wheel. Other researchers have used experimental data to identify attributes that can help archaeologists recognize dung-tempered ceramics (London 1981), the firing temperature of particular ceramics (Harry 1996), or the firing temperature and atmosphere of ceramics in general (Gosselain 1992). In contrast to these studies, which have focused on the ceramics themselves, Blinman and Swink (1993) have used experimental data to better understand how ceramic firing features were used and created. In their studies, they constructed and used several pit firing features and compared their physical characteristics after use with those of prehistoric features in the American Southwest.

Ceramic Technology and Vessel Function

Perhaps the most significant contributions of ceramic experimental studies have dealt with the relationship between manufacturing technology and vessel performance. These studies inform on how manufacturing choices may affect (a) the suitability of a vessel for a particular use, by either enhancing or detracting from certain performance characteristics; (b) the life of the vessel, by increasing or decreasing its resistance to the stresses it experienced; or (c) both.

Numerous studies have examined the effect of temper type, size, and shape on ceramic properties. Researchers have examined tempering effects on vessel strength (Bronitsky and Hamer 1986; Hoard et al. 1995; Schiffer and Skibo 1987; Skibo, Schiffer, and Reid 1989; Steponaitis 1984; Vekinis and Kilikoglou 1988), abrasion resistance (Schiffer and Skibo 1987; Skibo and Schiffer 1987; Skibo, Schiffer, and Reid 1989), thermal shock resistance (Bronitsky and Hamer 1986; Hoard et al. 1995; Schiffer and Skibo 1987; Steponaitis 1984), heating and cooling effectiveness (Schiffer and Skibo 1987; Skibo, Schiffer, and Reid 1989), vessel weight (Schiffer and Skibo 1987; Skibo, Schiffer, and Reid 1989), and the spalling of the fired ceramic body (Klemptner and Johnson 1985, 1986; Stimmell, Heimann, and Hancock 1982). Other researchers have examined the effects of various surface treatments on properties such as vessel strength (Harry et al. 2009; Wallace 1989), abrasion resistance (Skibo, Schiffer, and Butts 1997), heating effectiveness (Harry et al. 2009, in press; Pierce 1999; Schiffer 1990a, 1990b; Schiffer et al. 1994), and vessel decomposition (Harry et al. in press; Schiffer et al. 1994). Other vessel attributes studied in relationship to vessel performance include the effect of firing temperature on impact strength (Mabry et al. 1988; Skibo, Schiffer, and Reid 1989) and abrasion resistance (Schiffer and Skibo 1989; Skibo, Schiffer, and Reid 1989) and the effect of vessel shape on impact resistance (Helton 2001).

Addressing Production Challenges

The choices made in the manufacturing process may be influenced not only by the desired characteristics of the finished vessel but also by the limitations and challenges faced during the production process. Several studies have experimentally evaluated the effects of different tempers on the workability of different types of clay. Experiments have shown that the handling of excessively plastic clays can be improved through the addition of burned shell (Million 1975) and limestone (Hoard et al. 1995), whereas clays lacking sufficient plasticity may be made improved by the addition of dung (London 1981). The effects of adding salt to clay bodies have been experimentally evaluated by Owen Rye (1981) and Carole Stimmell and colleagues (1982), who have demonstrated that the presence of salt can inhibit the decomposition of calcium carbonates. Thus, they hypothesize that potters working with pastes containing calcium carbonate inclusions (for example, caliche grains or shell or limestone temper) may have intentionally added salt to minimize degradation of the vessel wall. Other researchers have evaluated the effects of firing temperature on particular clays and tempers and suggest that, in some cases, lower firing temperatures may have been preferred over high-firing ones because of the problems (such as bloating and lime spalling) some clays exhibit when fired at high temperatures (Harry 1996; Hoard et al. 1995). Kathy Hensler and Eric Blinman (2000:377–378) reported on experiments conducted to assess the behavior of different clays and pigments at differing firing temperatures. Based on the results of these experiments, they proposed that morphological differences between prehistoric kilns of the Rio Grande Valley and the Colorado Plateau reflect different firing requirements of clays from each region. They further proposed that the organic paint technology of the Rio Grande Valley may have been adopted to overcome problems associated with using mineral paint on the region's ash-rich clays. Experiments by James Skibo and colleagues (1989) demonstrate that manure-tempered pastes have greater wet strength than pastes tempered with other materials. Based on this finding, Skibo and colleagues (1989) proposed that organic-tempered pastes may have been advantageous for mobile groups because they would have required less drying time during the manufacturing process. Finally, my colleagues and I have examined how pottery production in a cool, wet environment affected the technological choices potters made. Specifically, we have argued that the highly porous, fragile vessels found in the

Arctic region were a result of technological choices necessitated by the climatic challenges the potters faced (Frink and Harry 2008; Harry et al. 2009, in press).

The Social Context of Production

Although most experimental studies have dealt with issues of function, our understanding of how ceramic production was organized can also be improved through the use of experimental data. Experimental firings have provided information on such variables as how many vessels could have been fired per episode in a particular type of firing feature and how much fuel such firings would have required. Colm O'Brien (1980) found that using the bonfire method, 12–16 vessels could be fired in 1.5 hours using 40–50 kg of fuel. Similarly, Blinman and Swink (1993) have shown that an average of 15 vessels can be fired per square meter of a trench kiln. Extrapolating from the size of the prehistoric kilns found in the Anasazi region of the American Southwest, the latter researchers calculate that, prehistorically, the number of vessels fired per episode varied from 25 to 200. When compared against household ceramic assemblages and use-life data, these data indicate that the largest kilns could produce vessels for as many as 80 households. These same experiments suggest that the participation of multiple individuals would have been needed for a successful trench kiln firing. From these and other data, Blinman and Swink (1993) conclude that the trench kiln firings likely reflect the collaboration of several households. Their experiments further indicate that the trench kilns would have required about 100 kg of fuel per square meter (or about twice as much per vessel as that required with the bonfire method; see O'Brien 1980). Hensler and Blinman (2000) propose that this high fuel requirement explains why trench kilns were not located near habitation sites, insofar as it was easier to construct the kiln near the fuel sources than carry the fuels back to the settlement.

Working in southern Arizona, I have used experimental data to examine why specialized ceramic production developed at a particular location (Harry 2000). Based on the results of tests designed to evaluate the workability and strength of various clay and temper combinations, I postulated that the presence of high-quality clays contributed to the development of ceramic specialization. The results from additional experiments suggested that the relatively simple ceramic technology the potters used (i.e., the lack of kilns) may have resulted in part from how the clays and tempers reacted during open versus kiln firings.

Finally, my colleagues and I relied on the results of experiments to examine why pottery was adopted in certain areas of the Arctic but not in others (Harry and Frink 2009). Contrary to expectations derived from other areas of the world, the adoption of pottery in this region had little to do with dietary food-processing requirements. Because Arctic foods were parboiled rather than cooked for long periods, indirect cooking (that is, stone boiling) with non-ceramic containers would have been sufficient to prepare the food. Compared with cooking directly over the fire with ceramics, however, our experimental data indicated that such methods would have required the use of larger fires. Because of the difficulties associated with acquiring fuel wood and having fires inside Arctic sod homes, we concluded that in this case the adoption of pottery related more to the need to conserve fuel resources and to preserve the livability of the homes rather than to any improvements in the nutritional quality of the foods being prepared.

THEORETICAL ISSUES

Several theoretical issues underlie the use of experimental data for interpreting prehistoric ceramic manufacture. These issues have to do with how we move from experimental observations—made under conditions that can never precisely match those of the past—to credible interpretations of the archaeological data. This question, of course, is fundamental to all areas of archaeological inquiry. Nonetheless, certain issues are especially relevant to the interpretation of ceramic experimental data, and these issues are discussed here.

Interpretive Challenges

The long-term objective of a comprehensive ceramic experimental program is to construct a body of correlates from which robust archaeological inferences can be derived. The process of correlate building requires a commitment to ongoing experimental studies that collectively and incrementally increase the body of available knowledge (Clark 2002; Schiffer 2003; Schiffer et al. 1994). In the past, the results of isolated experiments were often prematurely applied to the archaeological record, leading to interpretations not supported by additional research. Several reasons exist to explain why the results of isolated experiments might not apply to particular archaeological situations.

First, because of the wide range of variables involved in ceramic production and use, no single experiment can account for all the conditions underlying the manufacturing process. The results of experimental studies prove simply that the findings occurred under the conditions characterizing the test; the degree to which they apply to other situations can only be inferred. Experimental outcomes result from a complex interplay of factors, including the type and proportion of clay(s) and temper(s) used, the techniques used to prepare these materials, and the conditions (temperature, atmosphere, and firing length) under which the ceramics were fired. Therefore, in interpreting the results of any single experiment, consideration must be given to how closely the manufacturing conditions match those of the archaeological assemblage. For example, experiments conducted by Gordon Bronitsky and Robert Hamer (1986) showed that test tiles made with fine-grained shell temper were stronger than those made with coarser-grained shell inclusions. In contrast, the opposite results were obtained by James Feathers (1989), whose experiments involved the use of different clays, forming techniques, and firing temperatures. Similar issues affect experiments undertaken to evaluate the quality of various clays, tempers, and pigments for pottery production. A clay that performs poorly under one set of conditions may be of excellent quality when prepared differently (i.e., ground or aged)[1] or mixed with a different type of temper. Similarly, studies have shown that the quality of paint may depend as much on the underlying slip as it does on the pigment itself (Swink 1993).

Second, experimental results may not apply to archaeological situations because of differences introduced by the actual use of the ceramics. For example, early experiments demonstrated that vessel permeability is negatively correlated with the heating effectiveness of cooking vessels (Schiffer 1990a, 1990b; Schiffer and Skibo 1987; Schiffer et al. 1994; Skibo 1992). Specifically, these studies found that under laboratory conditions it took longer to bring water to boil in vessels that lacked interior surface treatments than it did in vessels having such interior finishes (such as resin coatings or polished surfaces), which reduced permeability. Based on these findings, one might be tempted to conclude that cooking vessels in archaeological assemblages would exhibit interior surface treatments. Later studies, however, established that under conditions more closely mimicking actual use, the differences in boiling time disappear. These results occur because, during cooking, food residues quickly clog the pores of the vessels, making even untreated and relatively porous vessels largely impermeable (Pierce 1999; Schiffer et al. 1994).

Third, even if a program of ongoing experiments identifies a consistent relationship between variables, it does not necessarily indicate that earlier potters recognized the relationship. For example, experiments conducted by Skibo and colleagues (1989) identified differences in impact resistance for tiles tempered with different materials. Although these differences were statistically significant, they were also minor. As a result, Skibo and his colleagues concluded that prehistoric potters would have been unaware of these differences and that the properties are unlikely to have influenced manufacturing decisions.

Fourth, even if potters were aware of a particular technological effect, it does not automatically follow that their awareness determined the manufacturing technology. Rather, studies have indicated that final vessel design results from a series of technological compromises, necessitated by the fact that any one variable may have both positive and negative effects (see Schiffer and Skibo 1997). For example, all other factors being held constant, the more temper a clay body has, the more resistant it will be to cracking during drying and firing. At the same time, however, increased amounts of temper have the effect of weakening the fired clay body. Decisions about how much temper to add, therefore, necessarily involve tradeoffs between desired results. Similar compromises are involved with temper size. Large temper particles tend to have the undesired effect of weakening the overall tensile strength of fired ceramic bodies, but they have the presumably desired effect of halting crack propagation. Because cracks can weaken a ceramic body, large temper particles can ultimately both strengthen and weaken ceramic vessels. The size and amount of temper particles used may therefore depend on a variety of functional needs (will the pot be subject to repeated thermal stress? to repeated impacts?) as well as on how the temper and those needs intersect with other technical choices (are weak-firing or strong-firing clays being used? is a large or small vessel being constructed?). In short, a potter must take into account a dizzying array of factors when choosing the materials and techniques to be used in the manufacture of any particular vessel.

Finally, factors other than technological ones can influence manufacturing decisions. Technological studies are often predicated on the belief that human beings will strive to maximize vessel performance and manufacturing efficiency. However, some researchers have begun to question this implicit assumption (e.g., Sillar 2000; Sillar and Tite 2000; Smith 2000; Tite, Kilikoglou, and Vekinis 2001). These archaeologists stress that ceramic technology can be influenced by social and ideological factors as well as functional ones and correctly note that such factors should be taken into account in interpretations based on experimental data. Experimental archaeology, by its nature, is better suited to the examination of technological factors than of social ones. Through experimental techniques, we can obtain information on the engineering principles that underlie pottery manufacture. To understand the degree to which these principles played a role in the potter's decision-making process, however, information about the social and historical contexts of the pottery production and use must be obtained. Such information can be acquired from a variety of sources, including ethnoarchaeology, historical documents, and the archaeological contexts of the ceramics.

Laboratory versus Field Experiments

The issues raised previously illustrate the importance of considering how comparable the experimental conditions are to those to which the archaeological ceramics were subjected. To minimize problems associated with generalizing between different sets of conditions, Feathers (1989:580) has proposed that experiments be designed to replicate prehistoric manufacturing and use conditions as closely as possible. Other researchers, however, have noted that such replicative experiments do not provide the controls needed to fully investigate any single variable of interest (Schiffer et al. 1994; Young and Stone 1990). These researchers have advocated standardizing production methods so that all factors are held constant except the variable of interest. The different viewpoints in essence center around whether experiments are best conducted as controlled laboratory experiments, in which as many variables as possible are held constant, or as field experiments, in which "experimenters give up some control of the variables, imposed in the previous stage, to test hypotheses under more natural (i.e., behaviorally relevant) conditions" (Skibo 1992:22).

As Skibo (1992) has pointed out, there is room for both kinds of experiments in a successful experimental program. By incorporating both types of experiments, the researcher can take advantage of the strengths while overcoming the weaknesses of each approach. Furthermore, it is noted that the roles of the two types of experiments differ. Controlled laboratory experiments are generally undertaken to identify general principles "that explain or describe the relationship between a technological property or material item and some behaviorally meaningful unit" (Skibo 1992:22). Field experiments, in contrast, should be undertaken to determine how and whether this relationship is relevant to the interpretation of any particular archaeological situation.

Developing Credible Inferences from Ceramic Experiments

Given the issues raised previously, how can credible inferences be derived from ceramic experimental data? W. David Kingery (1982) has proposed that two conditions must be met. First, he argues, we must begin with a hypothesis or question that can be made more or less plausible by examining its consequences. Hypotheses are confirmed but not proven by consequences that increase their plausibility. Second, he proposes, we should obtain as many confirmations as possible, ones that are "as sure as possible . . . as different as possible, and [that] . . . verge on being incredible unless our conjecture is true" (Kingery 1982:43).

These confirmations can be sought through various avenues. First, we should conduct as many experiments as possible, during which we control for as many different variables as possible. Expectations generated from laboratory experiments should be tested against results obtained under more archaeologically relevant conditions. Second, knowledge obtained from ceramic experiments should be tested against other data. The plausibility of inferences is increased by repeated archaeological or ethnoarchaeological patterns. As an example, Michael Tite and colleagues (2001) used archaeological data to test the expectation, generated from ceramic experiments, that the need for high thermal shock resistance structured the manufacturing decisions of prehistoric potters. After identifying a consistent correlation between cooking pots and technological attributes that favored thermal shock resistance, Tite and his colleagues concluded that thermal shock resistance did indeed influence technological choice. Finally, researchers can increase plausibility by identifying and ruling out other factors that might explain the established patterns (e.g., Feathers 2003). In considering these other factors, the social, economic, and ideological contexts should be considered as well as technological ones.

DESIGNING CERAMIC EXPERIMENTS

Prior to initiating a ceramic experiment, several issues must be considered. The first, rather obvious step is to identify the project goals. Why is the experiment being initiated? Is its purpose to understand the effects of a specific technical choice on vessel performance? To identify the manufacturing techniques used to create a particular ware? Or perhaps to evaluate the time and effort required to produce a particular ceramic type? After the goals have been explicitly defined, the next step should be a comprehensive review of the relevant literature (i.e., the experimental, archaeological, and material science literature). Minimally, as a starting point, the researcher should determine what, if any, other similar experiments have been conducted and how those experiments were carried out. Because much of our knowledge about how to design experiments has been learned through trial and error, the researcher may pick up important time-saving tips by reviewing past experimental studies.

The researcher must then decide to what degree the experimental variables will be held constant. Does the research question call for a controlled laboratory experiment, or is a field experiment more appropriate? Or, perhaps, should both types of experiments be conducted? What manufacturing techniques should be used? To what degree should the researcher attempt to duplicate the prehistoric or historic manufacturing techniques of interest? At this stage of the research design, several issues must be addressed.

1. *What types of clays should be used? Will the experiment be conducted using commercial or naturally occurring clays?* Depending on the research issue(s) involved, there are both advantages and disadvantages to each clay type. Advantages of commercial clays are that they are relatively cheap and easy to acquire, they can be obtained pre-mixed so little or no additional preparation is needed, and they are more homogeneous than natural clays (thus introducing less variability into the experiment). However, because they have been prepared to meet the needs of modern potters, most commercial clays are finer grained and require a higher temperature to sinter than do natural clays. (Sintering refers to the cementing of the clay particles, which occurs as the clay body is heated. A clay is said to have "sintered" when the hardening process is irreversible.) Thus, if the goal is to find a clay similar to that used by most prehistoric potters, the archaeologist may wish to collect natural clays. Failing that, he or she should try to purchase the commercial clays that mature at the lowest temperatures possible. If natural clays are to be used, the researcher should test to ensure that they are suitable for ceramic manufacture. A simple, preliminary test that can be undertaken in the field is the "bend test," in which the clay is wetted, rolled into a coil, and bent into a U-shape. If the clay cracks as it is bent, it is not suitable for ceramic manufacture.[2]

2. *How, if at all, should the clay be prepared?* Should the clay be ground? Wetted and aged? Mixed with other clays or additives to improve or reduce plasticity? Levigated to remove unwanted silt? In general, pre-mixed commercial clays will require little or no preparation (other than wedging and perhaps adding tempering

materials), whereas natural clays may need some type of preparation (although not all natural clays will). There are no simple methods to determine how and whether a particular clay will need to be prepared, although there are some guidelines. If the clay contains large inclusions, they should be removed by hand prior to mixing the clay body. If the clay is too plastic to handle, the researcher may wish to add tempering materials or mix it with a less plastic clay. If the clay lacks sufficient plasticity, several steps may be taken to improve workability, including grinding the clay, aging it, levigating it, mixing it with more plastic clays, and adding vinegar or other types of acidic materials (Rice 1987:63). To grind the clays, mechanical or manual methods may be used. Mechanical grinding of large quantities or rock-hard clays is best accomplished using a ball mill, available from most ceramic supply stores. Alternatively, I have used an inexpensive electric coffee grinder to pulverize small amounts of clays (this method works well as long as the clays are not too hard). Manual grinding can be done using a mano and metate or a mortar and pestle.[3] Regardless of the preparation technique used, the researcher would be wise to experiment with different methods before initiating the experiment to determine which method obtains the best results.

3. *What, if any, type(s) of tempers should be added to the clay, and in what proportion? How, if at all, should the temper(s) be prepared?* In rare cases, the addition of tempering materials is unnecessary. For example, some natural clays are essentially "self-tempered" because they contain appropriate inclusions. Pre-mixed commercial clays have generally already been tempered, although the tempers are often too small for archaeological purposes. (However, clays designed for large sculptures often contain large quantities of sand temper.) Almost any type of material can serve as a tempering agent. In prehistoric and historic sherds, archaeologists often find tempering materials as diverse as shell, bone, rock, sand, ground sherds, grasses, fibers, and hairs. The type and proportion of temper to be used will again depend on the research question being asked. If the goal is to replicate materials used prehistorically, the researcher should examine the archaeological sherds of interest to determine what was used in that assemblage. Additionally, he or she should note the texture of the tempers for clues as to how they should be processed. For example, sands may be collected from major streambeds (in which case they should be well-worn and rounded) or from closer to their sources (in which case they should be more angular and less worn). Sharply angular sand tempers may indicate that they were ground before being added to the clay body. If grog (i.e., ground sherd) is to be used, the researcher may wish to either grind fired ceramics or—to save time and effort—fire the ground clays themselves (Clint Swink, personal communication 2003).

4. *What form should be produced, and what forming techniques will be used?* Will the experiment be conducted on a ceramic vessel? Or a test tile? If a vessel is to

be made, what forming technique will be used? Many experiments require the use of vessels, ideally produced in the same manner as those found in the archaeological assemblage. However, few archaeologists have the skills necessary to produce such replicas. Because of this lack of skill and because many experiments require that the objects be of a standardized size and shape, archaeologists often prefer to experiment on test tiles or on vessels made using coil extruders, molds, or both to minimize unwanted variation (see Schiffer 1990b; Schiffer et al. 1994; Young and Stone 1990). Other archaeologists have hired modern-day potters to produce replicas using more traditional techniques (e.g., Courty and Roux 1995; Pierce 1999; Young and Stone 1990).

5. *What, if any, surface treatments will be added?* Will the object be slipped? Polished? Glazed? Painted? Smudged? Slipping consists of applying a thin fluid of clay suspended in liquid to the surface of the vessel. Although thin slips can be easily applied to wet or even bone-dry clays, thicker slips are best applied when the green ceramic is partially dried (but not yet to the leather-hard stage); care should be taken, however, not to apply thick slips too heavily, or they may crack or spall during drying and firing. Polishing, in contrast, should be conducted on leather-hard ceramics and is done by rubbing the ceramic surface repeatedly with a smooth object, such as a river-worn pebble. Glazes can be applied to the leather-hard surfaces of greenware but are more commonly applied to bisque-fired wares. Paints can be applied at virtually any stage prior to the final firing. Smudging is a process whereby the surface of the pottery is permanently blackened by exposing it to carbon. To smudge a ceramic, the object is removed from the fire while it is at its peak temperature and is placed in contact with a fine-grained organic material such as sawdust, pine needles, or manure. If only the interior of the vessel is to be smudged, it can be filled with the organic substance and placed upside down in a bed of sand until the vessel cools. If the entire ceramic object is to be smudged, it should be completely smothered by the organic material. When firing with an open fire, the organic material can simply be piled on top of the ceramic to completely smother it. When using a kiln, the ceramic should be removed while at its highest temperature and buried in a metal can filled with organics. (For an alternative method of smudging, see Bell 1994.) If the ceramic is to be removed from the kiln at its red-hot stage, safety precautions must be used to ensure that the researcher is not burned. Tongs should be employed to remove the ceramic object, and fire-resistant gloves and aprons should be worn (these can be purchased from most ceramic supply stores).

6. *How will the ceramic be fired?* Once the ceramic is fully dried, it is ready to be fired. (Note: if it is not fully dried, it will likely explode during the firing process.) At this point, the experimenter faces the decision of how it should be fired. Again, if the goal is to replicate prehistoric or historic conditions, the archaeologist should examine the sherds and other aspects of the archaeological record for clues about

the firing temperature and atmosphere. How closely should these conditions be copied? Is it more important to replicate the exact firing technology or to maintain control over the firing process? For example, although in many cases an outdoor open firing may be more authentic, such firings are characterized by highly variable and unpredictable conditions. If open firings, trench kiln firings, or simple kiln firings are to be used, the researcher may wish to monitor the variability by using a thermocouple and an oxygen probe to measure changes in the temperature and atmosphere. However, if tight control over the firing temperature and atmosphere is important, the use of a commercial kiln may be more appropriate. Most commercial kilns are electric and fire in an oxidizing atmosphere, although reducing kilns or raku kilns can be used to achieve a reducing or neutral atmosphere. Such kilns must be adequately ventilated, however, and the researcher should check with the kiln manufacturer for ventilation guidelines.

7. What, if any, specialized tests will be conducted? If strength tests are to be conducted, should they be designed to measure impact strength or tensile strength?[4] What type of testing device is most appropriate? (For information on strength testing devices and methods, see Beck 2002; Bronitsky and Hamer 1986; Feathers 1989; Mabry et al. 1988; Neupert 1994.) If thermal shock resistance is to be measured, what techniques should be used? (See Bronitsky 1986; Schiffer et al. 1994; Skibo, Schiffer, and Reid 1989; Tite, Kilikoglou, and Vekinis 2001 for information regarding various methods that have been used.) Which method of measuring heating and cooling effectiveness is most appropriate (see Pierce 1999; Schiffer 1990a, 1990b; Young and Stone 1990)? Which technique should be used to measure abrasion resistance? (Compare Skibo, Schiffer, and Reid 1989 and Vekinis and Kilikoglou 1998 for information on different methods.)

Regardless of the specific methods selected, the researcher should be prepared to run several tests. Some experiments may require different runs to systematically manipulate different variables. In other cases, it may take several runs just to determine which methods are most appropriate. Schiffer and colleagues (1994) recommend that prior to the initiation of the full-scale experiment, the researcher employ limited trials in which a small sample is used to run through the entire experiment. Such trials, they propose, enable the researcher to develop the skills and knowledge needed to conduct the actual experiment and minimize the amount of wasted effort.

Finally, the materials and methods used should be reported on as carefully and in as much detail as possible. For example, not only the type of temper is relevant, but the researcher should also report on the amount used and how it was mixed with the clay. If one part temper was added to two parts clay, were the proportions measured while the clay was dry or wet? Do measurements reflect volume or weight? Similarly, not only should the maximum firing temperature be reported, but the time taken to achieve that temperature and its holding time should also be noted. In short, report, report, and report! To aid in accurate reporting, the experimenter should keep a detailed laboratory notebook that is maintained throughout the experiment and updated at every stage as the experiment progresses.

EXPERIMENTAL DESIGN: CASE STUDIES

In this section I present two case studies that utilize experimental research to address archaeological problems. Neither study results in definitive answers to the questions posed. Rather, the projects are presented as examples of how (and how not) to design experimental projects and to explore some of the issues involved in the interpretation of experimental results. The first study was initiated more than a decade ago, when I directed excavations at a site known to have been a prehistoric ceramic production center. To investigate factors that may have contributed to the development of this craft specialization, a series of ceramic experiments was conducted. In retrospect, it is apparent that those early experiments contained design flaws, which I attempt to address here. The second study was undertaken to investigate whether ceramic smudging inhibits the growth of bacteria and fungi, as some researchers have suggested. The results of this study contribute to our understanding of how smudged vessels might have been used and whether they would have exhibited any advantages over non-smudged vessels for food storage.

Evaluating the Quality of Clays: The West Branch Project

The West Branch site represents the remains of a prehistoric Rincon phase (AD 900–1100) Hohokam village located in the Tucson Basin of southern Arizona. In 1993, while serving as a project director for Statistical Research, Inc. (SRI), I was fortunate to participate in the excavation of a portion of this large site. The initial set of experiments reported on here was conducted as a part of that project.

Earlier research had suggested that the residents of the village had specialized in ceramic production (Huntington 1986). The results of that research, combined with data obtained from more recent studies, indicate that a relatively high proportion of the pottery used and discarded in the basin during the Rincon phase was manufactured at the West Branch settlement (for a summary of these data, see Harry 2000; Heidke, Miksa, and Wallace 2002). To investigate what factors may have contributed to the development of this part-time craft specialization, in 1994 I initiated a set of ceramic experiments designed to evaluate the quality of the local clays. Specifically, the investigations focused on evaluating whether the clays located adjacent to the West Branch site exhibited more desirable qualities than clays found elsewhere in the basin.

The experiments were conducted in two stages. During the first stage, various clays were collected from around the Tucson Basin, and their manufacturing properties (i.e., ease of preparation, plasticity and handling, and drying and firing behavior) were evaluated. Laurel Thornberg, a professional potter skilled in hand-building techniques, was hired to make these assessments. Thirteen clay samples were submitted to her, including two collected from the riverbank adjacent to the West Branch site. Sample numbers were assigned to the clays, but she was not told the location from which each sample was collected. Thornberg processed all samples using a mortar and pestle, made them into test tiles, and fired them in a wood-burning kiln. Of the thirteen clays tested, Thornberg recognized only five as exhibiting the qualities needed for ceramic manufacture. The two West Branch clays were identified as having the best manufacturing qualities (for a summary of her findings, see Harry and Whittlesey 2004:table N.2).

The results support, but do not prove, the hypothesis that the West Branch residents were located near unusually high-quality clays compared with other residents of the basin. Because alluvial clays are ubiquitous along the various waterways that cross the basin, it is not feasible to test and evaluate all of the clays that would have been available prehistorically. Furthermore, these tests represent but a first step of evaluation, even for those clays that were sampled. The tests provide a first impression of the workability of the clays but do not inform on all manufacturing properties. For example, unresolved is how well each of the clays would perform during the manufacture of actual vessels. To what degree is each clay capable of supporting the weight of wet vessel walls during the manufacturing process? Do pigments and slips interact well with the clay, so that the desired colors are clearly visible after the firing process? Does the clay retain a polished surface and high gloss after firing? To resolve these and other issues, additional tests are necessary.

The second stage of experiments was designed to investigate whether the West Branch clays may have produced more durable (i.e., stronger) vessels than those made of other clays. To evaluate this question, seven clays collected from various areas of the basin were made into test tiles that were strength tested. These tiles were intended to mimic the manufacturing technology of the Hohokam sherds as closely as possible. Accordingly, attributes of Rincon phase sherds guided the manufacturing decisions. Tiles were made by adding one part sand temper to two parts wet clay, the ratio and temper type approximating those observed in the archaeological sherds. Clays were collected dry, ground in an electric coffee grinder, and mixed with water to make the wet clays. Clays were not aged but were used immediately. All of the tiles were tempered with sands collected from a secondary drainage running through the West Branch site. The sands were sieved, so the proportion of the various size ranges added to the clays approximated that found in the prehistoric sherds. After the clay and sands had been thoroughly mixed, the paste was flattened with a rolling pin to a uniform thickness of 7.9 mm and cut into circular tiles measuring 4 cm in diameter.[5] The round tiles were dried in a drying oven overnight and then fired to a temperature of 625°C with a twenty-minute soak (i.e., holding time) in an electronic oxidizing kiln. Although the Hohokam fired their ceramics in open fires, an oxidizing kiln was used for these experiments to minimize introduced variability.

For the purposes of these experiments, all variables were held constant except the clays. Twenty-five test tiles were made from each clay sample.

These initial strength tests were conducted in 1994 using the ball-on-three ball tester described by Mark Neupert (1994). To compare the strength of the test samples, the modulus of rupture (MOR) formula was used (see Neupert 1994:appendix B). This formula standardizes the test results obtained for different-sized specimens and was used because, despite the fact that the wet test tiles were all manufactured to the same specifications, slight size differences existed after firing.

The strength tests results are presented in Figure 2.1. These data show that the two strongest test tile groups are those made from the alluvial clays (Samples #12 and #20) collected from the riverbank adjacent to the West Branch site. With the exception of the test tiles made from Clay Sample #50, none of the other MOR values is encompassed within the 95 percent confidence intervals exhibited by the West Branch clay tiles. Significantly, Clay Sample #50 differed in texture from all the other clay samples. Unlike the others, this sample consisted of extremely fine, sticky clay that could not have been worked unless a far greater quantity of temper was added.

Based on these results, I speculated that vessels produced at the West Branch settlement may have been stronger than those produced elsewhere (Harry 2000). But is this speculation based on sound experimental design? In an effort to keep all variables constant other than the clays, I elected to use the same tempering materials for all test tile groups. Subsequently, however, it was suggested to me that by using sands recovered from within the West Branch site, I had "stacked the deck" in favor of the West Branch clays (James Heidke, personal communication 1996). This prospect was raised because of the expectation that West Branch sands would be more similar mineralogically to West Branch clays than to other clays. If true, the thermal expansion rate of those sands should closely mirror that of the West Branch clays, resulting in stronger test tiles for the West Branch groups.

Several lines of evidence suggest that Hohokam potters used locally available sands when tempering their clays (see Abbott 2000; Miksa and Heidke 1995). Thus, there is no reason to believe that prehistoric potters would ever have combined clays collected from one area of the basin with sands collected from another. In retrospect, therefore, it is clear that a more appropriate research design would have been to mix each clay sample with sands collected from the same vicinity as the clays. Regardless, it is unclear whether the West Branch sands are indeed more similar mineralogically to the West Branch clays than to other clays because the sands and the clays do not derive from the same bedrock source. The sands used in the test tiles originated from the bedrock formation underlying the West Branch site; the riverbank clays, however, originated at some unknown distance to the south and were re-deposited by flowing river waters.

To evaluate whether the West Branch sands were responsible for the results obtained earlier, ideally one would make additional test tiles using clays and sands

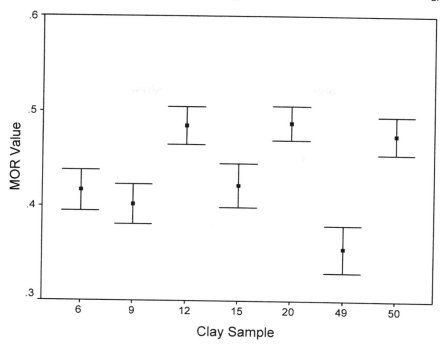

FIGURE 2.1 | Graph showing the results of the 1994 strength tests. Black squares indicate the mean MOR value obtained from each ceramic paste group. Error bars indicate the 95 percent confidence interval for the population mean. All test tiles were tempered with sands collected from the vicinity of the West Branch site. The two clays recovered from near the West Branch site are Samples #12 and #20. Sample size for all groups is twenty-five.

collected from the same area. Unfortunately, in the decade since the original strength tests were conducted, virtually all of the riverbanks in the Tucson Basin have been paved over, making it impossible to collect additional clays. Additionally, records from the original experiment did not indicate the speed at which the load was applied during the strength tests. Thus, even if we had enough clay to conduct new experiments with more appropriate sands, we would not have been able to compare our newly obtained results with those obtained in 1994.

This project illustrates several important points. First, in designing an experiment, the researcher should consider the implications of controlling as many of the variables as possible versus those of more closely replicating the prehistoric technology used. In the present case, my attempts to minimize variation initially led to the use of inappropriate tempering materials. Additionally, by adding the same proportion of sands to all the clays, I did not factor in the possibility that different clays would require different amounts of temper. In particular, although

Sample #50 produced relatively strong test tiles, the results are irrelevant because the paste recipe was unsuitable for ceramic manufacture. Second, the project results provide a somewhat humbling lesson about the importance of rigorous reporting. The failure to maintain files regarding the details of the strength testing conditions make it impossible to compare results from redesigned tests with those obtained earlier.

The project also illustrates the advantages and disadvantages of using experimental archaeology to address research questions. The experiments reported on here were undertaken to examine whether clay quality may have contributed to the development of the ceramic specialization. Although only partially evaluated here, an experimental approach has the capability to inform on whether the clays located nearest to the West Branch site exhibit better manufacturing qualities than do clays located elsewhere.[6]

As Kingery (1982) recommended, the research question addressed here is testable; that is, it can be made more or less plausible through additional research. The workability tests conducted by Laurel Thornberg support the hypothesis that the West Branch clays are easily worked compared with many other clays. The strength tests are considered inconclusive at this time. Further testing—using both experimental and archaeological data (for example, strength testing of the sherds)—could further increase or decrease the plausibility of the hypothesis.

Even if additional tests demonstrate that the vessels made at West Branch are of a higher quality than those made elsewhere, however, it does not prove that the quality of the clays was solely or even primarily responsible for the development of craft specialization. Elsewhere (Harry 2000), I have argued that the distribution of firewood and water in the basin also played a role. Additionally, nonfunctional factors may have been important. Finally, even if strength differences between the clays do exist, additional tests are needed to determine whether those differences were significant enough to have been detected by the people using the vessels. The experimental data play but a limited, albeit an important, role in beginning to address these questions.

Evaluating the Effects of Smudging on Food Preservation

Ceramic smudging refers to the process of permanently blackening the surface of pottery by causing the pores to become impregnated with carbon. Although variations can be employed (for example, see Bell 1994:54), most techniques involve waiting until the vessel being fired reaches its maximum heat and then covering it with a fine-grained organic substance such as powdered manure, sawdust, or rice chaff (LeFree 1975:63–65; Longacre, Xia, and Yang 2000; Shepard 1956:88). This process causes smoke, generated by the incomplete combustion of the fuel, to be deposited into the pores of the ceramic wall. Smudged vessels are often—although not always—highly polished, leading to a lustrous and decorative effect.

Several researchers (i.e., Crown 2000:255; Rogers 1980; Tankersley and Meinhard 1982) have proposed that smudging may have promoted the freshness of foods. Carbon, of course, is well recognized for its filtering properties; it has long been used to remove contaminants and impurities from various materials. As a result of this well-known property, it might be expected that the growth of fungi and bacteria would be delayed in smudged vessels and that foods stored in such containers would last longer. The experiments described in this section were undertaken to evaluate this hypothesis.

The objective in this case was to test the validity of a hypothesized principle rather than to evaluate whether smudging acted in a particular way in any particular setting. Accordingly, I had substantial leeway in designing this experiment, in terms of the type of pottery to be used, the food to be stored in the containers, and the climatic conditions under which the foods were to be stored. However, because I was most interested in understanding the potential role of smudging in prehistoric North American pottery, I elected to use ceramic containers that closely mimicked the general ceramic attributes reflected in that pottery.

The experiment consisted of placing food and liquids into containers from two groups, one of which consisted of smudged vessels and one of which consisted of unsmudged ones. In selecting the vessels, I had two goals in mind. First, I wanted the vessels to be as consistent in size, shape, thickness, porosity, and clay type as reasonably possible. Second, I wanted the vessels to have been hand built and fired under low temperatures, so that their porosity and hardness values would be similar to those exhibited by prehistoric North American sherds. Although I was capable of hand building and firing such vessels, I knew that any containers I might make would vary widely in size, shape, and thickness. Therefore, I elected to purchase completed vessels and re-fire them to make them smudged. The vessels used were flat-bottomed, terra cotta jars exhibiting restricted necks and openings. The owners of the business from which I purchased the jars indicated that they had been made in Mexico but had no information concerning how they were manufactured. Nonetheless, visual observation indicated that they were constructed by hand and fired at fairly low temperatures, probably in a wood-burning kiln. The hardness of the vessels and the ringing sound made when struck suggested that the degree of sintering between these wares and most prehistoric North American wares was similar.

I purchased fifteen pots, six larger vessels and nine smaller ones.[7] Within each of these two size groups the size, shape, and thickness of the pots were remarkably consistent. Prior to initiation of the smudging experiments, a single vessel was re-fired in an electronic oxidizing kiln to 1,000°C, at which temperature it was held for twenty minutes. This piece served as a "test piece" to determine the appropriate firing temperature to be used for the remaining pieces. The pot was removed immediately after the twenty-minute holding time and set out at room temperature to cool. Once it had cooled, the vessel was examined to see how it compared with the

FIGURE 2.2 | Ceramic vessels in the process of smudging. Pots are removed from the kiln at their peak temperature and inverted over sawdust in a bed of sand. Once the pots are cooled, they are turned upright and the sawdust is removed.

other vessels. Observations indicated that the vessel was redder and harder than the others, suggesting that its initial firing temperature had been much lower. Because I wanted the vessels to remain fairly porous so the carbon could easily impregnate the vessel walls, I decided to re-fire the remaining vessels at a lower temperature. This pot was not used in the remainder of the experiments.

The remaining fourteen vessels were re-fired in the same electronic oxidizing kiln to a temperature of 600°C. The pots were held at that temperature for twenty minutes, at which point they were immediately removed from the kiln with fire-resistant gloves. The pots that were not to be smudged were set aside to cool. The remaining pots were immediately filled with fine-grained sawdust, turned upside down, and then embedded in sand to ensure that the smoke would not escape (Figure 2.2). After the vessels had cooled, they were removed and emptied of any remaining sawdust. These smudged vessels were then scrubbed with water to remove any specks of debris that might remain and dried overnight in a drying oven at 125°C. This process created a heavily smudged interior for these vessels (Figure 2.3).

Two separate but related experiments were conducted to evaluate whether smudging enhances food preservation. In these experiments, foods were stored in the smudged and unsmudged vessels, and their conditions were monitored over the course of a few days. In these initial experiments, the goal was simply to assess the

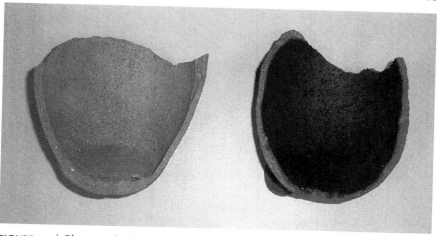

FIGURE 2.3 | Photograph showing the interior of the jars used in the ceramic experiments. Vessel on the left is plain; vessel on the right was smudged.

effects of smudging in general rather than to evaluate its effect on any particular foodstuffs or within any particular environmental setting. In selecting which foods to use, I avoided foods that might mildew at different rates even when stored in similar conditions. Thus, small, moist fruits, such as berries, were not used because of the likelihood that some berries would be riper than others. Instead, fruit juice, apples, and cheese were used. Pieces of apple were sectioned from a single apple, and those sections were then placed randomly in the various jars. The pieces of cheese also came from a single block cut and were placed randomly in the jars.

In the first experiment, the six larger vessels were filled with pasteurized juice, capped with ceramic lids (in this case, terra cotta planter bases purchased at a local garden store), and left in my garage for observation. (Note: these experiments were conducted in Las Vegas in the summer, so conditions were hot and dry.) After the first day I noticed that some of the apple juice had leaked out of the jars, so I again filled each jar to the brim. No other leaking occurred, indicating that the apple juice had plugged up the open pores. No attempt was made to control the climatic conditions under which the juice was stored, but a temperature and humidity gauge indicated that the daytime temperatures in my garage averaged in the low to mid-90s, and the humidity was around 18–20 percent. The contents of the jars were examined at twenty-four-hour intervals and my visual observations were recorded. These observations, summarized in Table 2.1, reveal no patterned differences between the conditions of the juice stored in the two groups (i.e., smudged and unsmudged) of jars.

In the second experiment, solid foods were placed in each of the eight smaller vessels. Initially, I placed apple sections in the vessels and stored the vessels in my

Table 2.1. Results of smudging experiments for vessels containing apple juice.

Vessel	Day 2	Day 4	Day 6
Smudged Vessels			
Vessel #1	A little scum forming on juice; no mold on jar interior	Abundant scum on juice; no mold on jar interior	Very nasty; scum on juice is very thick, though still no mold on jar interior
Vessel #2	Juice is clear; a small patch of mold forming on jar interior	Juice is still clear, but mold on jar interior is spreading	Very nasty; abundant scum on juice, mold is thick on jar interior
Vessel #3	Juice is clear; no mold on jar interior	Juice is still clear, but mold is starting to form on jar interior	Very nasty; abundant scum on juice, mold is spreading on jar interior
Plain Vessels			
Vessel #4	Juice is clear; small patches of mold forming on jar interior	Juice is still clear, but mold is starting to form on jar interior	Juice is still clear, but mold is expanding on jar interior
Vessel #5	Juice is clear; lots of mold on jar interior	Juice is still clear, but mold on jar interior is expanding	Very nasty; abundant scum on juice, mold on jar is quite thick
Vessel #6	Moderate amount of scum on juice; small amount of mold on jar interior	Moderate amount of scum on juice; mold on jar interior is now abundant	Very nasty; scum on juice is moderately thick and mold on jar interior is quite thick

garage. After four days, however, the apples were only slightly limp and showed no signs of mold or rotting. Accordingly, I abandoned that attempt and began the experiment again. This time I cut a block of cheddar cheese into eight equally sized pieces, which were set inside each jar. To facilitate the growth of mold, I created a humid environment by covering the jars with plastic wrap and placed them in an enclosed Rubbermaid tub filled with about ¼-inch of water. The jars were placed on stands to ensure that their bases did not rest in the water. Again, the condition of the cheese was observed every twenty-four hours. No change was observed for the cheese (other than sweating, or pooling of water on the surface) until Day 6. At that time, some small patches of mildew were observed. A subjective rating of 1 through 3 was assigned to the condition of each piece, with 1 reflecting the presence of light mildew and 3 reflecting fairly advanced mildew. The results of this experiment are presented in Table 2.2. Again, the data show no marked difference between the preservation of the cheese stored in the smudged versus the unsmudged vessels.

The results of these two sets of experiments contradict the expectation that smudging would have preserved stored foods. Theoretically, the carbon deposited by smudging should act as a desiccant, which should keep the food drier and inhibit

Table 2.2. Results of smudging experiments for vessels containing cheese.

Vessel	Day 6	Day 7
Smudged Vessels		
Vessel #1	A few small pea-size dots of mildew are visible (rating = 1)	A few small pea-size dots of mildew are visible (rating = 1)
Vessel #2	A few small pea-size dots of mildew are visible (rating = 1)	A few small pea-size dots of mildew are visible (rating = 1)
Vessel #3	Mildew is relatively abundant (rating = 1.5)	Mildew has grown, is now "hairy" (rating = 2)
Vessel #4	A few small pea-size dots of mildew are visible (rating = 1)	Mildew is very bad (rating = 3)
Plain Vessels		
Vessel #5	A few small pea-size dots of mildew are visible (rating = 1)	A few small pea-size dots of mildew are visible (rating = 1)
Vessel #6	A few small pea-size dots of mildew are visible (rating = 1)	Mildew is relatively bad (rating = 2)
Vessel #7	A few small pea-size dots of mildew are visible (rating = 1)	Mildew is very bad (rating = 3)
Vessel #8	A few small pea-size dots of mildew are visible (rating = 1)	Mildew is very bad (rating = 3)

the development of bacteria and mold. However, the amount of carbon deposited is likely to be insufficient to result in behaviorally noticeable effects. Although carbon is one of the best materials for adsorbing molecules, in its ordinary state its capacity is low. To overcome this problem, modern-day companies that use carbon filters "activate" the carbon through a complex process that substantially increases its surface area and absorption capacity. The inactivated carbon deposited during the smudging process, in contrast, likely would have been relatively quickly loaded. Furthermore, once loaded, it would be unable to adsorb additional molecules unless heated again almost to a red heat (Henry Bungay, professor of chemical and environmental engineering, Rensselaer Polytechnical Institute, personal communication 2001).

The conclusions reached here are strongly suggestive but not yet definitive. In these experiments, the carbon penetrated about 9 mm into the base of the vessel but only about 1.5 mm into the side walls. This relatively thin layer of smudging is typical of that found in many prehistoric Southwestern ceramics. However, in some prehistoric and historic wares, smudging can penetrate the entire thickness of the wall (Ellis 1992; Rogers 1980:2). It is possible that thicker smudging would have resulted in noticeable results. Additional experiments should be undertaken to investigate this possibility. Even if significant results are obtained, however, experiments should be repeated within the same vessel to determine how long the vessel maintains its preservation characteristics. Finally, additional tests should be made comparing unpolished and polished smudged wares. As noted, smudged vessels are typically also highly polished. However, this polishing process will close off pores, which may inhibit the adsorptive capacity of the carbon (Henry Bungay, personal communication 2001).

CONCLUDING THOUGHTS

Ceramic experimental archaeology is entering an exciting new phase. Early experimental work demonstrated the ability of such projects to contribute to our understanding of archaeological ceramics. More recent experiments have shown how far we still have to go. We are beginning to understand the complexity of ceramic behavior, and it has become clear that answers cannot be acquired easily from single and quickly conducted experiments. The need for an ongoing program of experiments that builds upon the knowledge obtained from earlier experiments is apparent. This statement is not intended to discourage researchers from conducting individual experiments; on the contrary, the more researchers involved in ceramic experimental research, the more rapidly we will be able to expand our knowledge. Rather, such experiments should be designed so they build upon work previously conducted by others, and they should be fully reported to enable others, in turn, to build upon them.

I close with two appeals. First, I encourage archaeologists to continue to conduct archaeological experiments and to communicate with other archaeologists regarding their experiences, methods, and findings. Because so much of what we know has been learned through trial and error, it is essential that archaeologists collaborate with one another and share the lessons learned in their own experiments. Second, I argue that archaeologists need to develop greater skills to allow them to design and carry out experiments using traditional techniques. I encourage students who wish to pursue archaeological ceramic analysis both to take ceramics classes and to work with (or apprentice under) practitioners of traditional technologies to learn the methods.

NOTES

1. Grinding or aging of clays generally increases their plasticity.

2. It may be possible, however, to make the clay workable by levigating a sample to remove the coarser sediments (see Rice 1987:118; Rye 1981:18). Levigation refers to a method of separating fine from coarser material by mixing it with water and letting the coarser material settle at the bottom. The finer-grained sediments are then removed and used in the clay body.

3. When grinding clays or working with them in their powdered state, wear a mask to avoid inhaling the silica dust. Inhalation of silica dust can cause serious damage to the lungs

and increases the likelihood of certain types of diseases, such as silicosis, bronchitis, tuberculosis, and lung cancer.

4. Impact strength refers to the ability of the ceramic to resist fractures from an applied blow to a small area. Tensile strength refers to the ability of the ceramic to withstand slow applied pressure under a bending load.

5. To achieve a uniform thickness, the clay was rolled out between two thickness strips measuring 7.9 mm. Thickness strips of various sizes are available at most ceramic supply stores. The circular tiles were cut using a round cookie cutter.

6. The research reported on here does not begin to exhaust this issue. Additional tests are needed to more fully evaluate the clay qualities. To better evaluate this issue, experiments are needed that include the use of more clays and explore additional performance characteristics not yet investigated, such as the ability of the clay to hold a polish and to maintain its shape during manufacture (to name but two). Furthermore, the various clays might perform differently under different manufacturing conditions—for example, using a different combination of clay and temper or different methods of processing the clay.

7. The larger vessels averaged 6½ inches tall and 4½ inches wide (at the widest point). The smaller vessels averaged 4½ inches tall and 4¼ inches wide (at the widest point). Two different sizes of pots were purchased for the simple reason that the store's inventory contained no more than nine vessels of any one size.

REFERENCES CITED

Abbott, D. R.
2000   *Ceramics and Community Organization among the Hohokam*. University of Arizona Press, Tucson.

Arnold, P. J., III
2000   Working without a Net: Recent Trends in Ceramic Ethnoarchaeology. *Journal of Archaeological Research* 8(2):105–133.

Beck, M. E.
2002   The Ball-on-Three Ball Test for Tensile Strength: Refined Methodology and Results for Three Hohokam Ceramic Types. *American Antiquity* 67(3):558–569.

Bell, J.
1994   Making Pottery at Mata Ortiz. *Kiva* 60(1):33–70.

Bjørn, A.
1969   *Exploring Fire and Clay*. Van Nostrand Reinhold, New York.

Blinman, E., and C. Swink
1993   Technology and the Organization of Anasazi Trench Kilns. In *Ceramics and Civilization*, vol. 7: *The Prehistory of Ceramic Kilns*, ed. P. Rice, 85–102. The American Ceramic Society, Westerville, Ohio.

Braun, D. P.
1983   Pots as Tools. In *Archaeological Hammers and Theories*, ed. A. Keene and J. Moore, 107–134. Academic Press, New York.

Bronitsky, G.
   1986   The Use of Materials Science Techniques in the Study of Pottery Construction
            and Use. *Advances in Archaeological Method and Theory* 9:209–276.

Bronitsky, G., and R. Hamer
   1986   Experiments in Ceramic Technology: The Effects of Various Tempering Mate-
            rials on Impact and Thermal-Shock Resistance. *American Antiquity* 51(1):89–
            101.

Chiang, Y., D. P. Birnie III, and W. D. Kingery
   1997   *Physical Ceramics.* J. Wiley & Sons, New York.

Clark, J. E.
   2002   Ancient Technology, Justifiable Knowledge, and Replication Experiments. In
            *Traditions, Transitions, and Technology: Themes in Southwestern Archaeology,
            Proceedings of the 2000 Southwest Symposium*, ed. S. H. Schlanger, 259–271.
            University Press of Colorado, Boulder.

Costin, C. L.
   2000   The Use of Ethnoarchaeology for the Archaeological Study of Ceramic Produc-
            tion. *Journal of Archaeological Method and Theory* 7:377–403.

Courty, M. A., and V. Roux
   1995   Identification of Wheel Throwing on the Basis of Ceramic Surface Features and
            Microfabrics. *Journal of Archaeological Science* 22:17–50.

Crown, P. L.
   2000   Women's Role in Changing Cuisine. In *Women and Men in the Prehispanic
            Southwest: Labor, Power, and Prestige*, ed. P. L. Crown, 221–266. School of
            American Research Press, Santa Fe.

Ellis, L. W.
   1992   Technological Style in Upper Texas Coastal Ceramics: A Case Study from
            41HR616, Harris County, Texas. MA thesis, Department of Anthropology, Uni-
            versity of Texas at Austin.

Feathers, J. K.
   1989   Effects of Temper on Strength of Ceramics: Response to Bronitsky and Hamer.
            American Antiquity 54(3):579–588.
   2003   Comments on M. S. Tite, V. Kilikoglou and G. Vekinis, "Review Article:
            Strength, Toughness and Thermal Shock Resistance of Ancient Ceramics, and
            Their Influence on Technological Choice," *Archaeometry* 43(3) (2001), 301–
            324, Comments I: Accounting for Ceramic Change. *Archaeometry* 45(1):163–
            169.

Frink, L., and K. G. Harry
   2008   The "Beauty" of Ugly Eskimo Cooking Pots. *American Antiquity* 73(1):103–
            120.

Gosselain, O. P.
   1992   Bonfire of the Enquiries: Pottery Firing Temperatures in Archaeology: What
            For? *Journal of Archaeological Science* 19:243–259.

Grimshaw, R. W.
  1971   *The Chemistry and Physics of Clays and Allied Ceramic Materials*, 4th ed. Iley-
             Interscience, New York.

Harry, K. G.
  2000   Community-Based Craft Specialization: The West Branch Site. In *The Hohokam
             Village Revisited*, ed. D. E. Doyel, S. K. Fish, and P. R. Fish, 187–220. South-
             western and Rocky Mountain Division of the American Association for the
             Advancement of Science, Fort Collins, Colo.
  2004   Investigations into Ceramic Technology. In *Archaeological Investigations at the
             SRI Locus of the West Branch Site, Tucson, Arizona,* vol. 2: *Synthesis and Inter-
             pretations,* ed. S. M. Whittlesey, 271–282. Statistical Research, Inc., Technical
             Series 80. Statistical Research, Inc., Tucson.

Harry, K. G., and L. Frink
  2009   The Arctic Cooking Pot: Why Was It Adopted? *American Anthropologist* 111(3):
             330–343.

Harry, K. G., L. Frink, A. Charest, and B. O'Toole
  2009   How to Make an Unfired Clay Cooking Pot: Understanding the Technological
             Choices Made by Arctic Potters. *Journal of Archaeological Method and Theory*
             16(1):33–50.

Harry, K. G., L. Frink, C. Swink, and C. Dangerfield
  In press   An Experimental Approach to Understanding Thule Pottery Technology. Ms.
             submitted to *North American Anthropology.*

Harry, K. G., and S. Whittlesey (editors)
  2004   *Pots, Potters and Models: Archaeological Investigations at the SRI Locus of the
             West Branch Site,* vol. 1: *Feature Descriptions, Material Culture, and Specialized
             Analyses.* Statistical Research, Inc., Technical Series 80. Statistical Research,
             Inc., Tucson.

Hegmon, M.
  2000   Advances in Ceramic Ethnoarchaeology. *Journal of Archaeological Method and
             Theory* 7:129–137.

Heidke, J. M., E. J. Miksa, and H. D. Wallace
  2002   A Petrographic Approach to Sand-Tempered Pottery Provenance Studies:
             Examples from Two Hohokam Local Systems. In *Ceramic Production and Cir-
             culation in the Greater Southwest: Source Determination by INAA and Comple-
             mentary Mineralogical Investigations,* ed. D. M. Glowacki and H. Neff, 152–
             178. Cotsen Institute of Archaeology Monograph 44. University of California,
             Los Angeles.

Helton, C. K.
  2001   The Pointed Pot Phenomenon: Testing Strength. Paper presented at the 66th
             Annual Meeting of the Society for American Archaeology, New Orleans.

Hensler, K. N.
  1999   Anasazi Ceramic Traditions: A View from the Cove. In *Anasazi Community
             Development in Cove–Redrock Valley: Final Report on the Cove–Red Valley*

Archaeological Project along the N33 Road in Apache County, Arizona, ed. P. F. Reed and K. N. Hensler, 551–686. Navajo Nation Papers in Anthropology 33. Navajo Nation Archaeology Department, Window Rock, Ariz.

Hensler, K. N., and E. Blinman
2000   Experimental Ceramic Technology: Or, the Road to Ruin(s) Is Paved with Crack(ed) Pots. In *Traditions, Transitions, and Technology: Themes in Southwestern Archaeology, Proceedings of the 2000 Southwest Symposium,* ed. S. H. Schlanger, 366–385. University Press of Colorado, Boulder.

Hoard, R. J., M. J. O'Brien, M. G. Khorasgany, and V. S. Gopalaratnam
1995   A Materials-Science Approach to Understanding Limestone-Tempered Pottery from the Midwestern United States. *Journal of Archaeological Science* 22:823–832.

Holstein, H. O.
1973a   Pottery Reproduction: A Technical Study. *Pennsylvania Archaeologist* 43(2): 39–50.
1973b   Replication of Late Woodland Ceramics from Western Pennsylvania. *Pennsylvania Archaeologist* 43(3–4):75–87.

Huntington, F. W.
1986   *Archaeological Investigations at the West Branch Site: Early and Middle Rincon Occupation in the Southern Tucson Basin.* Anthropological Papers no. 5. Institute for American Research, Tucson.

Kilikoglou, V., G. Vekinis, Y. Maniatis, and P. M. Day
1998   Mechanical Performance of Quartz-Tempered Ceramics: Part I, Strength and Toughness. *Archaeometry* 40(2):261–279.

Kingery, W. D.
1960   *Introduction to Ceramics.* J. Wiley & Sons, New York.
1982   Plausible Inferences from Ceramic Artifacts. In *Archaeological Ceramics,* ed. J. S. Olin and A. D. Franklin, 37–45. Smithsonian Institution Press, Washington, D.C.

Klemptner, L. F., and P. F. Johnson
1985   An Analytical Approach to the Technological Development of Mississippian Pottery. In *Ceramics and Civilization,* vol. 1: *Ancient Technology to Modern Science,* ed. W. D. Kingery, 101–112. The American Ceramic Society, Columbus, Ohio.
1986   Technology and the Primitive Potter: Mississippian Pottery Development Seen through the Eyes of a Ceramic Engineer. In *Ceramics and Civilization,* vol. 2: *Technology and Style,* ed. W. D. Kingery, 250–271. The American Ceramic Society, Columbus, Ohio.

LeFree, B.
1975   *Santa Clara Pottery Today.* University of New Mexico Press, Albuquerque.

London, G.
1981   Dung-Tempered Clay. *Journal of Field Archaeology* 8:189–195.

Longacre, W. A., J. Xia, and T. Yang
  2000   I Want to Buy a Black Pot. *Journal of Archaeological Method and Theory* 7(4): 273–293.

Mabry, J., J. M. Skibo, M. B. Schiffer, and K. Kvamme
  1988   Use of a Falling-Weight Tester for Assessing Ceramic Impact Strength. *American Antiquity* 53:829–839.

MacIver, R.
  1921   On the Manufacture of Etruscan and Other Ancient Black Wares. *Man* 21:86–88.

Miksa, E., and J. M. Heidke
  1995   Drawing a Line in the Sands: Models of Ceramic Temper Provenance. In *The Roosevelt Community Development Study: Ceramic Chronology, Technology, and Economics*, vol. 2, ed. J. M. Heidke and M. T. Stark, 133–206. Anthropological Papers no. 14. Center for Desert Archaeology, Tucson.

Million, M.
  1975   Ceramic Technology of the Nodena Phase Peoples. *Southeastern Archaeological Conference Bulletin* 18:201–208.

Neupert, M. A.
  1993   Strength Analysis of the Transwestern Ceramic Assemblage. In *Ceramic Interpretations*, ed. B. J. Mills, C. E. Goetze, and M. N. Zedeño, 279–300. Across the Colorado Plateau: Anthropological Studies along the San Juan Basin and Transwestern Mainline Expansion Pipeline Routes, vol. 16. Office of Contract Archeology and the Maxwell Museum of Anthropology, University of New Mexico, Albuquerque.
  1994   Strength Testing Archaeological Ceramics: A New Perspective. *American Antiquity* 59(4):709–723.

O'Brien, C.
  1980   An Experiment in Pottery Firing. *Antiquity* 54:57–59.

Pierce, C. D.
  1999   Explaining Corrugated Pottery in the American Southwest: An Evolutionary Approach. PhD dissertation, Department of Anthropology, University of Washington, Seattle. UMI Microfilms, Ann Arbor, Mich.

Plog, S.
  1986   Understanding Cultural Change in the Northern Southwest. In *Spatial Organization and Exchange: Archaeological Survey on Northern Black Mesa*, ed. S. Plog, 310–338. Southern Illinois University Press, Carbondale.

Rice, P. M.
  1987   *Pottery Analysis: A Sourcebook*. University of Chicago Press, Chicago.

Rogers, R. N.
  1980   The Chemistry of Pottery Smudging. *Pottery Southwest* 7:2–4.

Rye, O. S.
  1981   *Pottery Technology: Principles and Reconstruction*. Taraxacum, Washington, D.C.

Schiffer, M. B.
   1990a   Technological Change in Water-Storage and Cooking Pots: Some Predictions from Experiment. In *The Changing Roles of Ceramics in Society: 26,000 B.P. to the Present*, ed. W. D. Kingery, 119–136. The American Ceramic Society, Westerville, Ohio.
   1990b   The Influence of Surface Treatment on Heating Effectiveness of Ceramic Vessels. *Journal of Archaeological Science* 17:373–381.
   2003   Comments on M. S. Tite, V. Kilikoglou and G. Vekinis, "Review Article: Strength, Toughness and Thermal Shock Resistance of Ancient Ceramics, and Their Influence on Technological Choice," *Archaeometry* 43(3) (2001), 301–324, Comments II: Properties, Performance Characteristics, and Behavioural Theory in the Study of Technology. *Archaeometry* 45(1):169–172.

Schiffer, M. B., and J. M. Skibo
   1987   Theory and Experiment in the Study of Technological Change. *Current Anthropology* 28(5):595–622.
   1989   A Provisional Theory of Ceramic Abrasion. *American Anthropologist* 91:102–116.
   1997   The Explanation of Artifact Variability. *American Antiquity* 62(1):27–50.

Schiffer, M. B., J. M. Skibo, T. Boerlke, M. Neupert, and M. Aronson
   1994   New Perspectives on Experimental Archaeology: Surface Treatments and Thermal Response of the Clay Cooking Pot. *American Antiquity* 59:197–217.

Shepard, A. O.
   1956   *Ceramics for the Archaeologist*. Carnegie Institution of Washington Publication 609. Carnegie Institution, Washington, D.C.

Sillar, B.
   2000   Dung by Preference: The Choice of Fuel as an Example of How Andean Pottery Production Is Embedded within Wider Technical, Social and Economic Practices. *Archaeometry* 42(1):43–60.
   2003   Comments III: Technological Choices and Experimental Archaeology. *Archaeometry* 45(1):173–181.

Sillar, B., and M. S. Tite
   2000   The Challenge of "Technological Choices" for Materials Science Approaches in Archaeology. *Archaeometry* 42(1):2–20.

Skibo, J. M.
   1992   *Pottery Function: A Use-Alteration Perspective*. Plenum, New York.

Skibo, J. M., and M. B. Schiffer
   1987   The Effects of Water on Processes of Ceramic Abrasion. *Journal of Archaeological Science* 14:83–96.

Skibo, J. M., M. B. Schiffer, and T. Butts
   1997   Ceramic Surface Treatment and Abrasion Resistance: An Experimental Study. *Journal of Archaeological Science* 24:311–317.

Skibo, J. M., M. B. Schiffer, and K. C. Reid
  1989   Organic-Tempered Pottery: An Experimental Study. *American Antiquity* 54(1): 122–146.

Smith, A. S.
  2000   Processing Clay for Pottery in Northern Cameroon: Social and Technical Requirements. *Archaeometry* 42(1):21–42.

Stark, M. T.
  2003   Current Issues in Ceramic Ethnoarchaeology. *Journal of Archaeological Research* 11(3):193–242.

Steponaitis, V.
  1984   Technological Studies of Prehistoric Pottery from Alabama: Physical Properties and Vessel Function. In *The Many Dimensions of Pottery*, ed. S. van der Leeuw and A. Pritchard, 79–121. University of Amsterdam, Netherlands.

Stimmell, C., R. B. Heimann, and R.G.V. Hancock
  1982   Indian Pottery from the Mississippi Valley: Coping with Bad Raw Materials. In *Archaeological Ceramics*, ed. J. S. Olin and A. D. Franklin, 219–228. Smithsonian Institution Press, Washington, D.C.

Swink, C.
  1993   Limited Oxidation Firing of Organic Painted Pottery in Anasazi-Style Trench Kilns. *Pottery Southwest* 20:1–5.

Tankersley, K., and J. Meinhard
  1982   Physical and Structural Properties of Ceramic Materials Utilized by a Fort Ancient Group. *Midcontinental Journal of Archaeology* 7(2):225–231.

Tite, M. S., V. Kilikoglou, and G. Vekinis
  2001   Strength, Toughness and Thermal Shock Resistance of Ancient Ceramics, and Their Influence on Technological Choice. *Archaeometry* 43(3):301–324.

Vekinis, G., and V. Kilikoglou
  1998   Mechanical Performance of Quartz-Tempered Ceramics: Part II: Hertzian Strength, Wear Resistance and Applications to Ancient Ceramics. *Archaeometry* 40(2):281–292.

Wallace, D.
  1989   Functional Factors of Mica and Ceramic Burnishing. In *Pottery Technology: Ideas and Approaches*, ed. G. Bronitsky, 33–39. Westview, Boulder.

Young, L. C., and T. Stone
  1990   The Thermal Properties of Textured Ceramics: An Experimental Study. *Journal of Field Archaeology* 17:195–203.

CHAPTER THREE

Ceramic Vessel Use and Use Alteration: Insights from Experimental Archaeology

Margaret E. Beck

○ ○ ○
○ ○ ○
○ ○ ○

What happened here? Archaeologists answer this question in increasingly sophisticated ways, squeezing more and more information about human behavior from used and discarded tools. Because different activities physically and chemically alter tools in different ways, these alterations suggest how the tools were used. This chapter addresses the use alteration of ceramic vessels. Alteration patterns may reveal if a vessel was used for cooking, storage, or transport; whether it was directly or indirectly heated; how it was handled and how heavily; and something about the nature of its contents. Vessel form is another important line of evidence for intended use (Henrickson and McDonald 1983), but alteration develops from actual use and may indicate multiple functions or reuse for other purposes (Schiffer 1989).

Valuable overviews of ceramic use alteration appear in James Skibo (1992a), who describes use-alteration processes, and Michael Schiffer (1989), who compares use-alteration studies between the fields of ceramic analysis and lithic analysis and defines basic terms. This chapter summarizes the current state of ceramic use-alteration research, incorporating recent publications, and also points out areas for future experimental work. Although the focus of this chapter and the volume overall is on experimental archaeology, it is impossible to completely separate experimental from ethnoarchaeological research on ceramic use alteration (Skibo 1992b). Both avenues of investigation belong to the actualist strategy of behavioral archaeology (Reid, Schiffer, and Rathje 1975; Schiffer 1976; Schiffer et al. 2001).

PREVIOUS RESEARCH

Archaeological inferences, including the interpretation of use-alteration patterns, require an understanding of cause and effect. Dynamic activities must be linked to their static material traces so that when the end product alone is visible, the processes or events that created it can be inferred. These links, or correlates (Schiffer 1995:36), can only be formulated in the present, either by observing the ongoing behavior of others or by mimicking the behavior in experiments under controlled conditions (Schiffer 1995:70). The study of the relationship between "behavior and material derivatives" has been termed middle-range research (Binford 1981:29).

Ceramic use-alteration studies may use data from both strategies: (1) observations of behavior and the resulting material patterns, and (2) experimental replication. Dorothy Griffiths (1978:70), in her study of attrition on historical period ceramics, found it "most useful to examine the use-marks on modern ceramics in constant, specialized use at home and in restaurants." The actual alteration-producing behavior was not directly observed, but Griffiths believed she was already sufficiently familiar with it. Other early studies that do not specify how they link alteration to the degree and type of use (e.g., Bray 1982; Fenner 1977) probably involve similar informal comparisons between generalized behavior and the expected material patterns. The most reliable data of this type come from systematic ethnoarchaeological observations of vessel use accompanied by detailed descriptions of the resulting alteration (Arthur 2000, 2002, 2003; Kobayashi 1994; Reid and Young 2000; Skibo 1992a).

Used vessels, however, only reveal how alteration occurs in one setting, involving one type of ceramic technology and a limited range of specific behaviors. To generalize from these cases to others requires an understanding of alteration processes under varying conditions. Experiments provide this by allowing researchers to systematically alter individual variables. For example, Skibo (1992a:157) conducted experiments on soot deposition and removal, a line of research started by David Hally (1983), to see what variables contributed to the soot patterns on his ethnoarchaeological vessels. In other cases, researchers attempt to predict what alteration should result from different activities based on ethnographic descriptions of use (Beck 2001; Jones 1989:358). Because such behaviors may no longer be directly observable anywhere in the world, experiments are ideal for testing hypothesized alteration patterns.

The middle-range research concerned directly with vessel use is limited, although multiple use-alteration analyses draw upon this work (e.g., Arthur 2001; Hally 1986; Hardin and Mills 2000; Henrickson 1990; Sassaman 1993; Skibo and Blinman 1999). Most of the experimental work, allied with materials science, focuses on how ceramic surfaces are modified and how the same alteration process may produce different results on different ceramic materials. It addresses general processes such as abrasion (Schiffer and Skibo 1989; Skibo and Schiffer 1987; Skibo, Butts, and Schiffer 1997), thermal damage (Schiffer et al. 1994), salt erosion (O'Brien 1990), and freeze-thaw action (Skibo, Schiffer, and Reid 1989) and includes alteration that may be natural rather than cultural in origin. This work, although less frequently cited in use-alteration studies, is equally important for accurate interpretations of alteration.

Forms of use alteration can be divided into accretion and attrition (Skibo 1992a:39–42). Accretion includes both carbon deposition and accumulation of residues from contents. Attrition, or "wear," includes abrasion, scratches, chipping, and pitting. These forms of alteration and their major causes are described next.

Carbon Deposits

Carbon deposits have been used to infer the functions of vessels that are thousands of years old (Sassaman 1993; Skibo and Blinman 1999). They result "from combustion of organic material and deposition of the resultant carbonized matter on or in some cases into the porous and permeable ceramic wall" (Skibo 1992a:147). Carbon deposits are the best way of identifying vessels used for cooking and may be the most common, or at least the most easily interpreted, form of ceramic use alteration. Therefore, carbon deposits are described more extensively here than are other forms of use alteration. Deposits may develop during use or during the original firing of the vessel. Subsequent heating may remove previous carbon deposits or add more, depending upon the availability of oxygen in the environment and the temperature reached. In all of these cases, the processes involved are similar, and it is important to understand them to distinguish use from non-use alteration.

Carbon deposition on the vessel surface may first occur, intentionally or unintentionally, during firing. One source of carbon is naturally occurring organic matter in pottery clays. Owen Rye (1981:115–118) describes the appearance of vessels under varying firing conditions and with or without organic matter in the clay. During vessel firing, carbon in the paste starts to oxidize to CO and CO_2 at about 200°C and moves to the surface from within the wall. Temperatures above 600°C and the circulation of oxygen are necessary to visibly remove the carbon (Rice 1987:88). Temperatures as high as 1,000°C may be needed for clays with high levels of organic matter (Johnson et al. 1988). In a reducing atmosphere, with insufficient oxygen, carbon monoxide forms, and carbon "will usually remain in the pores of vessels" (Rye 1981:108).

The circulation of oxygen is often not uniform across vessels, creating firing clouds (Rye 1981:120). Firing clouds appear wherever the flow of oxygen was restricted, generally where fuel touched vessel surfaces, where vessels touched one another during firing and cooling (often on vessel sides), and inside the neck and upper body of the interior or on the entire interior.

Potters may intentionally produce a black surface by use of a reducing atmosphere near the end of firing. Known as smudging, this process involves the deposition of additional carbon (Rice 1987:158; Rye 1981:115; Shepard 1985:88–90) by covering hot, just-fired pots with a layer of manure, chaff, sawdust, or other fine combustible material that adds carbon and cuts off the flow of oxygen. Some modern potters in the Philippines still use this surface treatment (Longacre, Xia, and Yang 2000).

Use of the vessel for cooking also produces exterior and interior carbon deposits. Exterior carbon deposits, or soot, result from placement over an open fire. Carbon, resins, and other materials are released from the burning fuel and, under the right conditions, are deposited on the vessel surface (Rice 1987:235; Skibo 1992a:152). While the initial, black "fluffy" soot layer can be wiped off, the underlying layer is durable (Skibo 1992a:159). Sooting and the deliberate surface treatment of smudging are "not readily distinguishable" but generally differ in placement, thickness, and the appearance of fine cracking in thicker soot deposits (Hally 1983:9). Use-related interior carbon deposits are charred food residues (Kobayashi 1994:144; Skibo 1992a:148). Their patterning results not only from the presence of food but also from the vessel wall temperature, which is affected by the distance to the heat source and the presence of water within the vessel.

Oxidation, or heating in the presence of abundant oxygen, removes carbon both within and on vessel walls and can happen during use as well as firing (Hally 1983:11; Rye 1981:108; Skibo 1992a:159). During cooking, oxidation might remove not only exterior carbon but also organic matter in the vessel wall, "possibly leaving a patch that would be lighter in color than the original ceramic surface" (Skibo 1992a:159).

Masashi Kobayashi (1994) and Skibo (1992a) have described carbon deposition from vessel use in the Kalinga community of Guina-ang in the Pasil River Valley, northwestern Luzon, the Philippines. Their research focused on differences between the two local cooking vessel types, the *oppaya* and *ittoyom*. An *oppaya* is short, with a wide mouth for stirring vegetables while they boil. An *ittoyom* is taller, with a narrower rim and neck to help keep steam inside for cooking rice. Both types are used for cooking over an open fire, and the exteriors of both kinds quickly accumulate soot deposits that become more extensive with age.

Two kinds of soot have been identified on ethnoarchaeological, experimental, and archaeological vessels: glossy soot and dull soot (Hally 1983; Skibo 1992a). Sooting experiments (Hally 1983:8–12; Skibo 1992a:157–162) have demonstrated that temperature controls which types of soot will be deposited on the surface (Figure 3.1). As noted previously, the vessel surface may be oxidized where the heat is greatest, directly above the flames. The soot accumulating higher on the vessel body includes "fluffy" dull black soot that can be removed by washing and

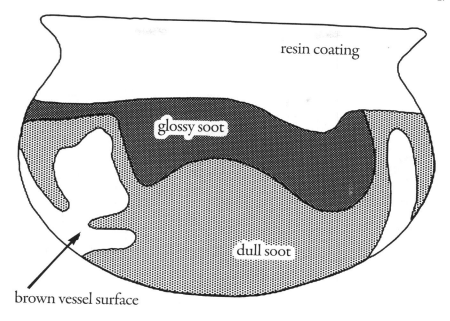

resin coating

glossy soot

dull soot

brown vessel surface

FIGURE 3.1 | Distribution of glossy and dull soot on an *oppaya*. Ethnographic vessel no. 88-77-9, Arizona State Museum, University of Arizona, Tucson (profile adapted from Skibo 1992a:figure 7.2).

glossy soot that cannot (Skibo 1992a:159–161). The glossiness of the permanent soot depends on "resin droplets [from the burning wood] that solidify" (Skibo 1992a:162), which can only solidify on a relatively cool surface. When water is in the ceramic vessel it cools the vessel surface, resulting in the absence of a carbonized patch on the bottom and permitting glossy soot to form (Skibo 1992a:164; see Beck et al. 2002:figure 15).

The nature of the contact between the soot and the vessel surface is poorly understood. Some observation suggests (Skibo 1992a:147) that soot penetrates into the vessel wall to a certain extent, while in other cases soot appears to be flaking off from intact vessel surfaces (Skibo 1992a:154; see Sassaman 1993:figure 29). This contact may change depending upon the type of soot; glossy soot formed while vessels contained water, for example, might be more prone to form a separate layer on top of the vessel surface.

On the inside, carbon accumulates differently depending upon the contents (Kobayashi 1994; Skibo 1992a:148–152). When vegetables, meat, or both are boiled with water, as in an *oppaya*, food residues build up at the top of the water, producing a brown oily stain and an accumulation of carbon around the middle interior (Figure 3.2; Kobayashi 1994:figure 12). The water keeps the food from

FIGURE 3.2 | Interior carbon pattern on an *oppaya*. Ethnographic vessel no. 88-77-106, Arizona State Museum, University of Arizona, Tucson. Photograph by Janelle Weakly.

sticking to, and burning on, the bottom. Rice cooked in an *ittoyom*, however, absorbs the water in the pot as it cooks. *Ittoyom* develop more interior carbon more quickly than *oppaya* do. The interior carbon on *ittoyom* also covers a greater area of the lower vessel body and often includes patches of burned food on the base and lower sides (Figure 3.3; Kobayashi 1994:figure 12). These interior carbon patterns should be useful in other regions to infer the texture of vessel contents. The spatial patterning of interior carbon on vessels may indicate whether the food usually cooked in that pot was a thick porridge (more like rice in consistency) or whether it was only boiled in water.

The appearance of interior carbon changes over the life of a cooking vessel. Kobayashi (1994:146) defines four interior carbon types, distinguished by color and thickness: (1) light brown, resembling an oily stain on the vessel; (2) black, with no buildup on the surface; (3) black, with a thin carbon layer on the surface; and (4) black, with a thicker carbon layer (over 0.3 mm). Interior carbon may not be visible on vessels that are relatively new and accumulates over time to Stage 3 or 4.

Many damaged or worn-out Kalinga vessels were also used as *linga*, or roasting vessels. Vessels are placed over the fire at an angle, so that the contents to be roasted

FIGURE 3.3 | Interior carbon pattern on an *ittoyom*. Ethnographic vessel no. 88-77-180, Arizona State Museum, University of Arizona, Tucson. Photograph by Janelle Weakly.

rest on the middle interior of the vessel (Skibo 1992a:72, figure 4.18). This form of reuse leaves an unusually large oxidized patch on the base (Skibo 1992a:162) because tilting exposes new areas slightly higher on the vessel body to the oxidizing effect of the fire. As I observed firsthand in another Kalinga community (Beck 2003), roasting also adds carbon to the middle interior, obscuring the interior carbon patterns that distinguish *oppaya* and *ittoyom*.

Residue Analysis

Residues from vessel contents accumulate on and within vessel walls during use, and studies such as Mary Malainey and colleagues (2001) illustrate the contribution their identification can make to archaeological interpretation. Given the complexity of this topic, only a brief overview is provided here. Those interested should consult the works cited and collaborate with researchers in chemistry.

Although pollen and phytolith residues have been studied (e.g., Jones 1993), absorbed residues (Evershed 1993; Evershed et al. 1992; Heron and Evershed 1993) receive more attention, perhaps because of their more secure association with vessel contents. Many analyses identify lipids with gas chromatography–mass spectrometry (Skibo 1992a; Skibo and Deal 1995), although maize has been identified in lipids using carbon stable isotope analysis (Reber and Evershed 2004). Immunological identification of plant residues by crossover immunoelectrophoresis has also been tried (Leach 1998). Phosphorus concentrations serve at least as an indicator of organic content (Cackette, D'Auria, and Snow 1987; Duma 1972).

Experiments create a library of known substances for comparison with archaeological samples (Malainey, Przybylski, and Sheriff 1999a), determine how residues are acquired by the vessel and how they can be extracted (Cackette, D'Auria, and Snow 1987; Charters et al. 1993, 1997; Deal and Silk 1988; Duma 1972; Evershed, Charters, and Quye 1995), and determine how they degrade (Evershed, Charters, and Quye 1995; Malainey, Przybylski, and Sheriff 1999b) or are susceptible to contamination (Heron, Evershed, and Goad 1991). The ceramics in these experiments include used vessels from ethnoarchaeological settings (Cackette, D'Auria, and Snow 1987; Skibo 1992a), experimentally used vessels (Malainey, Przybylski, and Sheriff 1999b), and test tiles (Deal and Silk 1988). This background work is necessary before these analyses can be successfully applied to archaeological material (e.g., Malainey, Przybylski, and Sheriff 1999c).

James Skibo and Michael Deal (1995:326) suggest that "[r]ealistic cooking experiments should be done in which both exterior encrustation residues as well as those absorbed within the ceramic can be examined immediately after cooking and after periods of burial in simulated depositional conditions." The experimental work of Malainey and colleagues (1999b:96–97), guided by ethnographic descriptions of cooking behavior from the project area, approaches this ideal.

Attrition

Many use-alteration studies of archaeological ceramics focus on physical abrasion (Bray 1982; Crown 1994; Griffiths 1978; Hardin and Mills 2000; Henrickson 1990; Jones 1989). In addition to the presence of water in the abrading environment (Skibo and Schiffer 1987), the type and amount of temper (Skibo, Schiffer, and Reid 1989; Vaz Pinto et al. 1987), firing temperature (Skibo, Schiffer, and Reid 1989), and ceramic surface treatment (Skibo, Butts, and Schiffer 1997) all affect the abrasion rate.

Attrition, or surface removal, also includes other processes besides physical abrasion (Skibo 1992a:106–110), such as pitting or spalling from water vaporization within the vessel wall, salt erosion, and activity from organisms such as yeast. As summarized elsewhere (Beck 2001), nonabrasive attrition is often identified on both ethnoarchaeological and archaeological vessels (Arthur 2000, 2002, 2003; Di Peso, Rinaldo, and Fenner 1974:86; Hally 1983:14–20; Simon 1997:334; Skibo 1992a; Skibo and Blinman 1999:182).

Skibo (1992a:134–136) has described the erosion of cooking vessel surfaces through thermal spalling, which appears only inside rice-cooking vessels in his vessel sample. In the final stages of rice cooking, rice has absorbed the water inside the vessel. If the vessel is heated too long afterward, water inside the vessel walls is driven through the interior wall and removes shallow spalls from the surface (Skibo 1992a:figure 6.20). In some cases these spalls cover the entire interior surface (Skibo 1992a:139–140). Thermal spalls occur only if water can reach wall interiors. Permeable surfaces allow walls to become saturated and therefore prone to spalling (Schiffer et al. 1994:205).

On vessels vulnerable to this type of alteration, thermal spalls should be produced not only by rice cooking but also whenever the cooking water is boiled off or absorbed by the vessel contents before heating stops. Possible cooking techniques for foods include steaming items within a vessel, during which the pot may accidentally be boiled dry, or preparing thick gruels that are relatively dry along the vessel interior surface.

Other possible causes of interior erosion are alkali processing of corn and the preparation of alcoholic beverages. Vessels used to hold a mixture of water and ashes, such as those used for soaking hominy or mixing an alkaline solution to add to bread or dumpling dough, may exhibit patterned salt erosion on the vessel interior (Beck 2001). Salt erosion is the disintegration of a porous material by the introduction of soluble salts into the fabric, which then exert pressure through volume expansion by crystallization, hydration, or thermal expansion. Experiments have shown a mixture of mesquite ash and water to cause salt erosion on ceramic test tiles (O'Brien 1990).

Among the Gamo of Ethiopia, vessels that contain yeast products such as beer or yeast dough exhibit considerable interior erosion from the yeast activity (Arthur 2000:203–206). Similar damage is present on the interiors of Tarahumara *tesguino,* or corn-beer brewing vessels, in the ethnographic collections of the Arizona State Museum (Beck 2001). It is not clear exactly how this damage is produced, and it resembles salt erosion as described and illustrated by Margaret Beck (2001).

Distinguishing between use-related and non–use-related attrition is difficult from observations of the damage alone. Salt erosion, for example, will look the same on the vessel wall regardless of the cause. Placement of the damage on the vessel may provide a valuable clue; use-related attrition should appear only where vessel contents touch the vessel wall, while non–use-related attrition should exhibit no such patterning.

THEORETICAL ISSUES

The Role of Experimentation

Cooking is a complicated, multi-step process, often involving geographically restricted ingredients and special utensils. It is not easy to replicate in a laboratory.

Neither is beer brewing or production of other alcoholic beverages, another common activity involving ceramic vessels. Experimental simulations of vessel use often stop at heating water (e.g., Beck et al. 2002; Longacre, Xia, and Yang 2000; Schiffer 1990; Schiffer et al. 1994). Fortunately, heating water at least provides information on exterior soot formation and thermal response. For more complicated alteration patterns, such as interior attrition (Arthur 2000, 2002, 2003; Reid and Young 2000; Skibo 1992a) and interior carbon patterning (Kobayashi 1994), use-alteration analysis is based not on experimental replication but rather on ethnoarchaeological collections and data.

Nonetheless, experiments contribute significantly to use-alteration research in several ways. First, experiments demonstrate how vessels with different pastes and surface treatments react to processes such as abrasion and heating. Second, experiments can replicate non-use alteration, which is difficult to observe directly. Because not all ceramic alteration is the result of use, non-use alteration must be considered in any analysis.

Use and Non-Use Alteration and Differences between Sherds and Vessels

Documented alteration patterns on ethnoarchaeological vessels are often similar to those on archaeological vessels and are useful for determining vessel function in these cases (Rice 1996). In other cases, alteration on the archaeological pieces does not match available comparative material or may be ambiguous. These differences may be caused by variation in use processes or resistance to alteration. They may also be the result of post-depositional or non-use processes (Schiffer 1987:158–162), potentially altering or obscuring the evidence of use (Schiffer 1989).

Prehistoric ceramics generally have more non-use alteration than do vessels collected from ethnographic settings, given their much longer and perhaps more complicated histories. Sherds already display post-use damage in the form of fragmentation, and one might assume that whatever information they might provide has been masked by a host of destructive processes. Even whole or reconstructed vessels are vulnerable to some processes. Schiffer (1989:190) and Skibo (1992a:42) have suggested that detailed use-alteration analysis should be restricted to whole vessels so the spatial patterns of damage can be used to distinguish use from non-use alteration.

Sherds are worth including in use-alteration studies, however, even if the analysis must be less detailed as a result. Whole or reconstructed vessels are often unavailable or do not provide a representative sample, depending upon the project area and research questions. Discarded cooking vessels, for example, are often moved one or more times as trash and eventually placed as secondary refuse into deposits such as middens. Fragments are subjected to a host of alteration processes at each step, including recycling, trampling, wet/dry cycles, or fluvial abrasion. Nonetheless, studies of food preparation should incorporate midden sherds in some way because the vast majority of cooking vessels probably became midden sherds. In one ethnoarchaeological study, the estimate of household vessels deposited into middens was as high as 73 percent (Beck 2006; Beck and Hill 2007).

Late Archaic ceramic assemblages from the U.S. Southeast and Midwest (5000–3000 BP) are examples of vessels with long post-use histories (Reid 1984a, 1984b; Sassaman 1993). They are generally recovered as sherds from middens and other contexts with some potential for surface exposure, and vessels are usually represented by isolated sherds. They are also highly susceptible to weathering, given low firing temperatures and high porosity as a result of voids left by fiber temper (Beck et al. 2002; Skibo and Schiffer 1987; Skibo, Schiffer, and Reid 1989). Nonetheless, Kenneth Sassaman (1993) was able to address significant questions about the function, adoption, and spread of these early ceramics based on presence-absence and frequency data for soot.

The primary impediment to use-alteration analysis is sherd size. Small sherds (less than 5 cm^2) have a significantly lower frequency of carbon than larger sherds in Kalinga middens (Beck 2003:table 5.10), although it is not clear why. The processes that reduce sherd size, such as abrasion, may also remove carbon, or larger surfaces may increase the chance of seeing traces of carbon. Almost all Kalinga midden sherds are too small to see carbon patterning that might indicate vessel function. The only exceptions are larger than 16 cm^2 (Beck 2003). These sherds are large enough to determine general vessel position and whether interior carbon accumulated only around the midsection or covered the base and lower walls.

Because non-use alteration cannot be completely avoided, analysts must learn to recognize it and account for its effects. It may even be the focus of attention in site formation studies (e.g., Skibo 1987). Several types of non-use alteration described later may be frequently observed on sherds and vessels, depending upon the environment of the project area.

Non-Use Carbon Deposition and Removal. Carbon deposits are commonly used for inferring prehistoric vessel function (Crown 1994; Hally 1983; Jones 1989; Kobayashi 1994; Sassaman 1993; Skibo 1992a). Carbonized organic material preserves well in a variety of environments and is really only vulnerable to mechanical damage (Miksicek 1987). Carbon is common on Kalinga midden sherds, although any carbon extending above the surface has usually been knocked off (Beck 2003; Skibo 1992a:154). Fortunately, it is the placement of carbon, rather than the thickness, that is related to vessel function. Carbon on and within the vessel wall is relatively resistant to abrasion, and traces will often be present even on abraded surfaces (Beck et al. 2002).

Limited evidence suggests that carbon may be removed by prolonged exposure to water. For example, water leaking through the base of an old rice-cooking pot removed a patch of carbon from that area (William Longacre, personal communication 1999). Smudged test tiles I placed in running water for a month retained no trace of carbon.

Some carbon on vessel surfaces may have been deposited during manufacture as firing clouds and is not evidence of use. Confusion between use-related carbon and firing clouds is less likely with whole vessels because the location, size, and shape of the carbon cloud or patch suggest its origin (James Skibo, personal communication 1998). It is useful to examine unused complete vessels to see what firing clouds on vessels with no use alteration look like and compare them to carbon patches resulting from use. Firing clouds tend to be light gray, diffuse, or patchy.

Damage to the Vessel Surface. Erosion from wet-dry cycles, freeze-thaw cycles (Skibo, Schiffer, and Reid 1989), and salts in the burial environment (O'Brien 1990) may remove the use-altered vessel surface or be initially mistaken for use-related abrasion. Salt erosion is of special concern to conservators working with ceramics from arid regions because it may continue to damage whole vessels even during curation (Cronyn 1990:103–104; Odegaard and Jacobs 1989; Sease 1994:41–42). Beck (2001) illustrates and describes three manifestations of salt erosion: bloom and crystal growth, "powdering" of the vessel surface, and wedge spalls.

Acid Leaching. Acid leaching, or leaching of iron, is a common post-depositional alteration in relatively acid soil environments and results in a lighter color (Rye 1981:120; Schiffer 1987:160). This color change may interfere with recognizing color changes related to use, such as a lighter oxidized patch on a vessel base. Because it only occurs under particular circumstances, those circumstances are briefly described here.

The mobilization of iron in fired clay may occur in a similar manner to the mobilization of iron in soil, discussed in detail elsewhere (Allen and Hajek 1989; Ponnamperuma 1972; Schulze 1989; Schwertmann 1988, 1993; Schwertmann and Taylor 1989). Iron, present in soils after release from primary minerals during weathering, occurs as Fe^{3+} under oxidizing (aerobic) conditions. Ferric iron (Fe^{3+}) is almost entirely insoluble. However, iron can move in solution in three situations (Ellis, Knazek, and Jacobs 1983:118–119): (1) when iron is chelated by organic acids, (2) when Fe^{3+} is reduced to Fe^{2+} (ferrous iron) under anaerobic conditions, or (3) when Fe is mobilized under very acidic conditions.

Areas for Future Research

Thanks to experimental studies and ethnoarchaeological observations, use-alteration patterns can now be used to infer aspects of vessel use. The presence and placement of exterior carbon indicate whether a vessel was used over an open fire and its spatial relationship to the fire. Interior carbon patterns and the presence or absence of thermal spalling suggest the consistency of vessel contents, which may be a watery soup or liquid in which food is boiled or a thick gruel or other food in which all of the water is absorbed or boiled away. We can identify, or at least narrow the possibilities for, vessel contents by analysis of residues either on the vessel wall (such as pollen or phytoliths) or in the vessel wall (such as absorbed lipids). Certain ingredients also cause attrition on vessel interiors; the destructive effects of yeast and salt are two examples.

More experimental work is necessary to verify and refine these patterns and to apply the resulting correlates to archaeological vessels, which may have been used in ways never observed ethnographically and may also have suffered non-use alteration. Skibo and Deal's (1995:326) call for "many more behaviourally relevant experiments," although it was in reference to organic residue analysis, applies to use-alteration research in general. Simple experiments with limited numbers of variables are ideal for understanding isolated alteration processes. They may also have little in common with actual cooking behavior. Much could be learned from attempts to prepare food in ceramic vessels, following ethnographic or ethnoarchaeological descriptions as appropriate, although it may be difficult to completely standardize the process and hold variables constant. These attempts may be most productive when used in conjunction with idealized experiments.

Two alteration processes in particular need more research: nonabrasion attrition and post-depositional carbon removal. The effects of yeast, acids, and salts on ceramic vessels during food and beverage preparation are still poorly understood. Post-depositional carbon removal also deserves more attention, not least because so many archaeological use-alteration analyses rely on carbon frequency and distribution on ceramic vessels and fragments.

EXPERIMENTAL METHODS: SOME CONSIDERATIONS

Schiffer and his colleagues (1994) have explained their approach to experimentation and the difference between archaeological experiments and experimental archaeology. While archaeological experiments "tend to be one-shot affairs," studies in experimental archaeology "do not exist in isolation, but draw expertise and technology from the program's tradition and, in turn, contribute to its elaboration" (Schiffer et al. 1994:198). They describe the experimental tradition at the Laboratory of Traditional Technology at the University of Arizona, but researchers elsewhere can place their work within this tradition and body of literature (or another) and conduct studies that contribute to long-term research goals.

When designing your study, think about how your experiment will contribute to families of related principles (Schiffer et al. 1994:198). This means building upon previous work and structuring your own work so that other studies can build upon it. What questions remain to be answered from previous studies? What predictions can you make about your own research question, based on the conclusions of earlier studies? Can you adopt the same or similar methods as previous studies so your results will be directly comparable? By contacting the authors of a particular study, it may be possible to visit them or borrow the equipment they used.

Be clear about your methods so that you can interpret your experimental results and others can replicate them. Follow procedures for note taking during experiments from other disciplines, such as chemistry. James Zubrick (1997:11–24) provides a good description, and other introductory laboratory manuals summarize the steps involved. Methods obviously include the technology used for conducting experiments. Any equipment manufactured or adapted for a particular experiment should be described (e.g., Neupert 1994; Schiffer et al. 1994) so that others can make copies for their own use, if necessary.

If your experiments are designed to help you interpret alteration on a particular vessel collection, your background research should address human behavior as well as materials science. You should consider in your research design (and address in the background section of your paper) these questions:

How were these vessels manufactured, and what materials were used? How might manufacture and materials affect alteration patterns by making vessels more or less resistant to modification? You may or may not have any comparative data available on vessel composition, firing temperature, or strength. If you do, you can use them to make predictions about the behavior of your sample by referring to existing experimental literature.

One phase of your study may be devoted to collecting such information. For example, Beck and her colleagues (2002) used radiographic and dilatometry analyses to determine the method of vessel construction and firing temperature of several Late Archaic fiber-tempered vessels. Such vessels were primarily built with a technique other than coiling and were fired to temperatures between about 500 and 700°C. This information was then used to select the construction method and firing temperature of test tiles and vessels for experimental work. Use of replicated vessels may produce additional useful information. When fiber-tempered vessels are used for boiling liquids, liquid absorption into the porous and permeable paste and subsequent evaporation on the exterior reduce the heating effectiveness (Schiffer 1990; Skibo, Schiffer, and Reid 1989:129–132). Liquid leaking from the large pores of the vessel during use also creates a very smoky fire (Beck et al. 2002). Organic vessel coatings, often observed ethnographically (Rice 1987:163–164), would have been necessary to make fiber-tempered cooking vessels more watertight.

Will the experiment use vessels, sherds, or test tiles? Once you have selected an appropriate paste and firing temperature, you still need to choose a shape for the experimental pieces. Large ceramic slabs, small test tiles, and vessels have all been used (e.g., O'Brien 1990; Schiffer et al. 1994; Skibo 1992a), and the choice depends largely on the research questions.

You may decide to use several shapes for comparison. Beck and her colleagues (2002), in their study of soot removal on sherds by abrasion, used both test tiles and sherds. The goal was to establish sampling procedures for use-alteration analysis, focusing on fiber-tempered, low-fired ceramics. Abrasion not only removes soot but also leaves diagnostic wear on the sherd, particularly on the edges. The results suggest that if carbon was removed from the sherd surface through abrasion, the sherd will appear abraded and can be removed from the sample.

The first phase of the experiment used test tiles, similar in shape and size to tiles for other ceramic experiments at the Laboratory of Traditional Technology. Test tiles were abraded to calculate the rate of material loss for this ceramic material and to observe overall changes in shape at different abrasion intervals. Tiles with uniform shape and thickness can be quickly measured, and changes are easily observed and quantified.

Irregular vessel fragments will be abraded differently, however, and these differences are important for applying experimental results in archaeological analysis. Sherd edges are rough, and the rounding of numerous small peaks and troughs is one guide to the degree of abrasion. The curved shape of sherds from a rounded vessel will also affect the way abrasion removes the surface (see Beck et al. 2002: figures 2, 5, 7).

Once general patterns for low-fired, fiber-tempered tiles were established, three experimental vessels were made from the same paste, fired to the same temperature, and then used once to heat water. Sherds from these vessels were then abraded to observe soot removal. Depressions in the sherd surface and more rounded vessel portions were more likely to retain soot. Rounded areas were apparently more protective of soot than flat areas were because on rounded surfaces, one point took the brunt of the abrasion, sparing adjacent areas.

How were similar vessels used, in your project area or elsewhere? Beck (2001), Hally (1986), and Reid (1989, 1990), among others, contain examples of ethnographic vessel use descriptions relevant for their archaeological research questions and project areas. Reid illustrates an important point, often lost in the ethnoarchaeological focus on village potters and residents: not all containers used for cooking are ceramic, and not all cooking is performed over an open flame. Vessels should not have soot from use on the exterior unless they were placed over an open fire.

Hunter-gatherer cooking techniques have been divided into dry ("broiling, roasting, baking, and parching") and wet ("simmering, boiling, and steaming") categories (Reid 1990:9). Most types of dry cooking do not require ceramic vessels, although parching might be done using coals in a shallow bowl (Bowen and Moser 1968:122). Although the wet cooking methods of simmering and boiling use a container, the container might be a hide bag, hide-lined pit, basket, or bark container (Sassaman 1993:135–136; Wissler 1910:26). The contents are then heated with hot stones dropped inside.

Even when ceramics were used for cooking, they may not have been used over an open flame. Flat-bottomed, wide-mouthed ceramic vessels were sometimes used ethnographically for stone boiling and may have been more effective than other containers for this purpose because they "functioned as a kind of primitive thermos" (Reid 1990:16). Vessels were also placed beside the fire or over embers (Reid 1990:12).

Are any similar used whole vessels available in museum collections or published works so you can compare experimental patterns with actual use? Fragments of used, unpainted vessels dominate many archaeological collections, but collectors and the viewing public generally prefer painted vessels in good condition. As a result, plain ware vessels tend to be underrepresented in ethnographic and historical period museum collections, and heavily used vessels are even less common. Some examples do exist, however, such as historical period and modern tortilla griddles (*comales*) and Tarahumara *tesguino* jars from the U.S. Southwest and northern Mexico, curated at the Arizona State Museum in Tucson. The ethnoarchaeological vessel collection analyzed by Skibo (1992a) and Kobayashi (1994) in their use-alteration research is also curated at the Arizona State Museum. One hundred and eighty-nine Kalinga vessels were collected in 1988 from the community of Guina-ang in the Pasil River Valley, northwestern Luzon, the Philippines (vessels 88-77-1 through 88-77-190). Beck (2003:tables 5.4, 5.5) summarizes carbon patterns and the resin removal stage (related to the number of use events) for individual vessels in the catalog.

CONCLUDING THOUGHTS

Ceramic use-alteration data are important for any research question involving vessel use, including the question of why ceramics were initially adopted (Longacre 1995; Skibo and Blinman 1999). The simplest conclusions from use-alteration analysis, such as the presence or absence of cooking vessels, help reveal site function or intra-site variation in activity areas. But more detailed use-alteration studies should also be performed because different cooking methods may reflect intensive processing of agricultural staples, rituals or other community events, social identity and socioeconomic stratification, and task scheduling and the organization of household labor (Arthur 2002, 2003; Beck 2001; Brumfield 1991). Vessel use can be combined with other evidence into a larger picture of household activities (Meadows 1999).

None of this is worth pursuing, though, if ceramic use-alteration patterns are not a respected line of evidence. We need confidence that observed patterns represent a particular activity and should be able to eliminate cultural and noncultural alternatives. We also need to recognize and control for the effects of non-use alteration, or the universe of artifacts for analysis will be very small. Additional experimental work, as outlined previously, will make significant contributions toward these ends.

REFERENCES CITED

Allen, B. L., and B. F. Hajek
    1989   Mineral Occurrence in Soil Environments. In *Minerals in Soil Environments*, ed. J. B. Dixon and S. B. Weed, 99–278. Soil Science Society of America Book Series 1. Soil Science Society of America, Madison, Wis.

Arthur, J. W.

2000   Ceramic Ethnoarchaeology among the Gamo of Southwestern Ethiopia. PhD dissertation, Department of Anthropology, University of Florida, Gainesville.

2001   A Functional Analysis of Early Pithouse Period Ceramics. In *Early Pithouse Villages of the Mimbres Valley and Beyond: The McAnally and Thompson Sites in Their Cultural and Ecological Contexts*, ed. M. W. Diehl and S. A. LeBlanc, 69–76. Peabody Museum of Archaeology and Ethnology, Harvard University, Cambridge, Mass.

2002   Pottery Use-Alteration as an Indicator of Socioeconomic Status: An Ethnoarchaeological Study of the Gamo of Ethiopia. *Journal of Archaeological Method and Theory* 9:331–355.

2003   Brewing Beer: Status, Wealth, and Ceramic Use-Alteration among the Gamo of Southwestern Ethiopia. *World Archaeology* 34:516–528.

Beck, M.

2001   Archaeological Signatures of Corn Preparation in the U.S. Southwest. *Kiva* 67:187–218.

2003   Ceramic Deposition and Midden Formation in Kalinga, Philippines. PhD dissertation, Department of Anthropology, University of Arizona, Tucson.

2006   Midden Ceramic Assemblage Formation: An Ethnoarchaeological Case Study from Kalinga, Philippines. *American Antiquity* 71:27–51.

Beck, M. E., and M. E. Hill Jr.

2007   Midden Ceramics and Their Sources in Kalinga. In *Archaeology as Anthropology: Perspective on Method and Theory*, ed. J. M. Skibo, M. W. Graves, and M. T. Stark, 111–137. University of Arizona Press, Tucson.

Beck, M. E., J. M. Skibo, D. Hally, and P. Yang

2002   Sample Selection for Ceramic Use-Alteration Analysis: The Effects of Abrasion on Soot. *Journal of Archaeological Science* 29(3):1–15.

Binford, L. R.

1981   *Bones: Ancient Men and Modern Myths*. Academic Press, Orlando.

Bowen, T., and E. Moser

1968   Seri Pottery. *Kiva* 33(3):89–132.

Bray, A.

1982   Mimbres Black-on-White, Melamine or Wedgewood? A Ceramic Use-Wear Analysis. *Kiva* 47:133–150.

Brumfiel, E.

1991   Weaving and Cooking: Women's Production in Aztec Mexico. In *Engendering Archaeology*, ed. J. Gero and M. Conkey, 224–254. Basil Blackwell, Oxford.

Cackette, M., J. M. D'Auria, and B. E. Snow

1987   Examining Earthenware Vessel Function by Elemental Phosphorus Content. *Current Anthropology* 28:121–127.

Charters, S., R. P. Evershed, L. J. Goad, A. Leyden, P. W. Blinkhorn, and V. Denham
   1993   Quantification and Distribution of Lipid in Archaeological Ceramics: Implications for Sampling Potsherds for Organic Residue Analysis and the Classification of Vessel Use. *Archaeometry* 35:211–223.

Charters, S., R. P. Evershed, A. Quye, P. W. Blinkhorn, and V. Reeves
   1997   Simulation Experiments for Determining the Use of Ancient Pottery Vessels: The Behaviour of Epicuticular Leaf Wax during Boiling of a Leafy Vegetable. *Journal of Archaeological Science* 24:1–7.

Cronyn, J. M.
   1990   *The Elements of Archaeological Conservation*. Routledge, London.

Crown, P. L.
   1994   *Ceramics and Ideology: Salado Polychrome Pottery*. University of New Mexico Press, Albuquerque.

Deal, M., and P. Silk
   1988   Absorption Residues and Vessel Function: A Case Study from the Maine-Maritimes Region. In *A Pot for All Reasons: Ceramic Ecology Revisited*, ed. F. R. Matson, C. C. Kolb, L. M. Lackey, and M. Kirkpatrick, 105–125. Laboratory of Anthropology, Temple University, Philadelphia.

Di Peso, C. C., J. B. Rinaldo, and G. J. Fenner
   1974   *Casa Grandes: A Fallen Trading Center of the Gran Chichimeca*. Vol. 6, no. 9 of the Amerind Foundation Series Technical Reports. Northland, Flagstaff, Ariz.

Duma, G.
   1972   Phosphate Content of Ancient Pots as Indication of Use. *Current Anthropology* 13:127–130.

Ellis, B. G., B. D. Knazek, and L. W. Jacobs
   1983   Movement of Micronutrients in Soils. In *Chemical Mobility and Reactivity in Soil Systems*, ed. David Kral, 109–122. SSSA Special Publication 11. Soil Science Society of America and American Society of Agronomy, Madison, Wis.

Evershed, R. P.
   1993   Biomolecular Archaeology and Lipids. *World Archaeology* 25:74–93.

Evershed, R. P., S. Charters, and A. Quye
   1995   Interpreting Lipid Residues in Archaeological Ceramics: Preliminary Results from Laboratory Simulations of Vessel Use and Burial. *Materials Issues in Art and Archaeology* 4:85–95.

Evershed, R. P., C. Heron, S. Charters, and L. J. Goad
   1992   Chemical Analysis of Organic Residues in Ancient Pottery: Methodological Guidelines and Applications. In *Organic Residues in Archaeology: Their Identification and Analysis*, ed. R. White and H. Page, 11–25. United Kingdom Institute for Conservation, Archaeology Section, London.

Fenner, G. J.
   1977   Flare-Rimmed Bowls: A Sub-Type of Mimbres Classic Black-on-White? *Kiva* 43:129–141.

Griffiths, D. M.
1978   Use-Marks on Historic Ceramics: A Preliminary Study. *Historical Archaeology* 12:68–91.

Hally, D. J.
1983   Use Alteration of Pottery Vessel Surfaces: An Important Source of Evidence for the Identification of Vessel Function. *North American Archaeologist* 4(1):3–26.
1986   The Identification of Vessel Function: A Case Study from Northwest Georgia. *American Antiquity* 51:267–295.

Hardin, M. A., and B. J. Mills
2000   The Social and Historical Context of Short Term Stylistic Replacement: A Zuni Case Study. *Journal of Archaeological Method and Theory* 7:139–163.

Henrickson, E. F.
1990   Investigating Ancient Ceramic Form and Use: Progress Report and Case Study. In *The Changing Roles of Ceramics in Society: 26,000 B.P. to the Present*, ed. W. D. Kingery, 83–117. The American Ceramic Society, Westerville, Ohio.

Henrickson, E. F., and M.M.A. McDonald
1983   Ceramic Form and Function: An Ethnographic Search and an Archaeological Application. *American Anthropologist* 85:630–643.

Heron, C., and R. P. Evershed
1993   Analysis of Organic Residues and the Study of Pottery Use. In *Archaeological Method and Theory*, vol. 5, ed. M. B. Schiffer, 247–284. University of Arizona Press, Tucson.

Heron, C., R. P. Evershed, and L. J. Goad
1991   Effects of Migration of Soil Lipids on Organic Residues Associated with Buried Potsherds. *Journal of Archaeological Science* 18:641–659.

Johnson, J. S., J. Clark, S. Miller-Antonio, D. Robins, M. B. Schiffer, and J. M. Skibo
1988   Effects of Firing Temperature on the Fate of Naturally Occurring Organic Matter in Clays. *Journal of Archaeological Science* 15:403–414.

Jones, B. A.
1989   Use-Wear Analysis of White Mountain Redwares at Grasshopper Pueblo, Arizona. *Kiva* 54(4):353–360.

Jones, J. G.
1993   Analysis of Pollen and Phytoliths in Residue from a Colonial Period Ceramic Vessel. In *Current Research in Phytolith Analysis: Applications in Archaeology and Paleoecology*, ed. D. M. Pearsall and D. R. Piperno, 31–35. MASCA Research Papers in Science and Archaeology, vol. 10. University of Pennsylvania Museum of Archaeology and Anthropology, Philadelphia.

Kobayashi, M.
1994   Use-Alteration Analysis of Kalinga Pottery: Interior Carbon Deposits of Cooking Pots. In *Kalinga Ethnoarchaeology: Expanding Archaeological Method and Theory*, ed. W. A. Longacre and J. M. Skibo, 127–168. Smithsonian Institution Press, Washington, D.C.

Leach, J. D.
    1998   A Brief Comment on the Immunological Identification of Plant Residues
             on Prehistoric Stone Tools and Ceramics: Results of a Blind Test. *Journal of
             Archaeological Science* 25:171–175.

Longacre, W. A.
    1995   Why Did They Invent Pottery Anyway? In *The Emergence of Pottery: Technol-
             ogy and Innovation in Ancient Societies*, ed. W. K. Barnett and J. W. Hoopes,
             277–280. Smithsonian Institution Press, Washington, D.C.

Longacre, W. A., J. Xia, and T. Yang
    2000   I Want to Buy a Black Pot. *Journal of Archaeological Method and Theory* 7(4):
             273–293.

Malainey, M. E., R. Przybylski, and B. L. Sheriff
    1999a   The Fatty Acid Composition of Native Food Plants and Animals of Western
             Canada. *Journal of Archaeological Science* 26:83–94.
    1999b   The Effects of Thermal and Oxidative Degradation of the Fatty Acid Compo-
             sition of Food Plants and Animals of Western Canada: Implications for the
             Identification of Archaeological Vessel Residues. *Journal of Archaeological Sci-
             ence* 26:95–103.
    1999c   Identifying the Former Contents of Late Precontact Period Pottery Vessels
             from Western Canada using Gas Chromatography. *Journal of Archaeological
             Science* 26:425–438.
    2001   One Person's Food: How and Why Fish Avoidance May Affect the Settlement
             and Subsistence Patterns of Hunter-Gatherers. *American Antiquity* 66:141–
             161.

Meadows, K.
    1999   The Appetites of Households in Early Roman Britain. In *The Archaeology of
             Household Activities*, ed. P. M. Allison, 101–120. Routledge, London.

Miksicek, C. H.
    1987   Formation Processes of the Archaeobotanical Record. In *Advances in Archaeo-
             logical Method and Theory*, vol. 10, ed. M. Schiffer, 211–247. Academic Press,
             New York.

Neupert, M. A.
    1994   Strength Testing Archaeological Ceramics: A New Perspective. *American An-
             tiquity* 59:709–723.

O'Brien, P.
    1990   An Experimental Study of the Effects of Salt Erosion on Pottery. *Journal of
             Archaeological Science* 17:393–401.

Odegaard, N., and M. Jacobs
    1989   Salt Problems in Hohokam Pottery. *Archaeological Conservation Newsletter* 1(1):
             5–7.

Ponnamperuma, F. N.
    1972   The Chemistry of Submerged Soils. In *Advances in Agronomy*, vol. 24, ed. N. C.
             Brady, 29–96. Academic Press, New York.

Reber, E. A., and R. P. Evershed
  2004   How Did Mississippians Prepare Maize? The Application of Compound-Specific Carbon Isotope Analysis to Absorbed Pottery Residues from Several Mississippi Valley Sites. *Archaeometry* 46:19–33.

Reid, A., and R. Young
  2000   Pottery Abrasion and the Preparation of African Grains. *Antiquity* 74:101–111.

Reid, J. J., M. B. Schiffer, and W. L. Rathje
  1975   Behavioral Archaeology: Four Strategies. *American Anthropologist* 77:864–869.

Reid, K. E.
  1984a   Fire and Ice: New Evidence for the Production and Preservation of Late Archaic Fiber-Tempered Pottery in the Mid-Latitude Lowlands. *American Antiquity* 49:59–76.
  1984b   *Nebo Hill: Late Archaic Prehistory on the Southern Prairie Peninsula.* Publications in Anthropology 15. University of Kansas, Lawrence.
  1989   A Materials Science Perspective on Hunter-Gatherer Pottery. In *Pottery Technology: Ideas and Approaches,* ed. G. Bronitsky, 167–180. Westview, Boulder.
  1990   Simmering Down: A Second Look at Ralph Linton's "North American Cooking Pots." In *Hunter-Gatherer Pottery from the Far West,* ed. J. M. Mack, 8–18. Nevada State Museum Anthropological Papers 23. Nevada State Museum, Carson City.

Rice, P. M.
  1987   *Pottery Analysis: A Sourcebook.* University of Chicago Press, Chicago.
  1996   Recent Ceramic Analysis: 1. Function, Style, and Origins. *Journal of Archaeological Research* 4(2):133–163.

Rye, O. S.
  1981   *Pottery Technology: Principles and Reconstruction.* Manuals on Archaeology 4. Taraxacum, Washington, D.C.

Sassaman, K. E.
  1993   *Early Pottery in the Southeast: Tradition and Innovation in Cooking Technology.* University of Alabama Press, Tuscaloosa.

Schiffer, M. B.
  1976   *Behavioral Archaeology.* Academic Press, New York.
  1987   *Formation Processes of the Archaeological Record.* University of New Mexico Press, Albuquerque.
  1989   A Research Design for Ceramic Use-Wear Analysis at Grasshopper Pueblo. In *Pottery Technology: Ideas and Approaches,* ed. G. Bronitsky, 183–205. Westview, Boulder.
  1990   The Influence of Surface Treatment on Heating Effectiveness of Ceramic Vessels. *Journal of Archaeological Science* 17:373–381.
  1995   *Behavioral Archaeology: First Principles.* University of Utah Press, Salt Lake City.

Schiffer, M. B., and J. M. Skibo
  1989   A Provisional Theory of Ceramic Abrasion. *American Anthropologist* 91:101–115.

Schiffer, M. B., J. M. Skibo, T. C. Boelke, M. A. Neupert, and M. Aronson
  1994   New Perspectives on Experimental Archaeology: Surface Treatments and Thermal Response of the Clay Cooking Pot. *American Antiquity* 59:197–217.

Schiffer, M. B., J. M. Skibo, J. L. Griffitts, K. L. Hollenbach, and W. A. Longacre
  2001   Behavioral Archaeology and the Study of Technology. *American Antiquity* 66:729–738.

Schulze, D. G.
  1989   An Introduction to Soil Mineralogy. In *Minerals in Soil Environments*, ed. J. B. Dixon and S. B. Weed, 1–34. Soil Science Society of America Book Series 1. Soil Science Society of America, Madison, Wis.

Schwertmann, U.
  1988   Occurrence and Formation of Iron Oxides in Various Pedoenvironments. In *Iron in Soils and Clay Minerals*, ed. J. W. Stucki, B. A. Goodman, and U. Schwertmann, 267–308. NATO Advanced Science Institutes Series. D. Reidel, Dordrecht.
  1993   Relations between Iron Oxides, Soil Color, and Soil Formation. In *Soil Color*, ed. J. M. Bigham and E. J. Ciolkosz, 51–69. SSSA Special Publication 31. Soil Science Society of America, Madison, Wis.

Schwertmann, U., and R. M. Taylor
  1989   Iron Oxides. In *Minerals in Soil Environments*, 2nd ed., ed. J. B. Dixon and S. B. Weed, 379–438. Soil Science Society of America Book Series 1. Soil Science Society of America, Madison, Wis.

Sease, C.
  1994   *A Conservation Manual for the Field Archaeologist*, 3rd ed. Archaeological Research Tools 4. Institute of Archaeology, University of California, Los Angeles.

Shepard, A. O.
  1985   *Ceramics for the Archaeologist*. Publication 609. Carnegie Institution of Washington, Washington, D.C. Reprinted by Braun-Brumfield, Ann Arbor, Mich.

Simon, A. W.
  1997   Plain, Red, and Other Ceramic Wares from U:4:33/132, the Cline Terrace Mound. In *A Salado Platform Mound on Tonto Creek, Roosevelt Platform Mound Study, Report on the Cline Terrace Mound, Cline Terrace Complex*, ed. D. Jacobs, 291–362. Roosevelt Monograph Series 7, Anthropological Field Studies 36. Arizona State University, Tempe.

Skibo, J. M.
  1987   Fluvial Sherd Abrasion and the Interpretation of Surface Remains on Southwestern Bajadas. *North American Archaeologist* 8(2):125–141.
  1992a   *Pottery Function: A Use-Alteration Perspective*. Plenum, New York.

1992b Ethnoarchaeology, Experimental Archaeology and Inference Building in Ceramic Research. *Archaeologia Polona* 30:27–38.

Skibo, J. M., and E. Blinman
1999 Exploring the Origins of Pottery on the Colorado Plateau. In *Pottery and People: A Dynamic Interaction*, ed. J. M. Skibo and G. M. Feinman, 171–183. University of Utah Press, Salt Lake City.

Skibo, J. M., T. C. Butts, and M. B. Schiffer
1997 Ceramic Surface Treatment and Abrasion Resistance: An Experimental Study. *Journal of Archaeological Science* 24:311–317.

Skibo, J. M., and M. Deal
1995 Pottery Function and Organic Residue: An Appraisal. In *Conference Papers on Archaeology in Southeast Asia*, ed. Y. Chun-tong and L. Wai-ling Brenda, 319–330. University Museum and Art Gallery, University of Hong Kong, Hong Kong.

Skibo, J. M., and M. B. Schiffer
1987 The Effects of Water on Processes of Ceramic Abrasion. *Journal of Archaeological Science* 14:83–96.

Skibo, J. M., M. B. Schiffer, and K. C. Reid
1989 Organic-Tempered Pottery: An Experimental Study. *American Antiquity* 54:122–146.

Vaz Pinto, I., M. B. Schiffer, S. Smith, and J. M. Skibo
1987 Effects of Temper on Ceramic Abrasion Resistance. *Archaeomaterials* 1:119–134.

Wissler, C.
1910 Material Culture of the Blackfoot Indians. *Anthropological Papers of the American Museum of Natural History* 5(1):1–175.

Zubrick, J. W.
1997 *The Organic Chem Lab Survival Manual: A Student's Guide to Techniques*, 4th ed. John Wiley and Sons, New York.

CHAPTER FOUR

Flake Debris and Flintknapping Experimentation

Philip J. Carr and Andrew P. Bradbury

○ ○ ○
○ ○ ○
○ ○ ○

Arguably, flintknapping experimentation is part of the core of modern lithic analysis. In addition to providing possible means for the manufacture of particular stone implements, exploring the effects of heat treatment on specific raw materials, and provisioning other experimenters with suitable tools for use in modern contexts such as studying use-wear, flintknapping experimentation has proved extremely valuable for the analysis of flake debris. Here, we briefly examine the variety of flintknapping experiments conducted in the past several decades aimed at understanding chipped-stone tool technologies. This is followed by a lengthier discussion of the qualities of a "good" flintknapping experiment designed to provide insight into the technological origin of flake debris. Subsequently, we review exemplars of different experimental approaches. We conclude with directions for future research in flake debris experimentation.

"Flake" is a generic term in archaeological lexicons, used most often in Americanist archaeology to refer to chipped-stone debris produced during tool manufacture but sometimes applied in a different sense to its practitioners, in a somewhat unkind manner. Michael Shott (1994:70) has pointed out that the term "flake," also applied to "breakfast cereals and ice crystals," is difficult to define and that archaeologists use a variety of other terms to refer to these artifacts, such as debitage, chips, and debris. In an attempt to add clarity, William Andrefsky (1998:9–10) employs the term "objective piece" in a lithics manual to refer to "stone items that have been hit, cracked, flaked, or modified in some way" and uses "detached pieces" for "stone items that have been removed from objective pieces during the modification process." Perhaps the new generation of lithic analysts will employ these terms, but we will follow Shott (1994) in using flake and flake debris, as opposed to detached pieces, because of the way we were trained in lithic analysis and how we conceptualize the flintknapping process.

It is easy to argue that flake debris constitutes the majority of the archaeological record prior to the modern age of mass production and a penchant for disposable items. Flakes were part of the toolkit of early hominids over 2.5 million years ago, and knapping stone for tools continued well into the historic period with the production of gunflints and, more recently, obsidian scalpels (e.g., Buck 1982; Disa, Vossoughi, and Goldberg 1993). Over this time span, innumerable archaeological sites were produced, from quarry sites with massive amounts of flakes to "temporary camps" at which the only artifacts remaining are a few flakes. Unlike stone tools, flake debris was rarely curated and therefore generally remains at the site of production. These characteristics—abundance and infrequently curated, combined with the fact that a flake retains evidence of the technology used in its production—spurred some lithic analysts in the 1970s and 1980s to consider this rather unimpressive artifact class in more detail. Andrefsky (2001:2) and others (Johnson 2001:18–19; Magne 2001:22) have pointed specifically to 1985, with the publication of "Debitage Analysis and Archaeological Interpretation" by Alan Sullivan and Kenneth Rozen (1985), as a major turning point in Americanist flake debris analysis because of the increased number and types of flintknapping experiments the article engendered and the desire to use flake debris to make behavioral inferences.

INTRODUCTION TO FLINTKNAPPING EXPERIMENTS

Experimental archaeology, middle-range theory building, and replicative studies are all terms that describe the present conduct of behaviors considered relevant for understanding the past. Textbooks that discuss this theoretical and methodological aspect of archaeology inevitably employ flintknapping as an exemplar (e.g., Feder and Park 2001:181–182; Hayden 1993:50–51; Renfrew and Bahn 1991:271–283; Staeck 2002:162–174; Thomas 1999:46). Flintknapping experiments have a long history in archaeology (i.e., Evans 1860; Nilsson 1868; cited in Johnson 1978) and illustrate for students how the archaeological record formed and how to make inferences from that record. However, textbooks generally focus on stone tools, not flake debris. John Staeck (2002:168–169) is an exception, as he provides a relatively detailed discussion of flake debris and the "reduction sequence" but fails to cite relevant discussions and experimental literature that have shown the primary-secondary-tertiary approach to flake debris analysis used in his discussion to be flawed (e.g.,

Bradbury and Carr 1995; Magne 1985; Sullivan and Rozen 1985). The general lack of discussion of flake debris in textbooks is perhaps a reflection of the fact that, until recently, this artifact class was largely ignored, perpetuating this situation by influencing students not to pursue flake debris studies. This artifact class continues to be underutilized in Americanist archaeology.

While experimentation has profoundly affected the analysis and interpretation of a wide range of artifact classes, perhaps none has benefited as much as flake debris (although much fruitful experimentation has been conducted for use-wear analysis; see Bamforth, this volume). In most cases, flake debris is not an effective diagnostic for making time or space designations. Therefore, flake debris has traditionally played little to no role in archaeological analyses and interpretations, despite its relative abundance at most prehistoric sites. Since the 1970s, new goals in the discipline, experimentation, and advances in computer technology have led to increased potential for flake debris studies. Contemporary lithic researchers recognize flake debris analysis as an essential component in the interpretation of chipped-stone assemblages (see Andrefsky 2001). Experiments have provided the necessary link between static flake debris excavated from the archaeological record and the dynamic behaviors that produced the debris. One lithic analyst put it this way: "In my opinion, our best insights into debitage variability, how variable it is and why, have come from experimentation" (Magne 2001:22). Today, lithic analysts are employing a variety of approaches in the analysis of flake debris, such as the organization of technology and *chaîne opératoire*, but they all involve experimentation.

Although there is support for, and pursuit of, flintknapping experimentation, there are also detractors. Flintknapping experiments have been criticized as representing a "circular" argument (Teltser 1991:366) and failing to demonstrate that the behaviors used to produce experimental debris are necessarily those that produced similar debris found in the archaeological record (Rozen and Sullivan 1989:171–173). As discussed by Shott (1994:83), both arguments are derived from the problem of equifinality, in which different explanations can account for the existence of a particular pattern. Likewise, Jan Simek (1994:119) suggests that from a scientific perspective, flintknapping experiments lack the controls needed to "evade equifinality."

There are several ways to tackle the potential problem of equifinality. We advocate employing multiple methods of analysis to identify the problem (Bradbury and Carr 1995, 1999; Carr and Bradbury 2000, 2001). If different experimentally developed means of analyzing flake debris produce ambiguous results, then it causes one to question whether the experiments adequately model the reduction process that produced the prehistoric lithic assemblage. Martin Magne (2001:23) has stated that "[m]ultiple lines of evidence can be more accurate indicators of reduction realities than any single line of evidence is encouraging, since redundant measures, to a reasonable amount, can serve as internal checks to reality." A thorough study of an archaeological chipped-stone assemblage should result in the analyst's ability to assess whether particular experimental assemblages adequately model that assemblage. Specific points of comparison might include material type, material quality, material size, core forms, tool types, percussors used, flake debris size, and flake debris morphology.

Similarly, Daniel Amick and his colleagues (1989:8) have suggested that "[t]he ability to work back and forth between experimental work and the archaeological record is essential for learning about the past." More recently, Jay Johnson (2001:17–18) reiterated this point in discussing the means of identifying flake attributes as indicators of assemblage characteristics and the "productive feedback between the analysis of archaeological assemblages and replicative assemblages." In addition, Simek (1994:119) suggested refitting—commonly conducted in Old World lithic analyses—as a means to avoid the problem of equifinality, and American researchers are increasingly using this approach (e.g., Bleed 2004; Franklin and Simek 2008; Morrow 1996). Finally, Shott (1994:83) has proposed that "replication studies in fact demonstrate that different results often follow from different causes, suggesting equifinality may not be a serious problem in the reduction process."

Without considering these various means to address equifinality in flake debris studies, Alan Sullivan (2001:205) has referred to the "ambiguity that arises from the equifinal results of lithic production," adding that "debitage analysis is something to be endured so that we can investigate vital problems in American archaeology." While equifinality remains an issue for consideration when conducting flake debris studies and applying experimental results to an archaeological assemblage, we do not see it as a reason to forgo such studies or experimentation.

FLINTKNAPPING EXPERIMENTS THROUGH TIME

The most comprehensive history of flintknapping experimentation, covering the time period 1838–1976, was written by Lucy Johnson (1978), but that overview makes no specific comparison of experimental results and does not focus on the understanding of flake debris. However, interesting tidbits of information throughout the article make it a worthwhile read for anyone interested in flintknapping experiments. For example, Johnson (1978:353), quoting Errett Callahan, emphasizes the variation in technique among three American knappers such that different "traditions" are apparent in the body movements used—such as the wrist, arm, and shoulder—in the knapping process. In commenting on Johnson's discussion, François Bordes (1978:359) states that "most of the time I can tell whether a stone has been worked by [Don] Crabtree, [Jacques] Tixier, or myself. Our styles are different, but do not ask me to say what the differences are! I feel them more than I see them. I suspect that flint-knapping will have to become a necessary part of the training of any archaeologist interested in prehistory." While Bordes's suspicion has come to general fruition in the sense that lithic analysts today are certainly familiar with flintknapping, few recognize the variable styles employed by individual knappers. An exception is Kimberly Redman (1998:76–81), who has argued that certain flake attributes in her study (curvature, flake length, maximum width, width at midpoint, platform width, and flake weight) were affected by idiosyncratic knapper behavior. Likewise, Phillip Shelley (1990; also see Nichols and Allstadt 1978) conducted experiments to determine if one could distinguish between novice and experienced knappers based on various flake attributes.

Amick and colleagues (1989:5–6) discuss flintknapping experimentation and trends over time, as well as examining experimentation more generally and its role in making archaeological inferences. They suggest that during the period 1870–1940, the focus was on distinguishing humanly modified stone from naturally flaked stone and reconstructing methods of stone tool manufacture. Between 1940 and 1970 the focus was again on methods of stone tool manufacture, and expert flintknappers—such as Bordes, Tixier, and Crabtree—"demonstrated plausible solutions to technical problems" (Amick, Mauldin, and Binford 1989:6). From their review, it seems that the 1970s represented the "breaking out" of flake debris experiments in the sense that a variety of goals were pursued. These flintknapping experiments are of three major types: technological, replicative, and highly controlled. The review by Amick and colleagues (1989) does not extend into the 1980s, but the volume in which their article appears continues to be a major impetus for flintknapping experiments that are technological in orientation and aimed at making inferences from flake debris.

A goal of certain flintknapping experiments during the 1970s and 1980s was to obtain technological information from flake debris, such as whether an archaeological assemblage represented core reduction or tool production. An early approach to deriving technological information from flakes, based on experiment, that continues to have importance today is size grading (e.g., Ahler 1975; Stahle and Dunn 1982, 1984; see papers in Hall and Larson 2004). In contrast to size-grading approaches, individual flake analysis methods are available that are also based on experimentation, such as the use of platform facets and dorsal scars as demonstrated by Magne (1985). We have shown through experimentation the utility of combining these two approaches and employing multiple lines of evidence as an important means of assessing results such that inferences are confirmed or ambiguities revealed (Bradbury and Carr 1995, 2004). Continued work in this area is necessary to corroborate findings and expand the coverage of established methods.

In contrast, the "replication" or "cognitive" approach, also popular in the 1970s, focused on identifying the specific process of how tools were produced and using these reduction techniques as "cultural markers" (Flenniken 1984). While J. Jeffrey Flenniken provided steps for determining the validity of a reduction technique as a cultural marker and emphasized the "careful identification of debitage," he did not discuss or demonstrate the importance of the results. He simply stated: "If valid, the replicator has reproduced a tangible aspect of prehistoric human behavior and demonstrated the reality of that behavior" (Flenniken (1984:197). This earned a negative response from David Hurst Thomas (1986:247–248), who suggested that those using the replication approach were out of synch with contemporary archaeology. Further, Amick and others (1989:6) have been critical of the underlying principles of this approach and the stated goals of identifying cultural markers. With regard to flake debris experimentation, it is important to replicate past reduction techniques accurately, and archaeologists should continue to appreciate the emphasis placed on this aspect of flintknapping experimentation.

The third type of experiment—highly controlled—was initially conducted in the 1970s to examine fracture mechanics (Speth 1972, 1975). While Lucy Johnson, in her overview of flintknapping experiments, tended to describe findings with little comment, she was critical of this type, stating that "Speth's experiments are so far from natural conditions and the mechanical variables are so poorly understood by engineers and physicists, that the applicability of these results to archaeological occurrences is questionable" (Johnson 1978:353). While it is important to recognize the "artificial" nature of highly controlled experiments, this approach is still useful because it examines the principles of how and why flakes form in the manner they do. This control allows examination of an individual variable while holding others constant.

Patterning in the size and shape of archaeological flake debris is determined with great confidence in highly controlled experiments. Seminal work in fracture mechanics has since been conducted by a number of researchers (e.g., Cotterell and Kamminga 1979, 1987; Dibble and Whittaker 1981; Speth 1972, 1975, 1981; Tsirk 1974, 1979) and continued into the 1990s (e.g., Dibble 1997; Dibble and Pelcin 1995; Pelcin 1997a, 1997b). However, a critical stance toward such experimentation continues to exist. "The simple fact is that controlled experiments, in spite of their elegance, objectivity and replicability, are only useful if the results obtained from them are directly applicable to archaeological materials" (Dibble 1998:611). For example, Harold Dibble and Andrew Pelcin (1995) examined the effects of the percussor's mass and velocity on the resulting flake mass and developed a formula for predicting flake mass based on platform thickness and exterior platform angle. Other authors examined these equations using flakes derived from less controlled flintknapping experiments (e.g., Bradbury, Carr, and Cooper 2008; Davis and Shea 1998; Shott et al. 2000) and provided additional insights.

Each of the three major types of flintknapping experiments identified for the 1970s—technological, replication, and highly controlled—has affected contemporary experiments. In our view, an important avenue for future research in flake debris analysis will be interweaving the results of these types of flintknapping experiments and the archaeological record, recognizing what each can contribute. Amick and his colleagues (1989:1) summed up the importance of experimentation:

> The critical aspect that distinguishes experimental studies from other approaches is explicit control over certain variables which are being investigated. By con-

trolling variables, it is possible to observe their effects and determine if those variables can be useful in describing the archaeological record. The primary goal of archaeology is to explain the archaeological record and this is a theoretical issue. Experimental research provides a method for improving descriptions of the archaeological record in terms which are relevant to these theoretical questions.

RELATION TO THEORY

In a discussion of what constitutes a "good" experiment, A. Franklin (1981) persuasively argued that a good experiment is "conceptually important," something he distinguishes from "technically good" experiments. Archaeology has much to gain from looking to traditional experimental sciences in developing a science of experimental archaeology. Franklin draws examples from physics and identifies three types of good experiments, classified by their relationship to theory as crucial, corroborative, and new phenomena. Crucial experiments provide evidence in support of one theory over another. Corroborative experiments "corroborate the basic or central ideas of a particular theory" (Franklin 1981:368) and are conducted as part of normal science (sensu Kuhn 1970). New phenomena experiments produce results that are "anomalous or unexpected on the basis of existing theory" (Franklin 1981:369); thus, they are vital to paradigm change. We will discuss aspects of technically good flintknapping experiments, but we first address the relation of flintknapping experiments to theory, examples of good flintknapping experiments, and how to design conceptually important flintknapping experiments.

When contemporary archaeologists think of theory, processualist versus postprocessualist probably comes to mind, as well as perhaps the long sequence of theories borrowed from cultural anthropology. How flintknapping experiments relate to such theories is not obvious; even less so is how flintknapping experiments might prove crucial, as Franklin discussed. Flintknapping experiments, even as a form of middle-range theory, may appear too far removed from archaeological theory to ever be conceptually important. This line of reasoning is based on a traditional view of theory and was challenged by Michael Schiffer (1988; see also Schiffer and Skibo 1987). He proposed a more complex view of archaeological theory in which flintknapping and other experiments can play conceptually important roles.

Schiffer divided archaeological theory into three realms: social theory, reconstruction theory, and methodological theory. Each is subdivided into various domains, consisting of low-, middle-, and high-level theories. For example, the realm of reconstruction theory includes the domains material-cultural dynamics, cultural formation processes, and natural formation processes. Schiffer employed lithic experimentation as the exemplar of material-cultural theory and suggested that "[t]he principles describing the conversion of lithic raw materials into usable tools comprise a fascinating corpus of experimental laws built up, primarily, by archaeologists" (1988:470). He suggested that principles derived from chemistry and physics will subsume these experimental laws. This indicates that the organization of technology approach employed by many lithic analysts (e.g., Amick 1999; Andrefsky 1994; Bamforth 1991; Bradbury, Carr, and Cooper 2008; Carr 2008) has its best fit in the domain of cultural formation processes. While this discussion may seem far removed from the conduct of flintknapping experimentation, we suggest that lithic analysts would greatly benefit from a more thorough consideration of theory. We are not able to fully explore this topic here, but we see the structure of archaeological theory outlined by Schiffer as having great potential for allowing lithic analysts to characterize the current state of their specialization and providing direction for future research.

Returning to Franklin's characterization of "good" experiments as conceptually important, we suggest that examples can be found of flintknapping experiments whose aim is a better understanding of flake debris. The categorization of a flake as primary, secondary, or tertiary based on the amount of cortex cover was the dominant form of flake debris analysis in the 1970s and 1980s. While not touted as such, the experiments reported by Magne (1985) were "crucial" in demonstrating that attributes other than cortex cover, such as platform facets and dorsal scars, were better able to classify a flake regarding the stage at which it was removed. A wide variety of experimental work resulted that was aimed at assessing methods and attributes for determining the technological origin of flake debris (e.g., see chapters in Amick and Mauldin 1989; Bradbury and Carr 1995; Morrow 1997).

Our own experiments, following a similar research design but using a particular type of chert, "corroborated" Magne's results regarding cortex cover (Bradbury and Carr 1995). We also corroborated the effectiveness of facets and scars over cortex cover and pointed out the need for increased accuracy in assigning flakes to stages (Bradbury and Carr 1995). Based on these findings, we suggested a multiple lines of evidence approach to better characterize the technological origin of flake debris. Archaeologists do not have a particularly good record of conducting corroborating experiments. Considering the complexity of the flintknapping process and the difficulty in controlling some variables, it is important to make the effort to corroborate experimental findings.

In contrast are experiments aimed at identifying new phenomena, such as establishing a specific technique for producing a flute on a Clovis or Folsom point (e.g., Crabtree 1966; Flenniken 1978) or examining the utility of new variables for the analysis of flake debris (e.g., Bradbury and Carr 1999; Morrow 1996; Odell 1989). Potentially, new phenomena are generated in the course of normal science during the conduct of what end up as corroborative experiments. These unexpected anomalies can lead to scientific revolutions (sensu Kuhn 1970). More corroborative experiments are needed in archaeology so that either previous results are confirmed or new phenomena are identified.

Archaeologists conducting any type of experiment, from lithic to pottery, can benefit from a consideration of the relation of their work to theory. We suggest that Schiffer's (1988) conceptualization of archaeological theory combined with Franklin's (1981) characterization of good experiments constitutes a useful means of framing experimental work. In particular, lithic analysts should see the significance of repeating established experiments so the new work will prove crucial or corroborative. Designing experiments to explore new phenomena is also critical for expanding our knowledge of the past and will require corroboration. Such cycles of experimentation would go far in better establishing material-cultural theory and cultural formation processes theory and would also provide a firm basis for making inferences from the archaeological record.

THE CONDUCT OF FLINTKNAPPING EXPERIMENTS

There are myriad ways to conduct flintknapping experiments, but certain procedures will lead to "technically good" experiments and others to questionable results. Experiments can be time-consuming. Magne (1985) reported an average of six months for his experiments, and we conducted one set of our own experiments (Bradbury and Carr 1999; Carr and Bradbury 2001) over a similar time frame, so it is critical to consider the research design carefully prior to beginning. Here, we discuss aspects of experimental research design (goals, scope, controls, assemblage size, and data analysis) that we have found important to consider in conducting technically good flintknapping experiments regarding methods of flake debris analysis. One overarching consideration we have found is that a single knapper working with at least one data recorder both speeds the process and helps ensure a technically good experiment.

A predetermined goal must be set prior to starting any experiment. The general goal is to examine sources of variability in flake assemblages related to technology. More specific goals dictate the particular conduct of the experiment. Such goals might include assessing the results of a previous experiment or a method of analysis (corroborative), developing a new method of analysis (new phenomena), and so on. If the goal is to assess previous experimental results, then the experimental design must be compatible with the previous experiment. If the goal is application to a specific archaeological assemblage, then the knapper must be familiar with that assemblage. The flintknapper should have previous experience with the raw materials present in the assemblage and have knowledge of the cores, finished tools, production rejects, and flakes debris so that appropriate manufacturing techniques are used in the experiment.

Lithic materials vary widely in characteristics such as toughness and inclusions, and familiarity with these and other characteristics will allow the experimental knapper to make informed decisions concerning percussor use, angle, amount of force, platform preparation, and similar factors. Consider, for example, someone who has only worked with obsidian conducting an experiment with quartzite, or vice versa. The amount of force needed to remove flakes in manufacturing a tool differs greatly for these materials. Knapping the material for the first time as part of a controlled experiment could lead to aberrant results. Conversely, if a knapper has previously worked with a material, this can help ensure that the resulting flake debris will more closely match that found in the archaeological record.

Another key consideration in the conduct of flintknapping experiments is the end product. In conducting our experiments, the knapper always stated the intended end product at the beginning of the experiment (e.g., the end goal is to produce large flake blanks from nodules or the goal is to produce a Kirk Corner Notched hafted biface). If the goal is unmet, then determinations are necessary regarding whether the experiment is truly representative of similar prehistoric tools and should be included in the final dataset. In some cases, a tool may be broken during the experiment. Such was also the case for prehistoric knappers, so in our work these items and the resulting debris were included in experimental datasets. In addition, one must consider whether to remove "usable" flakes from the experiments (e.g., Ahler 1989b:99) prior to the analysis to better reflect prehistoric behaviors. Greater discussion of these specific aspects of flintknapping experiments would aid others in determining both the comparability of different experiments and how well an experiment might model a specific archaeological assemblage.

The scope of our flintknapping experiments and those of many others involved two major approaches to flake debris analysis commonly employed in the United States: aggregate (e.g., Ahler's mass analysis) and individual flake (e.g., Magne's stages). The scope of the experiment may be limited to examining one of these methods individually, combining/comparing these methods, or developing a new approach, which has implications for the mode of collecting the experimentally produced flake debris. In conducting aggregate analysis experiments, it may be sufficient to collect the flake debris at the completion of each individual experiment—for example, collecting all flake debris produced while reducing a large flake with a hard-hammer percussor to a "roughed-out" biface (biface edging experiment). Notes concerning the experiment are recorded at its conclusion. Any further reduction of the produced piece, the roughed-out biface in this case, is a separate experiment.

If one is interested in studying individual flakes to examine a continuum model of biface production (e.g., Bradbury and Carr 1999; Ingbar, Larson, and Bradley 1989; Shott 1996), then each flake is collected as it is removed and notes are taken as the experiment proceeds. Bags can be prepared and labeled ahead of time, or small trays can be numbered so that each flake is placed in sequence after removal. When conducting experiments that require the collection of individual flakes, it is critical to have at least one person responsible for collection and note taking. This allows the knapper to continue uninterrupted. Obviously, time requirements for these experiments are exponentially greater than for those investigating aggregate methods.

For both types of experiments, knapping over a drop cloth is necessary to ensure that all debris is retained. In our experiments, we only individually bagged flakes larger than 0.25 inches and left smaller debris for collection en masse with each change in percussor. If it is important to have all debris associated with each individual removal action, then it is necessary to devise a system for easily and quickly replacing drop cloths to ensure minimal disturbance for the knapper. This may allow for a closer simulation of prehistoric stone tool manufacturing behavior, for which it is assumed that the knapper would work in an uninterrupted pattern and find what some knappers have described to us as a "flintknapping rhythm."

Perhaps the hallmark of the experimental tradition is control of variables. For the most part, archaeologists conducting flintknapping experiments recognize this, particularly for experiments aimed at investigating flake debris. Amick and his colleagues (1989:4) pointed out that the "aspect of control is essential to experimental studies." As previously discussed, experiments involving fracture mechanics necessitate strict control of variables. Those experiments in which a stone tool is produced or a core is reduced involve less control. Lack of controls can impact whether an experiment is technically good and can render results unreliable. The degree of control also affects the coverage of experimental findings.

Experiments involving a human flintknapper are usually designed to control certain variables and not others, or variables are considered "controlled" by establishing the knapper's skill. For example, regularly controlled variables include raw material type, percussor type, mode of reduction, and final product. Other variables such as the handedness of the knapper and knapping style are not controlled, as they are considered to be subsumed by the skill of the knapper. A highly accomplished knapper, whether left- or right-handed, is thought to produce a reliable and valid experimental flake assemblage because of skill level. Further exploration of these assumptions is necessary. Skill level was a variable Stanley Ahler (1989a) recorded in developing the impressive number of experiments involved in his mass analysis method.

Experiments that include one material type, one percussor, one reduction mode, one knapper, and one type of final product would have moderate control but low coverage. The applicability of the results alone to an archaeological assemblage is questionable. Obtaining consistent experimental results from a series of experiments in which variables are manipulated would provide for much greater coverage. Important questions arise regarding whether an experiment that results in an end product that deviates significantly from those recovered archaeologically should be included in an experimental database. Certainly, a subjective element is involved in determining whether a final product is valid. Objectivity is increased by determining if the end product fits the range of variability seen in prehistoric assemblages in attributes such as length, width, thickness, and weight.

Experiments must be designed so that a statistically sufficient sample size is obtained. Several experiments should be conducted for each reduction type to ensure that comparable datasets and not outliers are produced. For example, a single biface reduction experiment to model biface reduction would have low coverage and would unlikely produce an assemblage adequate for statistical consideration. If several biface reductions are conducted, then statistical comparisons can be made to determine the comparability of the results and to investigate effects of raw material type, percussor type, knapper skill level, and similar factors. Depending on the statistical methods, a large number of experiments may be required, and the experimental database will need to be built over several years.

A final important consideration is analysis of the resulting flake debris in terms of variables investigated and method of recording those variables. This subject is discussed too rarely as a formal part of experiments, but it is obviously vital for the usefulness of the results. The data analysis will vary from experiment to experiment. If the goal is to examine aggregate methods of flake analysis, then standard geologic sieves are needed, and the size-grade data should be entered into a database table. Are multiple people going to be involved in the analysis of the resulting debris? If so, inter-observer error is a consideration. Amick and colleagues (1989:3) included analyst bias as a consideration related to the reliability of experimental results. If two analysts are recording the same variable and they produce different data for the same flake, then the results are unreliable. George Odell (1989) established a 95 percent correspondence between lithic analysts as an appropriate level of performance, and we made sure to meet this standard on the variables used in our analyses (e.g., Bradbury and Carr 1995, 1999, 2004).

There are many appropriate ways to conduct technically good experiments, and such experiments have the potential to be theoretically good as well. However, specific aspects of the way an experiment is conducted may invalidate the results or prevent certain conclusions from being accurately drawn. In the first case, employing tools unavailable or unused by prehistoric knappers, such as copper billets or rock saws, invalidates inferences based on analysis of the resulting debris. An example of the second case would be failing to gather flake debris by reduction stage during the experimental flintknapping process and then attempting to "reconstruct" stages in a manner inconsistent with other experimenters, but still endeavoring to test their analytical method. Greater discussion of the experimental research design and description of the conduct of specific experiments are critical to judge the applicability of specific experimental results against other cases, both experimental and archaeological.

EXAMPLES OF EXPERIMENTS

Given the preceding discussion, it is now appropriate to examine specific flintknapping experiments. These examples illustrate the great variety of flintknapping experimentation involving flake debris. In particular, the scope ranges from examination of a specific problem to characterization of entire assemblages. Relating these experiments to theory helps illustrate the previous discussion. Many other experiments would serve for this endeavor, a testament to the vitality of flintknapping experimentation in modern flake debris analysis.

Our first example demonstrates the use of flintknapping experiments to address a specific question. During an archaeological survey, Bradbury (2001) noted the presence of mechanically produced flake debris (rock crusher producing road gravel) throughout the survey area. An examination of previous survey reports in the area suggested that mechanically produced flake debris was sometimes included with culturally produced debris when defining and analyzing sites. It was of interest to determine if mechanically produced flakes could be reliably differentiated from culturally produced flakes. A series of simple experiments was conducted using the same raw material (Blanding chert) used by prehistoric groups, which is also used today for producing road gravel. The experiments consisted of bipolar core reduction, freehand core reduction, and soft-hammer biface production—reflecting some of the common reduction techniques inferred from archaeological assemblages. Experimentally produced flakes were collected en masse at the end of each reduction, and collections of road gravel were also made. Several analytical methods were developed that allowed for distinguishing between the mechanically and humanly produced flakes. These methods were applied to archaeological materials. In addition, other factors (context of the materials, distance to roads, and similar factors) were considered in conjunction with the flake data. These experiments clearly fall under Schiffer's (1988) realm of reconstruction theory and in the domain of material-cultural dynamics. Also, these experiments could be considered corroborative (sensu Franklin 1981) in the sense that a variety of early flintknapping experiments (see Johnson 1978) were aimed at determining whether flakes produced in the manufacture of stone tools could be sorted from those produced in some other process, particularly natural processes.

In another vein, Bradbury and Carr (1999) used flintknapping experiments to assess different methods of flake debris analysis. We examined several variables used in analyses that employ a stage approach and studied flake debris analyses that rely on continuum-based models more specifically. Data from flintknapping experiments demonstrated that continuum-based models derived from one dataset could be successfully applied to other datasets and provide reliable results. In addition, this work complemented earlier studies by expanding on continuum-based models. Previous experiments (Ingbar, Larson, and Bradley 1989; Shott 1996) had only examined debris from bifacial tool manufacture. We included data from experiments involving core reduction and other types of tool production in the model. In this work, a means was developed to reliably separate flake debris into core and tool categories. Next, an equation was put forth that allowed flake debris resulting from tool production to be examined using a standardized scale that demonstrates what portion(s) of the continuum is represented in an assemblage. This scale allows for direct comparison between two assemblages. This work is best classified as material-cultural dynamics because it produces correlates by focusing on whether debris resulted from core reduction or tool production and further characterizing the tool debris. These experiments are also corroborative (sensu Franklin 1981) in relation to work by Eric Ingbar and his colleagues (1989) and Michael Shott (1996), as well as producing a new method that itself needs corroboration.

Ahler's (1989a, 1989b, 1975) mass analysis experiments are an example of new phenomena (sensu Franklin 1981) because they define "mass analysis" as a method based on the specific relationship of certain aggregate flake data to technological variables. His experimental program was conducted for over twenty years. Ahler's work provides an example of an extensive experimental program with great coverage. The experimental program's early focus was on Crescent Hills chert in an examination of Plains Village sites in South Dakota (Ahler 1975). The range of experiments and the raw materials employed expanded as Ahler's interests shifted. The experiments were updated continually and used multiple knappers and multiple raw materials. The design of the experiments remained essentially the same throughout the program. Individual experiments consisted of removing flakes from a core for further reduction, producing a biface from a flake, and producing unifacial tools, to name a few. Flake debris was collected en masse at the conclusion of each experiment. Analysis of the resulting debris was conducted by passing all flakes through a series of standardized geologic sieves. Counts and weights of flakes retained in each size grade and the number of flakes exhibiting cortex were recorded, along with information concerning the experiment. A discriminant function analysis was performed using the experimental data to provide classification equations for the examination of flake debris recovered from archaeological sites. Again, this work fits under material-cultural dynamics because it characterizes flake debris as to its technological origin and also represents new phenomena in terms of the specifics of how this characterization is accomplished. While some experimental work has corroborated certain aspects of mass analysis (Bradbury and Carr 1995, 2004, 2009), others have used experiments to demonstrate its limitations (Andrefsky 2007, 2009).

CONCLUDING THOUGHTS

It has been a decade and a half since Robert Kelly (1994:135) suggested that those interested in technological organization join flintknappers for a "week-long workshop . . . to hold experiments and collect data that could help us seriously evaluate things like the Sullivan/Rozen categories, the utility of mass analysis and size grade distributions, or the measurability of variables." While such a gathering would undoubtedly be both fun and rewarding, the fact that it has yet to occur speaks to the remote chance that it will ever happen. Flintknapping experimentation is likely to continue to occur in the manner described here: individuals or small teams of researchers will conduct limited experiments and publish their results. We hope our discussion will help spur future experimentation and provide useful guidelines for its conduct.

Over the years, we have "endured" and enjoyed countless hours of flake debris analysis and are convinced that significant patterning exists in archaeological lithic assemblages to allow us to infer a wide range of prehistoric behavior. Further, we remain positive of the former and future contributions flintknapping experimentation can and has provided for making these inferences. These contributions are more likely to be realized if those conducting the experiments carefully consider the relation of their work to theory and ensure that their experimental research design is technically good. For example, we see important implications deriving from the consideration of how to better integrate flake debris in models of technological organization (i.e., Carr and Bradbury n.d.; Nelson 1991).

Many areas for future investigation of flake debris can profitably employ experimentation. They include, but are not limited to, the role of idiosyncratic knapping behavior; further controlling variables by deconstructing knapper skill level; combining elements of highly controlled, replication, and technological experimental traditions, and so on. A great amount of work is necessary in corroborating the results of a wide range of experiments involving disparate flake variables (e.g., cortex cover, maximum length, platform facets) and analytical methods (e.g., aggregate, stage, continuum). While the amount of potential work appears daunting and conducting experiments is time-consuming, the benefits clearly outweigh the costs. If we are ever to "explain the archaeological record" with any accuracy, experimentation must play a key role.

ACKNOWLEDGMENTS

We thank Jeffrey Ferguson for asking us to contribute to this volume. Comments by Michael Schiffer and an anonymous reviewer allowed us to focus our thinking and clarify connections. That is, their comments greatly improved the chapter. We thank Sarah Price for her involvement in some of our more recent experimental work and for commenting on this chapter. We owe a final thanks to all the flintknappers we have observed, especially those who took the time to teach us this ancient art and science. Any errors or omissions are ours alone.

REFERENCES CITED

Ahler, S. A.
1975 Pattern and Variety in Extended Coalescent Lithic Technology. PhD dissertation, Department of Anthropology, University of Missouri, Columbia. University Microfilms, Ann Arbor, Mich.
1989a Experimental Knapping with KRF and Midcontinent Cherts: Overview and Applications. In *Experiments in Lithic Technology*, ed. D. S. Amick and R. P. Mauldin, 67–99. BAR International Series 528. Archaeopress, Oxford.
1989b Mass Analysis of Flaking Debris: Studying the Forest Rather than the Trees. In *Alternative Approaches to Lithic Analysis*, ed. D. O. Henry and G. H. Odell, 85–118. Archaeological Papers 1. American Anthropological Association, Arlington, Va.

Amick, D. S.
  1999   New Approaches to Understanding Folsom Lithic Technology. In *Folsom Lithic Technology: Explorations in Structure and Variation*, ed. D. S. Amick, 1–11. International Monographs in Prehistory, Ann Arbor, Mich.

Amick, D. S., and R. P. Mauldin (editors)
  1989   *Experiments in Lithic Technology*. BAR International Series 528. Archaeopress, Oxford.

Amick, D. S., R. P. Mauldin, and L. R. Binford
  1989   The Potential of Experiments in Lithic Technology. In *Experiments in Lithic Technology*, ed. D. S. Amick and R. P. Mauldin, 1–14. BAR International Series 528. Archaeopress, Oxford.

Andrefsky, W.
  1994   Raw-Material Availability and the Organization of Technology. *American Antiquity* 59(1):21–34.
  1998   *Lithics: Macroscopic Approaches to Analysis*. Cambridge University Press, Cambridge.
  2001   Emerging Directions in Debitage Analysis. In *Lithic Debitage: Context, Form, Meaning*, ed. W. Andrefsky Jr., 2–14. University of Utah Press, Salt Lake City.
  2007   The Application and Misapplication of Mass Analysis in Lithic Debitage Studies. *Journal of Archaeological Science* 34:392–402.
  2009   The Analysis of Stone Tool Procurement, Production, and Maintenance. *Journal of Archaeological Research* 17:65–103.

Bamforth, D. B.
  1991   Technological Organization and Hunter-Gatherer Land-Use: A California Example. *American Antiquity* 56:217–234.

Bleed, P.
  2004   Refitting as Aggregate Analysis. In *Aggregate Analysis in Chipped Stone*, ed. C. T. Hall and M. L. Larson, 184–198. University of Utah Press, Salt Lake City.

Bordes, F.
  1978   Comments on "A History of Flint-Knapping Experimentation, 1838–1976" by L. Lewis Johnson. *Current Anthropology* 19(2):359–360.

Bradbury, A. P.
  2001   Modern or Prehistoric: Experiments in Distinguishing between Culturally and Mechanically Produced Chipped Stone Artifacts. *North American Archaeologist* 22(3):231–258.

Bradbury, A. P., and P. J. Carr
  1995   Flake Typologies and Alternative Approaches: An Experimental Assessment. *Lithic Technology* 20(2):100–116.
  1999   Examining Stage and Continuum Models of Flake Debris Analysis: An Experimental Approach. *Journal of Archaeological Science* 26(1):105–116.
  2004   Combining Aggregate and Individual Methods of Flake Debris Analysis: Aggregate Trend Analysis. *North American Archaeologist* 25(1):65–90.

2009   Hits and Misses When Throwing Stones at Mass Analysis. *Journal of Archaeological Science* 36(12):2788–2796.

Bradbury, A. P., P. J. Carr, and D. R. Cooper
2008   Raw Material and Retouched Flakes. *In Lithic Technologies: Measures of Production, Use, and Curation,* ed. William Andrefsky Jr., 233–254. Cambridge University Press, Cambridge.

Buck, B. A.
1982   Ancient Technology in Contemporary Surgery. *Western Journal of Medicine* 136(3):265–269.

Carr, Philip J.
2008   Through the Lens of the Lithic Analyst: The Organization of Mississippi Delta Chipped-Stone Technologies. In *Time's River: Archaeological Syntheses from the Lower Mississippi River Valley,* ed. J. Rafferty and E. Peacock, 201–222. University of Alabama Press, Tuscaloosa.

Carr, P. J., and A. P. Bradbury
n.d.   Learning from Lithics: A Perspective on the Foundation and Future of the Organization of Technology. Submitted for publication in *Reduction Sequence, Chaîne Opératoire, and Other Methods: The Epistemologies of Different Approaches to Lithic Analysis.* Interdisciplinary Contributions to Archaeology Series. Springer, New York.
2000   Contemporary Lithic Analysis and Southeastern Archaeology. *Southeastern Archaeology* 19(2):120–134.
2001   Flake Debris Analysis, Levels of Production and the Organization of Technology. In *Lithic Debitage Analysis: Context, Form, Meaning,* ed. W. Andrefsky Jr., 126–146. University of Utah Press, Salt Lake City.

Cotterell, B., and J. Kamminga
1979   The Mechanics of Flaking. In *Lithic Use-Wear Analysis,* ed. B. Hayden, 97–112. Academic Press, New York.
1987   The Formation of Flakes. *American Antiquity* 2:675–708.

Crabtree, D. E.
1966   A Stone-Worker's Approach to Analyzing and Replicating the Lindenmeier Folsom. *Tebiwa* 9:3–39.

Davis, Z. J., and J. J. Shea
1998   Quantifying Lithic Curation: An Experimental Test of Dibble and Pelcin's Original Flake-Tool Mass Predictor. *Journal of Archaeological Science* 25:603–610.

Dibble, H. L.
1997   Platform Variability and Flake Morphology: A Comparison of Experimental and Archaeological Data and Implications for Interpreting Prehistoric Lithic Technological Strategies. *Lithic Technology* 22(2):150–170.
1998   Comment on "Quantifying Lithic Curation: An Experimental Test of Dibble and Pelcin's Original Flake-Tool Mass Predictor," by Zachary J. Davis and John J. Shea. *Journal of Archaeological Science* 25:611–613.

Dibble, H. L., and A. Pelcin
    1995   The Effect of Hammer Mass and Velocity on Flake Mass. *Journal of Archaeological Science* 22:429–439.

Dibble, H. L., and J. Whittaker
    1981   New Experimental Evidence on the Relation between Percussion Flaking and Flake Variation. *Journal of Archaeological Science* 8:283–296.

Disa, J. J., J. Vossoughi, and N. H. Goldberg
    1993   A Comparison of Obsidian and Surgical Steel Scalpel Wound Healing in Rats. *Plastic and Reconstructive Surgery* 92(5):884–887.

Evans, J.
    1860   On the Occurrence of Flint Implements in Undisturbed Beds of Gravel, Sand, and Clay. *Archaeologia* 38:280–307.

Feder, K. L., and M. A. Park
    2001   *Human Antiquity: An Introduction to Physical Anthropology and Archaeology.* McGraw-Hill, Boston.

Flenniken, J. J.
    1978   Reevaluation of the Lindenmeier Folsom: A Replication Experiment in Lithic Technology. *American Antiquity* 43:473–480.
    1984   The Past, Present, and Future of Flintknapping: An Anthropological Perspective. *Annual Review of Anthropology* 13:187–203.

Franklin, A.
    1981   What Makes a Good Experiment? *British Journal of Philosophical Science* 32: 367–379.

Franklin, J. D., and J. F. Simek
    2008   Core Refitting and the Accuracy of Aggregate Lithic Analysis Techniques: The Case of 3rd Unnamed Cave, Tennessee. *Southeastern Archaeology* 27:108–121.

Hall, C. T., and M. L. Larson (editors)
    2004   *Aggregate Analysis in Chipped Stone.* University of Utah Press, Salt Lake City.

Hayden, B.
    1993   *Archaeology: The Science of Once and Future Things.* W. H. Freeman, New York.

Ingbar, E. E., M. L. Larson, and B. A. Bradley
    1989   A Non-typological Approach to Debitage Analysis. In *Experiments in Lithic Technology,* ed. D. S. Amick and R. P. Mauldin, 67–99. BAR International Series 528. Archaeopress, Oxford.

Johnson, J. K.
    2001   Some Reflections on Debitage Analysis. In *Lithic Debitage: Context, Form, Meaning,* ed. W. Andrefsky Jr., 15–20. University of Utah Press, Salt Lake City.

Johnson, L. L.
    1978   A History of Flintknapping Experimentation, 1838–1976. *Current Anthropology* 19:337–372.

Kelly, R. L.
1994   Some Thoughts on Future Directions in the Study of Stone Tool Organization. In *The Organization of North American Prehistoric Chipped Stone Tool Technologies*, ed. P. J. Carr, 132–136. Archaeological Series 7. International Monographs in Prehistory, Ann Arbor, Mich.

Kuhn, T.
1970   *The Structure of Scientific Revolutions*, 2nd ed. University of Chicago Press, Chicago.

Magne, M.P.R.
1985   *Lithics and Livelihood: Stone Tool Technologies of Central and Southern Interior B.C.* Archaeology Survey of Canada, Mercury Series 133. N.p., Ottawa, Ont.
2001   Debitage Analysis as a Scientific Tool for Archaeological Knowledge. In *Lithic Debitage: Context, Form, Meaning*, ed. W. Andrefsky Jr., 21–31. University of Utah Press, Salt Lake City.

Morrow, T. A.
1996   Refitting and Archaeological Site Formation Processes: A Case Study from the Twin Ditch Site, Greene County, Illinois. In *Stone Tools: Theoretical Insights into Human Prehistory*, ed. G. H. Odell, 345–376. Plenum, New York.
1997   A Chip off the Old Block: Alternate Approaches to Debitage Analysis. *Lithic Technology* 22(1):51–69.

Nelson, M.
1991   The Study of Technological Organization. In *Archaeological Method and Theory*, vol. 3, ed. M. Schiffer, 57–100. University of Arizona Press, Tucson.

Nichols, J., and D. J. Allstadt
1978   Hinge Fracture Rates of Novice Flintknappers. *Lithic Technology* 7(1):1.

Nilsson, S.
1868   *The Primitive Inhabitants of Scandinavia*. Edited by John Lubbock. Longmans, Green, London.

Odell, G. H.
1989   Experiments in Lithic Reduction. In *Experiments in Lithic Technology*, ed. D. S. Amick and R. P. Mauldin, 163–197. BAR International Series 528. Archaeopress, Oxford.

Pelcin, A.
1997a   The Formation of Flakes: The Role of Platform Thickness and Exterior Platform Angle in the Production of Flake Initiations and Terminations. *Journal of Archaeological Science* 24:1107–1113.
1997b   The Effect of Indentor Type on Flake Attributes: Evidence from a Controlled Experiment. *Journal of Archaeological Science* 24:613–621.

Redman, K. L.
1998   An Experiment-Based Evaluation of the Debitage Attributes Associated with "Hard" and "Soft" Hammer Percussion. MA thesis, Department of Anthropology, Washington State University, Pullman.

Renfrew, C., and P. Bahn
    1991   *Archaeology: Theories, Method, and Practice*. Thames and Hudson, London.

Rozen, K. C., and A. P. Sullivan III
    1989   The Nature of Lithic Reduction and Lithic Analysis: Stage Typologies Revisited. *American Antiquity* 54:179–184.

Schiffer, M. B.
    1988   The Structure of Archaeological Theory. *American Antiquity* 53:461–485.

Schiffer, M. B., and J. M. Skibo
    1987   Theory and Experiment in the Study of Technological Change. *Current Anthropology* 28:595–622.

Shelley, P. H.
    1990   Variation in Lithic Assemblages: An Experiment. *Journal of Field Archaeology* 17:187–193.

Shott, M. J.
    1994   Size and Form in the Analysis of Flake Debris: Review and Recent Approaches. *Journal of Archaeological Method and Theory* 1:69–110.
    1996   Stage versus Continuum in the Debris Assemblage from the Production of a Fluted Biface. *Lithic Technology* 21:6–22.

Shott, M. J., A. P. Bradbury, P. J. Carr, and G. H. Odell
    2000   Flake Size from Platform Attributes: Predictive and Empirical Approaches. *Journal of Archaeological Science* 27(10):877–894.

Simek, J. F.
    1994   The Organization of Lithic Technology and Evolution: Notes from the Continent. In *The Organization of North American Prehistoric Chipped Stone Tool Technologies*, ed. P. J. Carr, 118–122. International Monographs in Prehistory, Ann Arbor, Mich.

Speth, J.
    1972   Mechanical Basis of Percussion Flaking. *American Antiquity* 37:34–60.
    1975   Miscellaneous Studies in Hard-Hammer Percussion Flaking: The Effects of Oblique Impact. *American Antiquity* 40:203–207.
    1981   The Role of Platform Angle and Core Size in Hard-Hammer Percussion Flaking. *Lithic Technology* 10:16–21.

Staeck, J. P.
    2002   *Back to the Earth: An Introduction to Archaeology*. Mayfield, Mountain View, Calif.

Stahle, D. W., and J. E. Dunn
    1982   An Analysis and Application of Size Distribution of Waste Flakes from the Manufacture of Bifacial Tools. *World Archaeology* 14:84–97.
    1984   *An Experimental Analysis of the Size Distribution of Waste Flakes from Bifacial Reduction*. Technical Paper 2. Arkansas Archaeological Survey, Fayetteville.

Sullivan, A. P., III
2001   Holmes's Principle and Beyond: The Case for Renewing Americanist Debitage Analysis. In *Lithic Debitage: Context, Form, and Meaning,* ed. W. Andrefsky Jr., 192–206. University of Utah Press, Salt Lake City.

Sullivan, A. P., III and K. C. Rozen
1985   Debitage Analysis and Archaeological Interpretation. *American Antiquity* 50: 755–779.

Teltser, P. A.
1991   Generalized Core Technology and Tool Use: A Mississippian Example. *Journal of Field Archaeology* 18:363–375.

Thomas, D. H.
1986   Contemporary Hunter-Gatherer Archaeology in America. In *American Archaeology Past and Future: A Celebration of the Society of American Archaeology 1935–1985,* ed. D. J. Meltzer, D. D. Fowler, and J. A. Sabloff, 237–276. Smithsonian Institution Press, Washington, D.C.
1999   *Archaeology: Down to Earth*. Harcourt Brace College Publishers, Fort Worth.

Tsirk, A.
1974   Mechanical Basis of Percussion Flaking: Some Comments. *American Antiquity* 39:122–130.
1979   Regarding Fracture Initiations. In *Lithic Use-Wear Analysis*, ed. B. Hayden, 97–112. Academic Press, New York.

CHAPTER FIVE

Conducting Experimental Research as a Basis for Microwear Analysis

Douglas B. Bamforth

○ ○ ○
○ ○ ○
○ ○ ○

This chapter focuses on how to design and execute programs of experimentation intended to help archaeologists interpret traces of use in the edges of ancient flaked stone tools. Archaeologists who specialize in such interpretation are referred to as "microwear analysts," and well-designed and executed experimentation is central to their training and research. Relatively few archaeologists self-identify as microwear analysts and pass through this training, but virtually all archaeologists who work on pre-metal periods of human history act as if they implicitly view themselves as at least basic microwear analysts, as evidenced by the near universality of distinctions between "used" and "unused" flakes—drawn in both the field and the lab. Many of the issues addressed here are as important to this kind of inference as they are to systematic, detailed study of use traces, although this reality is not widely appreciated in our field.

The term "microwear analysis" refers to the study of alterations to the edge of a flaked stone tool to infer something about how it was used. However, archaeologists have taken many approaches to drawing inferences about stone tool uses. I begin by briefly considering the range of such approaches to put systematic microwear analysis into its larger disciplinary context. I then discuss different kinds of microwear analysis and summarize what is currently known about their analytic potential. This background then provides a framework for my discussion of micro-wear experimentation.

APPROACHES TO INFERRING FLAKED STONE TOOL USES

Ancient people obviously manufactured stone tools to accomplish a variety of necessary tasks, and many archaeological analyses rely, implicitly or otherwise, on inferences about such tasks. For example, settlement pattern studies often depend on assertions about the distribution of ancient activities across the landscape, with these assertions typically based on the distributions of different kinds of artifacts, including stone tools. Similarly, discussions of craft specialization presuppose the ability to identify different kinds of craft production, often on the basis of inferences about the tools used in production. Explanations for many past techno-logical developments (such as the development of blade technology in the Upper Paleolithic or the shift to microlithic technology in the European Mesolithic) also depend on fairly detailed inferences of how tools were used.

Archaeologists have approached the issue of drawing inferences about tool use from a variety of perspectives. Most commonly, we often assume that at least general relations exist between tool forms and tool uses, with these relations implicit in our typologies: for example, "projectile points" are inferred to be weapon tips, "scrapers" are inferred to have been used in scraping, and "gravers" are inferred to have been used to incise grooves or lines. Examination of tool edge angles is a somewhat more subtle form of this kind of analysis, with lower or more acute angle edges generally thought to be useful for cutting and higher angle edges thought to be useful for scraping. Contextual data also inform inferences of tool use: large flakes found in bison bone beds on the Great Plains are taken to be butchery tools, and stone artifacts embedded in human or animal bone are taken to be projectile points.

However, with the exception of embedded points, all of these lines of evidence share common problems. First, they rely on assumptions about the potential uses of particular kinds of tools or parts of tools that derive largely from traditional archaeological usage and are rarely supported empirically. This is a particular problem with tool types ("utilized" flakes, gravers, denticulates, raclettes, and similar types) that can be produced equally well by human beings or by natural processes, such as trampling and subsoil sediment movements (McBrearty et al. 1998). Archaeologists are also demonstrably not very good at distinguishing use-modified from otherwise modified edges (Young and Bamforth 1990), implying that many identifications of these classes of "tools" are simply incorrect. Second, even in cases where our assumptions about the relation between tool form and function are correct (as they often are), knowing a tool's *potential* use is not the same as knowing its *actual* use or, indeed, knowing whether it was used at all. For example, measuring the angle of an edge to infer its use presupposes that it was used. In addition, none of these approaches to inferring tool uses provides very specific information regarding tasks: if a particular tool really is a scraper, what was it used to scrape? Finally, while context can provide important evidence, the complexity of site formation processes ensures that artifacts found together in a site will not always pertain to the same occupation of that site. Ethnoarchaeological data make it clear that tools used together in particular tasks are rarely discarded together as a group in their context of use in any event.

APPROACHES TO MICROWEAR ANALYSIS

Analysis of direct evidence of the uses to which individual tools were actually put—that is, microwear analysis—is the only presently available means of avoiding problems such as these. This work has a long history in archaeology, with at least informal observations of use traces made throughout most of the twentieth century (Olausson 1980). Systematic attention to microwear traces grew largely out of Sergei Semenov's (1962) work in the 1960s and accelerated with the development of systematic experimental programs in the United States and elsewhere since the 1970s (Ahler 1971; Kamminga 1982; Keeley 1980; Odell 1974; Odell and Odell-Vereecken 1980; Tringham et al. 1974; Vaughan 1985).

Existing work recognizes four general kinds of direct evidence of tool use (see also Keeley 1980; Vaughan 1985): edge damage (breakage along the working edge of a tool), striae (scratches on the tool's surface), polishes (alterations to the smoothness and brightness of a tool's surface), and residues (including both physical fragments and chemical traces of the material a tool was used on). The study of residues on tool edges is a specialization all its own and requires distinct techniques of analysis (see, for example, Shanks, Kornfeld, and Hawk 1999). This chapter therefore focuses on the first three of these, all of which are best examined microscopically. Edge damage can be studied at magnifications from 10× to 75× with either a binocular or an incident light microscope, while striation patterns and polishes are best examined with an incident light microscope at magnifications from 100× to 400×.

The archaeological literature often distinguishes between a "low-magnification" approach to microwear analysis focused primarily on edge damage and a "high-magnification" approach focused on polishes and striae. However, this dichotomy is misleading: accurate and detailed microwear inferences depend on integrating observations of all three of these kinds of traces, and microwear analysts must therefore work at a range of magnifications. At all levels of magnification, though, drawing accurate inferences depends on being able to recognize patterns on tool edges that result from use and not from some other process as well as patterns that result from different uses. Drawing such distinctions depends in turn on having observational standards, which can derive only from comparisons between archaeological patterns and patterns on artifacts with known use and taphonomic histories. Such comparisons depend on experimentation.

A NOTE ON MICROSCOPY

However, such comparisons also depend on being able to see relevant details of tool edges and surfaces. Different kinds of wear traces need to be studied using different kinds of equipment, and attention to issues of microscopy is thus essential. A wide variety of microscopes can be used to examine artifact surfaces, and detailing this variety is beyond the scope of this chapter. However, some basic distinctions are important.

Microwear analysis developed using optical microscopy, in which the analyst views the tool surface through a pair of lenses (the eyepiece and the objective lens). Optical microscopes can be *binocular* or *stereoscopic*. The latter are generally designed for work at relatively low magnifications and rely on light sources external to the instrument. They are truly stereoscopic, in that they have two eyepieces and two objective lenses and thereby bring a distinct image to each of the analyst's eyes. This gives them good depth of field, but the reliance on external light sources this typically requires means that much of the light directed on the surface being examined is scattered outside the microscope. This produces darker and darker images as magnifications increase and a smaller and smaller area of the examined surface is visible through the lenses, thus limiting the visibility of the surface.

In contrast, binocular microscopes have a single objective lens and use a prism to split the light from this lens in two, bringing identical images to each of the two eyepieces. These microscopes are generally designed for use at relatively higher magnifications, and many rely on light sources internal to the instrument (referred to as "incident" illumination). By keeping the light contained within the instrument, the image increases in brightness with increasing magnification by concentrating the same amount of light on a smaller and smaller area. This latter kind of microscope is generally required to work at magnifications above 100×. Importantly, most high-magnification work relies on metallurgical microscopes designed to examine surfaces. Microscopes designed to view thin sections have very short working distances, severely limiting the size of the object that can be placed on the stage, but even metallurgical microscopes equipped with special lenses have very small working distances (a centimeter or less) at magnifications of 200×. Most (although not all) optical microscopes also use movable stages and fixed lens systems, easing back strain for the analyst. However, movable stages are set below the optics, limiting their movement and hence object size.

The recent development of digital microscopes does not solve the problem of short working distances but can help dramatically with the problem of object size. A variety of such microscopes is available, many of which feed a digital image directly to a computer. This eliminates the use of eyepieces and makes it possible to mount the microscope on a flexible stand rather than a fixed stage, allowing examination of very large artifacts. Image-processing software can also enhance depth of field at high magnifications.

Aspiring analysts planning to purchase a microscope would do well to discuss the variety of instruments available with knowledgeable salespeople and particularly to emphasize the size of the object a given instrument can accommodate. Many microscopes suitable for high-magnification analysis, particularly optical microscopes, are expensive, and it is often worth the minimal effort involved to locate a dealer who refurbishes and sells used instruments.

A FRAMEWORK FOR EXPERIMENTATION: WHAT WE KNOW ABOUT THE POTENTIAL AND LIMITATIONS OF MICROWEAR ANALYSIS

Experimental programs can obviously be most effectively designed, and their outcomes most effectively assessed, within the framework of existing knowledge. It is particularly important to understand what past research has documented about both the potential of and the limits on the interpretive possibilities of microwear analysis.

What Kinds of Uses Can We See?

To begin, it is essential to understand the kind of information microscopic analysis offers. Human beings use tools to accomplish desired ends, and tools enter into the process of achieving these ends in a variety of ways: for example, people may need to scrape wood in many different contexts, and some of these contexts may involve a great many other kinds of tool uses in addition to scraping and a variety of materials in addition to wood. Analysis of the traces of use on the edge of any individual stone tool, then, tells us only about the way in which that specific tool was used and does not automatically place that use into any larger behavioral context. For example, Douglas Bamforth (1993) identified clear traces of reaming shell (that is, expanding an existing hole in a piece of shell) on tools from a Chumash town on the central California coast. By themselves, these traces identify the tools' specific use, but they do not tell us why such a use was necessary. However, consideration of the diameter of the holes that were made (based on the width of the reamers) and the kinds of shell artifacts in the Chumash area that contain holes of that size indicates that these tools were almost certainly used to manufacture abalone shell fishhooks.

The fact that contextual and other data are often required to make microwear analysis meaningful in human terms introduces the important conceptual distinction between the specific things individual stone tools were used to do, which we can call *tasks*, and the larger (and culturally more meaningful) interrelated sets of tasks we can call *activities*. Microwear analysis tells us about the first of these but provides only part of the information needed to reconstruct the second.

With this in mind, it is useful to recognize four increasingly specific levels of inference as basic goals for microwear analysis: (1) identifying the area(s) of a tool that were used, (2) identifying the mode of tool use (e.g., cutting, scraping, drilling), (3) identifying the general hardness of the material on which tools were used (also referred to as the "worked material" or the "contact material"), and (4) identifying specific kinds of contact material. These four inferences do not exhaust the kinds of behavioral information that can be obtained though microscopic examination of a tool surface, which can include evidence for hafting, scavenging of previously manufactured implements, reuse and recycling, heat alteration, and other aspects of ancient technological behavior. Microscopic study of tool surfaces can provide important taphonomic data as well. However, these four levels of inference do provide a means of organizing what is known about how well we can presently achieve the fundamental goal that has driven the development of microwear analysis.

Widely recognized modes of tool use include cutting or sawing, scraping, whittling, chopping, wedging or splitting, graving or incising, drilling (initiating a hole in a hard material), reaming (expanding an existing hole in a hard material), piercing or perforating, and projection. To date, the contact materials shown to produce well-documented distinctive microwear traces include wood, bone/antler/ivory, fresh hide, dry hide, plants, shell, and meat; in addition, butchering produces tools with combinations of polish and other traces characteristic of use on both meat and bone (Keeley 1980; Vaughan 1985; Yerkes 1983). There may also be systematic differences among traces produced by different kinds of plants (Unger-Hamilton 1985) and on burned and unburned wood (Binneman and Deacon 1986), although more work is needed to confirm, and possibly expand, this possibility. In addition, scaling fish produces distinctive striation patterns and an unusual residue, although the residue is usually destroyed by post-depositional processes (Bamforth 1993; Van Gijn 1984–1986). When this residue is absent, experiments indicate that tools used to process but not scale fish resemble tools used to cut meat. More limited experiments also suggest that tools used on stone (for example, in the production of soapstone bowls) and potsherds (for example, to drill repair holes in cracked pots) form distinctive traces.

Assessing Potentials and Limits: How Well Can We See Tool Uses?

Archaeologists regularly claim to be able to infer many aspects of past ways of life without providing concrete evidence to support those claims. However, in contrast to many (although not all) technical specializations in our field, microwear analysis has tested its assertions through blind tests, which provide a particularly powerful basis for assessing how accurate microwear inferences actually are. Bamforth's (1988) summary of the aggregate results of a number of blind tests provides a baseline for considering this issue, but, before summarizing those results, it is important to consider how we decide if an interpretation offered in a given blind test is correct.

The most straightforward way to evaluate blind test results is to tabulate correct and incorrect interpretations for each of the four levels in interpretation noted earlier. In most cases this is not difficult: tool edges are either used or unused, and most modes of use (scraping, cutting, and other modes) are fairly distinct from one another. However, some debate exists over scoring inferences at the most specific level, that is, contact material. In particular, Roger Grace (1996) has argued that Bamforth and his colleagues (1990) erred in treating an inference of "used on meat" as correct when the tool in question was actually used on fish. This critique highlights two distinct approaches to scoring blind tests. Grace's approach appears to rely on evaluating inferences against the kinds of differences he would like to be able to detect: salmon are not bison, and it would indeed be useful to be able to distinguish traces on tools used to process one from traces on tools used to process the other. After all, some human societies have exploited both of these creatures. Sadly, though, experimental evidence indicates that, absent the residue characteristic of processing fish and the striation pattern characteristic of scaling fish, such a distinction cannot be made. A second approach to scoring blind tests takes such problems into account. Essentially, this approach asserts that the categories used to assess whether an inference in a blind test is correct should be the categories empirically known to produce different kinds of wear traces, not the categories we wish would produce different kinds of wear traces.

Taking this second approach, Bamforth's (1988) tabulations of blind test results indicate—perhaps unsurprisingly—that analyses that rely on a wider range of traces, particularly those that incorporate information on all three major classes of trace, provide more accurate information at more specific levels of inference than do analyses that rely on a narrower range of traces (see also Keeley 1981). It is particularly clear that it is difficult or impossible to achieve even reasonably high rates of accurate interpretations of specific contact materials while relying only on low levels of magnification, although analysis conducted at such levels can provide accurate information at more general levels of inference.

However, blind tests and other experiments also make it clear that there are limits to all currently existing approaches to microwear analysis. Among the most important of these is that microwear traces do not develop instantaneously. Instead, they become increasingly distinct from one another over the course of prolonged use. Some blind test evidence suggests that it is also possible to predict which materials are most likely to be confused with one another when traces are poorly developed: for example, analysts in one test in which tools were used very briefly tended to confuse traces on tools used to work plants, wood, and bone/antler—all of which produce relatively bright, smooth polishes (Bamforth 1988). It is important to remember that briefly used tools often bear traces that indicate only that they were used or that they were used on a relatively hard or a relatively soft material and that even better-developed traces produced by some different uses can look similar. Analysts should expect to find that many tools will thus bear traces that cannot support the most specific levels of interpretation.

At least two additional important limits exist to the specificity of the inferences microwear data can support: the nature of the raw material from which a tool was made and the kind(s) of post-depositional processes to which it was exposed. Raw material is important for at least three reasons. First, some varieties of flakeable stone are more resistant to fracture than others, which means that tools used for the same task will accumulate edge damage at different rates. Similarly, varieties of stone that are mineralogically harder are more resistant to scratching and abrasion than are varieties of stone (such as obsidian) that are mineralogically softer, with similar results for striation patterns. Finally, microwear polishes form in part by dissolving microcrystalline silica from both the contact material and the tool surface, and part of the reason polished and unpolished parts of a tool's surface look different is that a visual contrast exists between the appearance of amorphous hydrolyzed silica dissolved during use and the crystalline structure of the original stone (Anderson 1980; Anderson and Whitlow 1983; Mansur-Franchomme 1983). Stones that lack silica, that contain silica in larger crystals whose low surface-to-volume ratio inhibits dissolution (for example, many kinds of quartzite), or that contain silica already in an amorphous form (i.e., obsidian) tend not to form diagnostic polishes, thereby limiting the specificity of the inferences that can be drawn from them on the basis of present knowledge (but see Lewenstein 1987; Sussman 1985).

Finally, post-depositional processes—including the physical and chemical effects of both exposure on the ground surface and extended burial—can damage the edges of stone artifacts, scratch and abrade them, and alter the brightness of their surfaces. Specific forces known to have such effects include trampling by humans or animals, wind and water abrasion, tumbling and re-deposition of artifacts by flowing water, expansion and contraction of sediments, movements of artifacts within sediments, exposure to a variety of chemicals (particularly soil carbonates), and rough or otherwise inappropriate handling by archaeologists in the field or the lab. As an example of this last case, strenuous brushing of tool edges with a nylon toothbrush can produce a *macroscopic* polish in sixty seconds. Although it is *not* the case that non-use forces necessarily produce random or unpatterned traces on stone tools, as has been suggested (i.e., Tringham et al. 1974; see McBrearty et al. 1998; Young and Bamforth 1990), such traces can often be distinguished from use traces because the latter tend to be restricted to limited parts of the edges, while the former tend to be present over most or all of a tool or its edges. The major exception is in the intermediate stages of some forms of chemical and physical weathering, which can remove microwear polishes without otherwise visibly altering the tool surface (Plisson 1983; Plisson and Mauger 1988); in this case, the operation of these processes can be invisible.

DESIGNING A PROGRAM OF MICROWEAR EXPERIMENTS

The range of factors identified in the previous section that have the potential to affect microwear inferences should make it clear that it is essentially impossible to carry out a "complete," or universal, program of experimentation in the formation of microwear traces. However, it is possible to define two distinct domains of microwear experimentation that deal with this problem in different ways. The first of these is to provide the set of material all microwear analysts must have to train themselves and to compare to archaeological pieces (and, in the process, to provide concrete experience making and using flaked stone tools). The second is to expand our knowledge of specific aspects of microwear analysis, such as the range of traces that can be formed, the rate(s) at which they form, and the effects of raw material differences or post-depositional processes on use traces. Before considering these factors, though, it is important to address some general issues.

General Issues in Experimental Design

First, microwear experimenters need to decide if they are designing their work to replicate the kinds of conditions under which ancient people used their tools or to derive rigorously controlled information on the formation of use traces (for example, an experimenter might try to quantify the rate at which use traces form). In the first case, experiments should be designed to accomplish a particular task, and tools should be used with this goal in mind. This would likely mean that an experimenter would use tools outside, with dirty hands, or both, and would adjust the details of his or her work (e.g., angle of attack, how the tool is held, the pressure exerted) in response to moment-to-moment changes in the progress of the task performed. In the second, experiments should be designed to control as many extraneous variables as possible. In the example just noted, an experimenter might design a machine to hold tools at an invariant angle to the contact material and to exert a fixed and constant pressure on that material, so that the effects of time on the formation of traces can be isolated from the effects of other factors (see also Keeley 1974).

The results of these two kinds of experiments are not necessarily interchangeable. For example, Boyce Driskell (1986) reports a blind test in which the microwear analyst trained himself on tools bearing wear traces produced by a machine rather than by a goal-oriented human tool user. Although the overall rate of correct inference in this test is fairly high, the correct interpretations offered were mainly in distinguishing use from non-use traces; rates of correct interpretation of specific uses were fairly low. This result probably reflects the facts that some of the test pieces were put to uses not included in the experimental collection and that the tests were done in a naturalistic way while the experimental controls were used artificially.

Second, as Lawrence Keeley (1974, 1980) discusses, a program of experiments needs to be designed so it can allow an analyst to infer that a given set of wear traces can be formed by a particular kind of use and also that those traces cannot be formed by other uses. An analyst might suspect that a particular class of tools was used, for example, to work wood and could replicate those tools and use them on wood. However, even if this experiment reproduced the traces on the archaeological specimens of interest, the analyst could not demonstrate that those specimens were woodworking tools unless he or she had also experimented on bone, hide, and other materials and shown that those materials formed different traces. This does not mean that all experimental programs need to incorporate tools used on all possible contact materials; we know enough to rule out some materials in many focused experimental programs and to use past experiments as comparisons for new ones (see, for example, Sliva and Keeley 1994). However, all programs of experimentation must grapple with this issue in one way or another.

The logical requirement of drawing adequate inferences from microscopic observations highlights the fact that, as with virtually all other archaeological inferences, those drawn by microwear analysts are imperfect. No published blind test has produced perfect results, and it is always possible that some unanticipated use might produce traces identical to those of a known use. However, the pre-metal world contains a limited range of possible materials, and while archaeologists clearly have not experimented with, for example, every species of wood or plant in existence, enough experiments have been carried out with a wide selection of materials to understand the basic pattern of variation in wear traces. This fact both underscores the continuing importance of experimentation to build on what we know at present and suggests some of the requirements of any new experimental program.

Basic Components of a Program of Microwear Experimentation

All microwear analysts need to be able to recognize the basic range of variation established by existing research because the range of uses already replicated includes many tasks that are likely to have been universal or nearly universal in the past (e.g., working hide, cutting meat, working wood) and because the existing framework of knowledge cannot be expanded without understanding what is already known. This means it is possible to define many of the elements of a basic program of experimentation designed to train novice microwear analysts. However, such a program should also be adapted to the likely circumstances in which such analysts will be working, meaning that even basic experimental programs will vary from case to case.

If an analyst hopes to learn to recognize traces of use on real tools used by real people to accomplish real tasks in the past, the issue of doing "real-world" versus highly controlled experiments is moot; experiments need to replicate realistic use contexts to the extent possible. This has implications for both the setting in which experiments are carried out and the way an experimenter should conduct his or her work. As noted earlier (see also Keeley 1974), working out of doors, where ancient people used many, and perhaps most, of their tools, is important, if only because modern interior spaces are much cleaner than the outdoors (although some archaeological labs may mimic outdoor conditions better than others).

Just as important, though, ancient tools were used to accomplish tasks, not to produce wear traces for archaeologists to study. This means that to produce traces that can be compared directly with those on ancient tools, experiments need to be carried out with the task in mind: hides should be fleshed to get them really clean, wood should be whittled to produce something useful (if only a pointed stick), and animals should be butchered to produce edible meat. Furthermore, while it is useful to have helpers in carrying out an experimental program and helpers can be essential for documenting experiments (discussed later), novice analysts should do as many experiments as possible themselves. This is not in order to control for individual patterns of tool use but to familiarize themselves with the great differences between using steel tools versus stone tools. This difference is particularly pronounced in the case of unhafted, handheld stone tools, and all experimenters—including experienced tool users—should keep a first-aid kit handy.

At a minimum, a "universal" experimental program should mirror those described by Keeley (1980) and Patrick Vaughan (1985) and should include experiments working all of the general classes of material shown to produce distinct use-wear patterns. As noted, these include wood, bone and antler, hide (both fresh and dry), meat, non-woody plants, and shell. Any of these general categories can be expanded: there are many kinds of wood, for example, and they vary in hardness; further, different kinds of non-woody plants do not necessarily all produce exactly the same use trace. However, for a training program, it is useful to think in terms of a series of progressively more focused phases of experimentation. The first task an analyst needs to accomplish is to train her or his eye to see patterns, and limiting initial experiments to a few examples of materials within these categories suffices for this purpose.

Tools can also be used in different ways, and distinguishing them is an important part of a microwear inference. Experiments working materials in different ways, then, are also important. However, these can often be limited by common sense (cf. Keeley 1980)—not all modes of tool use are relevant to all materials (it is unlikely that ancient or modern humans spent much time drilling or chopping meat, for example). Because use traces develop over time, it is also essential to learn to recognize poorly developed and otherwise undiagnostic traces; experiments in any given task should vary in duration of use, from a little as two minutes to as much as thirty minutes.

While these kinds of general guidelines are useful for all novice analysts, most such analysts already know the general archaeological context in which they plan to work. Once they have learned the basic skills, or even in the course of this learning, they should design experiments to address the specifics of their work. For example, raw materials vary greatly from region to region. While it is clear that essentially the same kinds of traces form on all microcrystalline silicates, it is also clear that such factors as the color and granularity of a given kind of stone can affect polish formation and appearance, and there is no doubt that granularity and resistance to fracture affect the formation of edge damage and striation patterns. Most analysts should therefore experiment with the kinds of raw material they will be analyzing.

This implies familiarity with the range of stone types an analyst will likely encounter, but it also implies attention to the possibility of intentional heat alteration of stone in the past. Heated stone is brighter than unheated stone under the microscope, and, because it is easier to flake, it accumulates edge damage more quickly. Experiments need to be done with heated and unheated examples of a given raw material if both were used in the past.

Local conditions also often indicate that particular contact materials or kinds of uses should be included or excluded from particular experimental programs. Shell beads were often drilled on the central coast of California, and central coast microwear analysts would do well to know what tools used in such drilling look like (Arnold 2001). Analogously, elephants were not present in most times and places, and working ivory is unlikely to be something analysts who work in elephant-free settings need to do. It is also true that people in many times and places made unusual, idiosyncratic, or diagnostic classes of tools, and many of these tools may have served very specific purposes (for example, "hollow scrapers" are known only from the Irish Neolithic [Bamforth and Woodman 2004; O'Hare n.d.]). Replication of such tools and experiments in using them for a variety of tasks are therefore likely to be important for analysts who expect to encounter them in their research.

A potentially infinite range of focused experimental projects can obviously be built on the overall framework a general program like the one just outlined can provide. Experiments to identify traces left by hafting (Anderson-Gerfaud and Mellars 1990; Rots 2003), to describe use traces on non-silicious or non-microcrystalline materials (Lewenstein 1987; Sussman 1985), or to attempt to distinguish finer categories of contact materials (Binneman and Deacon 1986) have all used this framework as background and expanded on it. Importantly, these more focused studies can often pursue a narrower range of experimental possibilities because existing knowledge can rule out some options a priori, as R. Jane Sliva and Keeley (1994) have shown. This does not mean focused experimentation is not subject to the kinds of requirements discussed earlier but rather that in many (but not all) cases it is possible to use what we already know to limit the range of experiments that must be done to answer a particular question.

Documenting Experiments

No matter what the purpose of a particular program of experimentation may be, it is always necessary to document both what an experimenter is doing and how this affects the tools used. Dorsal and ventral views (or other views that might be needed to record the traces that form during the experiment) of all tools should be drawn in advance of use, and the edges to be used should be examined under the microscope. At least a few photographs should be taken prior to experimentation to allow direct before-and-after-documentation; in this context, digital photographs have the great advantage of being both available for immediate inspection and easily storable. Methods of tool production should also be recorded, including whether tool edges are retouched and the material(s) of the tools used to produce/retouch them. It is particularly important to inspect retouched edges under the microscope to check for the presence of traces formed by flaking tools prior to experimental use and to photograph such traces and note their locations on the artifact drawing. Resharpening of tools during use should be documented in the same way, and it can be useful to collect and save resharpening flakes to the extent possible.

Experimental notes should record the duration of use, how the tool was used (e.g., direction of movement), and the number of strokes for which it was used. This last observation is difficult to record by oneself without either losing count of the strokes or losing focus on the task, and it is extremely useful to have someone other than the experimenter present to help with this task. Recording any problems encountered, the point at which a tool becomes too dull for additional use, and any other thoughts or information that seem relevant while an experiment is in progress is also important. Video recording of experiments can help tremendously with this and also offers the chance to comment on the experiment immediately while it is going on. Video recording also captures an unedited record of the experiment and can make it possible to return to the experiment to gather additional data that may not initially have seemed necessary. Descriptions of contact materials should also be as specific as possible: for example, if a tool was used on wood, experimental records should note the species, its condition (fresh or dry), and the parts of the wood contacted (bark, interior wood, knots, and similar elements). Some researchers may want to stop experiments periodically, perhaps at regular intervals, and inspect the tool under the microscope to document the development of traces. However, the need to clean tools of residues to see their surfaces can create a kind of artificiality that may affect the subsequent development of use traces because residues that may be involved in the formation of at least some microwear polishes need to be removed so tool edges can be inspected. It may be preferable to use a set of similar tools for differing lengths of time on the same material to avoid this problem.

CONCLUDING THOUGHTS

Despite the overall clarity of the fundamental goal of all microwear analysis (to derive information on stone tool uses), there are clearly many potential designs for programs of microwear experimentation. This diversity reflects, first, the difference between general experimental programs designed to train novice analysts and more focused or problem-oriented programs and, second, the tremendous potential diversity within the latter category.

Not all archaeologists will choose to specialize in microwear analysis, but it is worth reiterating that there are essentially no archaeologists working on Stone Age sites who do not at least sometimes act as if they are qualified microwear analysts despite having no training in the field. The available evidence (see especially

Bamforth 1998; McBrearty et al. 1998; Young and Bamforth 1990) tells us two things about microwear inferences—even very general inferences—drawn by archaeologists who have had no training in what use traces actually look like. First, virtually all archaeologists in this group interpret traces (mainly edge damage) the same way: damaged edges are classified as "used," and undamaged edges are classified as "unused." Second, virtually no archaeologists in this group can either accurately distinguish between edges damaged by use and edges damaged by non-use processes or identify edges used for tasks that do not produce macroscopically visible edge damage.

The result of the huge volume of inferences made by untrained analysts is thus a database that is likely consistent from place to place but that also simultaneously underrepresents certain kinds of uses and includes many—perhaps even a majority of—observations that are simply incorrect. It is difficult to imagine how such a database is useful to our field. This implies either that a general experimental program similar to the one designed for novice analysts should be a standard part of all graduate training in Stone Age archaeology or that such training should at least include systematic exposure to sets of tools generated as part of such a program.

REFERENCES CITED

Ahler, S.
    1971   *Projectile Point Form and Function at Rogers Shelter, Missouri.* Missouri Archaeological Society Research Series 8. College of Arts and Sciences, University of Missouri–Columbia, and the Missouri Archaeological Society, Columbia.

Anderson, H., and H. Whitlow
    1983   Wear Traces and Patination on Danish Flint Artifacts. *Nuclear Instruments and Methods in Physics Research* 218:468–474.

Anderson, P.
    1980   A Testimony of Prehistoric Tasks: Diagnostic Residues on Stone Tool Working Edges. *World Archaeology* 12:181–194.

Anderson-Gerfaud, P., and P. Mellars
    1990   Aspects of Behaviour in the Middle Palaeolithic: Functional Analysis of Stone Tools from Southwest France. In *The Emergence of Modern Humans: An Archaeological Perspective*, ed. P. Mellars, 389–418. Edinburgh University Press, Edinburgh.

Arnold, J.
    2001   *The Origins of a Pacific Coast Chiefdom: The Chumash of the Channel Islands.* University of Utah Press, Salt Lake City.

Bamforth, D. B.
    1988   Investigating Microwear Polishes with Blind Tests: The Institute Results in Context. *Journal of Archaeological Science* 15:11–23.

1993   Stone Tools, Steel Tools: Contact Period Household Technology at Helo'. In *Ethnohistory and Archaeology: Approaches to Postcontact Change in the Americas*, ed. D. Rodgers and S. Wilson, 49–72. Plenum, New York.

1998   Test Excavations at 5GA872, the Windy Ridge Quartzite Quarry. Report submitted to the USDA Forest Service, Routt National Forest, Steamboat Springs, Colo.

Bamforth, D. B., G. Burns, and C. Woodman

1990   Ambiguous Use Traces and Blind Test Results: New Data. *Journal of Archaeological Science* 17:413–430.

Bamforth, D. B., and P. Woodman

2004   Tool Hoards and Neolithic Use of the Landscape in Northeastern Ireland. *Oxford Journal of Archaeology* 23:21–44.

Binneman, J., and J. Deacon

1986   Experimental Determination of Use Wear on Stone Adzes from Bomplaas Cave, South Africa. *Journal of Archaeological Science* 13:219–228.

Driskell, B.

1986   *The Chipped Stone Tool Production/Use Cycle: Its Potential in Activity Analysis of Disturbed Sites*. British Archaeological Reports International Series. Archaeopress, Oxford.

Grace, R.

1996   Use-Wear Analysis: The State of the Art. *Archaeometry* 38:209–229.

Kamminga, J.

1982   *Over the Edge: Functional Analysis of Australian Stone Tools*. Occasional Papers in Anthropology 12. Anthropology Museum, University of Queensland, St. Lucia, Queensland.

Keeley, L.

1974   Technique and Methodology in Microwear Studies. *World Archaeology* 5:323–336.

1980   *Experimental Determination of Stone Tool Uses*. University of Chicago Press, Chicago.

1981   Reply to Holley and Del Bene. *Journal of Archaeological Science* 8:348–352.

Lewenstein, S.

1987   *Stone Tool Use at Cerros*. University of Texas Press, Austin.

Mansur-Franchomme, E.

1983   Scanning Electron Microscopy of Dry Hide Working Tools: The Role of Abrasives and Humidity in Microwear Polish Formation. *Journal of Archaeological Science* 10:223–230.

McBrearty, S., L. Bishop, T. Plummer, R. Dewar, and N. Conard

1998   Tools Underfoot: Human Trampling as an Agent of Lithic Artifact Edge Modification. *American Antiquity* 63:108–131.

Odell, G.
   1974   Microwear in Perspective: A Sympathetic Response to Lawrence H. Keeley. *World Archaeology* 7:226–240.

Odell, G., and F. Odell-Vereecken
   1980   Verifying the Reliability of Lithic Use-Wear Assessments by "Blind Tests": The Low Power Approach. *Journal of Field Archaeology* 7:87–120.

O'Hare, M.
   n.d.   Hollow Scrapers: Morphology, Function, and Distribution. MS in author's possession.

Olausson, D.
   1980   Starting from Scratch: The History of Edge-Wear Research from 1838 to 1978. *Lithic Technology* 9:48–60.

Plisson, H.
   1983   De la conservation des micro-polis d'utilization. *Bulletin de la Societé Prehistorique Francaise* 80:74–77.

Plisson, H., and M. Mauger
   1988   Chemical and Mechanical Alteration of Microwear Polishes: An Experimental Approach. *Helinium* 28:3–16.

Rots, V.
   2003   Towards an Understanding of Hafting: The Macro- and Microscopic Evidence. *Antiquity* 77:805–815.

Semenov, S.
   1962   *Prehistoric Technology.* Translated by M. Thompson. Cory Adams and MacKay, London.

Shanks, O., M. Kornfeld, and D. Hawk
   1999   Protein Analysis of the Bugas-Holding Tools: New Trends in Immunological Studies. *Journal of Archaeological Science* 26:1183–1191.

Sliva, R. J., and L. Keeley
   1994   "Frits" and Specialized Hide Preparation in the Belgian Early Neolithic. *Journal of Archaeological Science* 21:91–99.

Sussman, C.
   1985   Microwear on Quartz: Fact or Fiction? *World Archaeology* 17:101–111.

Tringham, R., G. Cooper, G. Odell, B. Voytek, and A. Whitman
   1974   Experimentation in the Formation of Edge Damage: A New Approach to Lithic Analysis. *Journal of Field Archaeology* 1:171–196.

Unger-Hamilton, R.
   1985   Microscopic Striations on Flint Sickle-Blades as an Indication of Plant Cultivation: Preliminary Results. *World Archaeology* 17:121–126.

van Gijn, A.
   1984–   Fish Polish, Fact or Fiction. *Early Man News* 9–11:13–27.
   1986

Vaughan, P.

 1985   *Usewear Analysis of Flaked Stone Tools*. University of Arizona Press, Tucson.

Yerkes, R.

 1983   Microwear, Microdrills, and Mississippian Craft Specialization. *American Antiquity* 48:499–518.

Young, D., and D. B. Bamforth

 1990   On the Macroscopic Identification of Used Flakes. *American Antiquity* 55:403–409.

CHAPTER SIX

Experimental Heat Alteration of Lithic Raw Materials

Robert J. Jeske, Daniel M. Winkler, and Dustin Blodgett

○ ○ ○
○ ○ ○
○ ○ ○

APPROACHES TO HEAT ALTERATION STUDIES

Some of the earliest research on the use of raw material for prehistoric tool production was Charles Willoughby's pioneering work at the famous Hopewell site
in Ohio's Scioto River Valley (Greber and Ruhl 1989). Willoughby attempted to
recreate the techniques of the artisans who left the elaborate grave goods associated
with Hopewell elites. A number of other nineteenth- and early–twentieth-century
scholars (e.g., Atwater 1820; Holmes 1971 [1919]) also discussed raw material in
their research. Some of these scholars mentioned reports of the use of heat and
water to flake lithic raw material into tools—describing unlikely scenarios such as
strategically dripping cold water onto heated stones to produce a shaped tool—and
disregarded their veracity (Pond 1930:25). It is possible that these unlikely early
descriptions of heat-breakage flintknapping came from two separate uses of fire in
the manufacture of stone tools: the use of fire to crack large blocks of stone at quarries into a usable size for transport or manual reduction and heat alteration of raw
material to impart higher-quality flaking attributes to the stone. This second use of
heat in raw material preparation is the subject of this chapter.

It is now widely accepted that heat was an important aspect of the tool-
manufacturing process for many prehistoric technologies, although archaeologists

still debate how and why heat alteration occurs (Andrefsky 2005). The systematic use of heat alteration during stone tool manufacturing varied through time and across space. Not all cultural groups who made stone tools used heat alteration in the process. Some altered materials fairly often, while others did so only with certain materials. This lack of uniformity in the use of heat alteration has long been an issue for discussion among archaeologists, who often focus on the economic and technological cost-benefits of the technique (cf. Jeske 1987; Lurie 1982; Rick 1978:54–55).

Perhaps disconcerted by the early improbable descriptions of fire in tool manufacture and reported results of experiments that seemed to show that heating chert caused uncontrolled cracking in flint (e.g., Pond 1930:25), North American archaeologists did relatively little formal work with heat alteration until the 1960s. Don Crabtree and B. Robert Butler (1964) and François Bordes (1969) are considered seminal works in the modern study of heat alteration. By the 1970s, systematic experimental and ethnographic efforts to recreate and understand the effects of thermal alteration on knappable stone were well under way (e.g., Anderson 1979; Bleed and Meier 1980; Collins and Fenwick 1974; Flenniken and Garrison 1975; Gould 1976; Hester 1972; Purdy 1974; Rick 1978). Yet even in the 1980s Jeske remembers some lithic analysts' skepticism concerning the actual use of heat alteration by prehistoric people—or at least archaeologists' ability to tell the difference between natural and cultural heat alteration. However, a number of archaeological studies at that time made it clear that deliberate heat alteration during manufacture, rather than post-depositional heating of stone, did occur at many sites and in many contexts (e.g., Akerman 1979; Anderson 1979; Bond 1981; Collins 1974; Flenniken and White 1983; Gregg and Grybush 1976; Hatch and Miller 1985; Jeske 1987, 1989; Joyce 1985; Lurie 1982, 1989; Mandville and Flenniken 1974; Price, Chappell, and Ives 1982; Purdy 1974; Robins et al. 1978). The misguided notion that post-depositional fires might confuse our ability to recognize cultural heat alteration, still occasionally heard today, was refuted because the major criteria for determining heat alteration in a tool—luster and color changes—are normally detectable only after the surface of the core/tool is flaked. The outside of a heat-altered core or tool blank looks heated, not heat-altered. Similarly, a flaked tool or flake burned in a fire post-depositionally generally looks burned, not heat-altered.

The experiments of archaeologists who followed up on Crabtree and Butler's work gave real force to the ideas that heat alteration was more than a trivial aspect of lithic production and that heat alteration was discernible from unintentional burning. In particular, Barbara Purdy's (1974) research laid the foundation for systematic understanding of the principles behind heat alteration, while John Rick's (1978) efforts with materials from the Illinois River Valley expanded and enhanced Purdy's findings, providing archaeologists with a true baseline for experimental results with lithic material from a wide range of geological contexts.

These baseline studies made it clear to archaeologists that chemical and physical changes occurred in siliceous rocks once they had been heated to circa 230–400°C and held at that temperature for a moderate period of time. Exactly what happened and the mechanics behind what happened were not entirely clear at first but have since been discussed in detail (e.g., Domanski and Webb 1992; Lavin 1983; Luedtke 1992). It was conjectured that the high temperatures caused micro-cracks to occur between hematite and quartz crystals (Schindler et al. 1982:535) or a recrystallization of silica (Crabtree and Butler 1964; Johnson 1985). Both Purdy and Brooks (1971) and Rick (1978) concluded that a melting of intra-crystalline impurities and a realignment of crystal structure through the fusion of silica molecules within the stone matrix resulted in the glossy or vitreous look associated with many heat-altered materials. It also appeared that interstitial water was lost, as controlled samples lost weight during the heating process (Rick 1978:62). The acoustic attributes of heat-altered cherts often changed when the cherts were struck with a hammer, sounding more like clinking glass than clunking stone. Through dehydration, oxidation, and decomposition, heating seemed to affect iron and other inclusions within the stone matrix, which often resulted in color changes (Luedtke 1992; Pavlish and Sheppard 1983). Depending upon the material, heat-altered cherts often displayed enhanced red color or highlights, but some types of heat-altered cherts yielded black, blue, and green highlights.

The amount and types of impurities within the silica matrix resulted in significant variation between and within chert types. The variation between one experimental result and others was so great that individual archaeologists interested in understanding the use of lithic raw material at a site were essentially obliged to conduct their own experiments with the materials available to the prehistoric occupants of the site under study (cf. Mandville and Flenniken 1974; Olausson 1983; Olausson and Larsson 1982; Patterson 1984; Schindler et al. 1982, 1984). Archaeologists, especially students, undertook a large number of unreported experiments to see how heat affected the lithic materials they found in their research area.

For example, between 1980 and 1986, Jeske (aided by numerous colleagues and students) used an outdoor charcoal fire method to conduct a series of heat alteration experiments on a variety of siliceous materials. These experiments were not designed for publication per se and were conducted with varying degrees of rigor. The primary purpose of the experiments was educational: an attempt to recognize changes in midwestern cherts that may have occurred under conditions less controlled than a kiln-based experiment. Other purposes included recognition of controlled versus uncontrolled heating, detection of fire crazing versus other types of breaks, and replication studies. In the charcoal method Jeske used, lithic blanks and small cores were measured and weighed using standard calipers and three-beam laboratory balance scales. Over the years, a wide variety of materials was used in the experiments, including several types of Burlington formation cherts from the Lower Illinois and Mississippi river valleys and their tributary streams, Silurian and

FIGURE 6.1 | Chert samples used in early heat alteration experiment.

Oneota cherts from the Upper Illinois River Valley and its tributaries, Moline chert from the Rock River Valley, Cobden cherts from southern Illinois, Flint Ridge cherts from Ohio, Alibates chert from Texas, and obsidian from Idaho. Samples were placed in a shallow pit on 5–6 cm of fine sand, covered by another 5–6 cm of fine sand. Approximately thirty pounds of charcoal briquettes were ignited over the pit to produce temperatures in the sand of 230–290°C (450–550°F), measured by a thermocouple. Peak temperatures lasted approximately four to six hours; a slow cooling phase lasting twelve to twenty-four hours brought the materials to near-ambient temperature. The chert samples were remeasured, reweighed, and tested for changes in workability (Figures 6.1, 6.2, and 6.3). Workability in this case was broadly defined as a flintknapper's ability to remove flakes from the blanks and cores in a controlled fashion.

The Burlington cherts samples used in the experiments closely replicated Rick's (1978) results and showed visible differences in color, graininess, luster, and workability. Although no size differences were recorded in any pieces, virtually all of the samples lost weight. Oneota cherts from northern Illinois also showed luster and color changes, as did Flint Ridge pieces. Other samples, including Alibates chert from Texas, northern Illinois Silurian chert from glacial deposits, and obsidian from Idaho, did not show significant changes in workability or became overly brittle and less workable.

Thin flakes and bifacial blanks, circa 10 cm or less in thickness, fared better overall than thicker cores, with more consistent alteration and less breakage. Although Jeske's heat alteration experiments themselves have never been published, some of the chert samples from those sessions were later used to facilitate an experi-

FIGURE 6.2 | Placement of samples in sand-lined pit for heat alteration.

FIGURE 6.3 | Thermocouple used to measure heating of samples.

ment in bipolar versus freehand percussion. Heat-altered cherts produced demonstrably different results from unaltered cherts in that knapping experiment (Jeske and Lurie 1993).

These projects demonstrated convincingly that (1) heating cherts, or at least certain kinds of cherts, altered the physical qualities of the rock so they were more consistently and easily knapped; (2) experimentally heat-altered cherts replicated very well examples of stone tools and debris recovered from archaeological sites; (3) uncontrolled burning, low-temperature heating, and post-knapping heating were clearly distinguishable from controlled heat alteration of tool blanks or cores; and (4) prehistoric heat alteration of cherts was a conscious effort by the knapper to bring about the physical changes associated with heating stone.

FUTURE APPROACHES TO HEAT ALTERATION STUDIES

The importance of heat alteration experimentation to almost any serious study of lithic technology is apparent, even for researchers studying sites where heat alteration does not appear to play a role in tool production. The possibilities described in this section are clearly interrelated and are by no means meant to be an exhaustive list of the kinds of questions or directions for research in heat alteration.

Since so many people at one time or another heat-altered stone, it is well worth asking, why did not everyone do it? Since experiments have shown that not all siliceous materials react the same way to heat alteration, it is worth finding out if the materials prevalent at any particular site under study could have been improved by the application of heat. The answer may lie in the nature of the raw materials, in the economic and political situation in which lithic tool users operated, or in some other social or environmental factor. If the materials are not helped or are actually harmed by heating, the lack of heat alteration is understandable. If materials are improved by heat alteration and the prehistoric knappers did not heat-alter the materials, then the researcher may focus on sociocultural and economic factors (rather than on function or manufacturing variables alone) to explain the lithic assemblage (e.g., Jeske 1987; Lurie 1982, 1989; Rick 1978).

Specific questions about the underlying chemistry and physics of heat alteration of siliceous materials are still poorly understood, at least in archaeological circles. For example, when one sees changes occur in different materials after heating, can we infer that the same chemical and physical processes were involved? How do differences in the chemical and crystalline composition of stone affect heat alteration? How does peak temperature relate to the period of heating to produce changes in materials? Experimental studies have begun to provide some of the answers to these questions (Luedtke 1992).

DESIGNING AN EXPERIMENT

The design of an experiment in thermal alteration begins like every other experiment. One begins with a series of criteria to be met.

1. A warrant, or reason to think the experiment is reasonable: Why is the experiment needed? What question does one seek to answer? Are there reasonable grounds to infer that what one sees experimentally may be connected to prehistoric behaviors? How probable is it that the experiment will provide an answer?

2. Technique: What is the most appropriate technique to use to answer the question? If the goal of the experiment is a fine-grained answer to a specific technical question (e.g., does heating a particular type of rock at a particular temperature result in chemical or physical changes to the lithic matrix?) strict controls on as many physical variables as possible must be maintained to obtain clear data and make secure inferences. On the other hand, if the objective is to look for lithic attributes that can be related to archaeological correlates of prehistoric behavior (e.g., does heating a particular type of stone using natural wood or charcoal fires produce the physical changes observed in archaeologically recovered artifacts made of the same material?), then actualistic studies with fewer controls may be necessary. While actualistic studies may have fewer imposed controls by the experimenter than many laboratory-based experiments do, they still require accurate, consistent, and objective recording and reporting of observations (Kowalewski and Labarbera 2004). Inferences derived from actualistic studies often form the basis for more technically controlled experimental work.

3. Materials: Does one have the appropriate material and equipment to apply the chosen technique to the question? The questions one asks and the techniques chosen to answer those questions will determine the appropriateness of materials and equipment.

4. Control: Can one ensure that a proper control sample is maintained for reference to the material used in the experiment? Control samples are important so comparisons can be made while interpreting the results of the experiment and also because experiments often create as many new questions as they answer. The ability to return to the original, unaltered material may be crucial to finding ways to answer these new questions. It is also important for replicating the experiment (discussed later).

5. Recording: Is it possible to record the activities and events that take place before, during, and after the experiment? Proper recording and maintenance of activity logs is necessary to ensure that all relevant variables are accounted for during and after the experiment. This criterion is arguably the most important, but least maintained, of all the criteria in archaeological experiments.

6. Replication: Can the experiment be performed in such a way as to allow for replication? While the results from one experimental run may be provocative, the

ability to replicate the results under similar conditions is crucial to demonstrate inferred relationships among the variables examined. The more times one can demonstrate consistency in results, the more convincing the results will be.

7. Alternatives: Are there other variables not controlled for in the proposed experiment that might also affect the observed results? Is it possible to run alternative versions of the experiment to compare and contrast with the results from the initial experimental design?

Once these criteria are met, one may proceed with the physical layout of the experiment. The following case study of one particular raw material—silicified sandstone—serves as an illustration.

AN EXPERIMENT IN THERMAL ALTERATION OF SILICIFIED SANDSTONES FROM WESTERN WISCONSIN

Orthoquartzites are formed when silica dissolved in groundwater is reconstituted within sandstones, where it forms a cement (Boszhardt 1998a:2; Withrow 1983:41). The cement appears to make the sandstone brittle enough to permit conchoidal fracture, allowing the stone to break through the sand grains rather than around them.

A number of distinct silicified sandstone sources are located in the Driftless region of southwestern Wisconsin, an area not covered by the ice sheets of the Wisconsinan Glaciation (Boszhardt 1998a:2, 1998b; Ebright 1987; Withrow 1983:37) (Figure 6.4). Discrete outcrops of silicified sandstones, also known as orthoquartzite, are widespread throughout the area (Boszhardt 1998a:2). Formed during the Cambrian period approximately 500 million years ago, the sandstone formations were covered by Ordovician limestone (Boszhardt 1998a:2; Porter 1961:78; Withrow 1983:37). The limestone has since eroded in this area, exposing the sandstone beds, including outcrops of orthoquartzite (Boszhardt 1998a:2).

In western Wisconsin, at least eleven distinct sources of prehistorically utilized silicified sandstones have been identified (Boszhardt 1998a:2). The identification of these sources is based on an outcrop and a nearby quarry or workshop site or as secondary deposits in stream valleys accompanied by a workshop site. The raw material quality at these exposures varies, with some varieties having small inclusions or vugs within the matrix, but it is generally high enough for tool manufacture (Boszhardt 1998b:89). The color and texture also vary, but honey color or white is the most common (Boszhardt 1998b:89).

Hixton is the best-known of the silicified sandstone outcrops in western Wisconsin, and the outcrop at Silver Mound is the largest prehistoric quarry site in the state (Behm 1980, 1997:36; Carr 2004:34; Withrow 1983:37). Until recently, almost all silicified sandstone found on archaeological sites in Wisconsin was clas-

FIGURE 6.4 | Locations of silicified sandstone deposits in Wisconsin.

sified as Hixton, but the recognition of new exposures and quarry sites outside the Hixton range calls many of these identifications into question. Hixton orthoquartzite is generally fine-grained and exhibits a wide range of colors. It is typically light gray, tan, white, or orange-brown, but dark brown, lilac, and reds are also found (Carr 2004: 33; Morrow 1994; Morrow and Behm 1985; Porter 1961:80; Withrow 1983). Other types of orthoquartzite in western Wisconsin—such as Alma, Arcadia Ridge, Belvidere Ridge, Browns Valley, Cataract, Stark Complex, and Walczak-Wontor—are superficially similar to Hixton, with a similar range of colors, but they are not as fine-grained.

Still other types of silicified sandstones from Wisconsin are easier to distinguish from Hixton. These types, exemplified by King Bluff and Kriss Bluff, have small inclusions of iron oxide that resemble small dots or speckles within the matrix of the stone. The speckled silicified sandstones are typically off-white or purplish in color and are usually not as fine-grained as Hixton.

Warrant: while unaltered Hixton from a quarry may be distinguished from unaltered orthoquartzites from other quarries in western Wisconsin, that does not mean that any quartzite found at archaeological sites may be readily distinguished from any others. Although Hixton orthoquartzite is generally naturally finer grained and relatively distinct in color compared with other Wisconsin materials, would heat alteration affect these variables? What color changes occur in Hixton and other silicified sandstones when they are heat-altered? Would color changes make the distinctions among silicified sandstone types harder or easier to make? Would heat alteration affect the graininess of Hixton and the other types of ortho-quartzite? Would it be more difficult to tell heat-altered Hixton from other varieties (natural or heat-altered)? Would other heat-altered varieties look more like Hixton (either natural or heat-altered)?

Based on previous experiments and archaeological analyses with heated chert materials (e.g., Purdy 1974; Rick 1978), it is likely that changes seen in experimentally heat-altered orthoquartzites can be used to make inferences about prehistorically recovered orthoquartzite materials from archaeological sites. The previous body of work concerning chert does not provide answers to the questions about orthoquartzite, but it does provide for preliminary expectations and a relative degree of security for making inferences from experimental data to archaeological samples.

Materials

Six of the silicified sandstones from western Wisconsin were thermally altered for this study: Hixton, Arcadia Ridge, Walczak-Wontor, Belvidere Ridge, Browns Valley, and King Bluff (Winkler and Blodgett 2004). The other five known types were not altered because of a small sample size of the material available at that time.

Technique

The technique chosen to answer the questions was modified from heat alteration experiments Jeske carried out on chert. The experimental study described here began by first splitting a large piece of silicified sandstone into two pieces using bipolar percussion (Winkler and Blodgett 2004). Next, one half of the fractured piece was removed as a control sample. The other half of the silicified sandstone samples was buried under approximately 5 cm of sand, and a fire was built above the stones using charcoal. The temperature of the fire was raised slowly to approximately 500°F, or 260°C, and was held there for five hours. During the thermal alteration process, the temperature was repeatedly measured using a thermocouple (Winkler and Blodgett 2004). After five hours at the desired temperature the coals were left to burn down; once the coals had cooled (circa twelve to fourteen hours), the lithic samples were removed from the sand.

Control

Each sample was split in half to provide for an experimental group and a control group.

Recording

Sample weights were recorded before and after alteration using standard laboratory scales. Temperatures were recorded every half hour using an Omega 871 digital thermometer. The colors of all chert samples were recorded using Munsell rock color charts before and after the thermal alteration.

Replication

Two heat alteration sessions containing both chert and silicified sandstone samples were run.

Alternatives

Changing several variables could have significant impacts on the results of this experiment. In this particular case, both samples were heated to the same level for replication. It is possible that subjecting a sample to higher heat levels may have altered our results. Increasing the length of time of the heating may also have affected the outcome of the experiment. In addition, thinner or thicker flake blanks would potentially change the outcomes of the heating experiment as we conducted it. These and other alternatives are fodder for future experimentation.

RESULTS OF HEAT ALTERATION

The five samples of Hixton that were thermally altered showed only slight color changes compared with the unaltered control samples after thermal alteration (Table 6.1). One piece did change color, from (10YR 5/4) moderate yellowish–brown to dark yellowish–brown and dark reddish–brown (10YR 4/2 with 10YR 3/4). The one sample of King Bluff speckled silicified sandstone showed no color change after thermal alteration.

The other four silicified sandstone types exhibited some color change after thermal alteration. Although two of the thermally altered pieces of Arcadia Ridge showed no color change or only a slight darkening, one piece did change from yellowish-orange (10YR 6/6) to a dark reddish color (10YR 3/4). The single sample of light brown Walczak-Wontor changed from pale yellowish–brown (10YR

Table 6.1. Munsell colors of unaltered and thermally altered silicified sandstones.

Type	Number	Color	Altered Number	Altered Color
Arcadia Ridge	10YR 6/6	Dark yellowish–orange	10YR 3/4	Dark reddish–brown
Belvidere Ridge	10YR 5/4	Pale yellowish–brown	10YR 6/2	Pale yellow–brown
Browns Valley	10YR 6/2	Pale yellowish–brown	5R 7/4	Mod. pink
	10YR 6/2	Pale yellowish–brown	5R 6/2	Pale red
	5Y 8/1	Yellowish gray	5R 8/2	Grayish-pink
Hixton	10YR 6/6	Dark yellowish–orange	10YR 6/6	Dark yellowish–orange
	5Y 8/1	Yellowish-gray	5Y 8/1	Yellowish-gray
	N9	White	N8.5	Grayish-white
	N9	White	N8.5 with 5R 7/4	Grayish-white with mod. pink
	10YR 5/4	Mod. Yellowish–brown	10YR 4/2 with 10R 3/4	Dark yellow-ish–brown/dark redish-brown
King Bluff	10YR 6/2	Pale yellowish–brown	10YR 6/2	Pale yellowish–brown
Walczak-Wontor	10YR 6/2	Pale yellowish–brown	5YR 5/2 with 5R 4/6	Pale brown with mod. red

Source: Numbers and colors from Munsell rock color chart.

6/2) to pale brown with moderate red (5YR 5/2 with 5R 4/6) after thermal alteration. The single Belvidere Ridge sample changed from a moderate yellowish–brown
(10YR 5/4) to dark reddish–brown (10YR 6/2). The single Browns Valley sample
changed from a pale yellowish–brown (10YR 6/2) and yellowish-gray (5Y 8/1) to
a moderate pink (5R 7/4), pale red (5R 6/2), and grayish-pink (5R 8/2) after thermal alteration. Overall, the Belvidere Ridge and Browns Valley silicified sandstone
samples showed the most visible changes in color when thermally altered.

According to Jeffrey Behm and Aleric Faulkner (1974), C. E. Brown reported
that some of the pieces near the quarry pits appeared to be smoked or blackened.
Neil Ostberg (personal communication 2005) had results similar to Brown's when
he experimentally heat-altered samples of Hixton orthoquartzite. It is possible that
some of the deep reds that occurred in the altered Belvidere Ridge and Browns
Valley samples in our experiments may not occur naturally in any of the silicified
sandstone bedrock deposits. Overall, at this time it appears that heat alteration has
a very moderate, if any, physical effect on the color of most orthoquartzites found
in western Wisconsin.

Samples were flaked after they were thermally altered, but there seemed to
be no change to the knapping quality of the material. The degree of difficulty in

removing flakes and the amount of control in flake removal qualitatively appeared unchanged. Microphotography of the edges of flakes showed little, if any, difference between altered and unaltered materials in the structure or morphology of silica grains.

CONCLUDING THOUGHTS

Our results with Wisconsin orthoquartzites essentially confirm Behm and Faulkner's (1974) more specific study of the thermal alteration of Hixton silicified sandstone. They found that some subtle physical changes occur in Hixton after heating to 245°C for several hours (Behm and Faulkner 1974). Their conclusion was that the most intensely hued colors of Hixton (dark red, brown, black, and honey) occur naturally but that iron oxides within lighter hues of the raw material may darken the stone as a result of thermal alteration (Behm and Faulkner 1974:273–275). Behm and Faulkner provided no criteria to distinguish between natural and thermally altered materials recovered archaeologically.

Behm and Faulkner (1974:275) could not find any evidence that thermal alteration significantly improved the flaking quality of the Hixton samples, in either hard-hammer or pressure flaking efforts. Some of the samples that were thermally altered became very fragile, and some behaved "differently" (Behm and Faulkner 1974:275).

Our study also indicates that heat alteration of orthoquartzite results in few significant changes in the ease or reliability of knapping. It appears that the heating of orthoquartzites at archaeological sites, if truly intentional, was designed to alter the color of the raw material. Also, heating may have been used as a quarrying technique to break up some of the large slabs of raw material, and archaeologically recovered specimens are artifacts of that process, rather than of deliberate heat alteration, in the production of a finished tool (Gregg and Grybush 1976).

Alternatively, further experimentation using higher temperatures may demonstrate that orthoquartzites are possibly enhanced by heat alteration. Rick (1978:18–21) indicates that temperatures of 230–290°C were sufficient to produce color changes but not luster changes in Burlington chert. Temperatures of more than 300°C were necessary for uniform luster changes, but temperatures of 370°C significantly increased the likelihood of raw material burning, decrepitation, and uncontrolled fracturing of material. Replicating our experiments while manipulating controllable variables such as peak temperature and length of heating will provide more complete answers to our questions in the future.

ACKNOWLEDGMENTS

We thank the anonymous reviewers, as well as Jeffery Ferguson and Douglas Bamforth, for numerous helpful comments and editorial suggestions that improved this chapter. Many thanks to the students, volunteers, and colleagues from Northwestern University and the Center for American Archaeology who spent much time and effort to conduct experiments at the Elgin field house from 1983 to 1988. In particular, Jeske thanks Rochelle Lurie, who provided the main impetus for his work in lithics. Finally, we thank Jeffery Behm and Robert "Ernie" Boszhardt for their advice and donations of lithic samples.

REFERENCES CITED

Ahler, S. A.
 1985   Heat Treatment of Knife River Flint. *Lithic Technology* 12:1–8.

Akerman, K. H.
 1979   Heat and Lithic Technology in the Kimberleys. *Archaeology and Physical Anthropology of Oceania* 14:1–8.

Anderson, D. G.
 1979   Prehistoric Selection for Intentional Thermal Alteration: Tests of a Model Employing Southeastern Archaeological Materials. *Midcontinental Journal of Archaeology* 4:221–254.

Andrefsky, W., Jr.
 2005   *Lithics: Macroscopic Approaches to Analysis,* 2nd ed. Cambridge University Press, Cambridge.

Atwater, C.
 1820   Description of the Antiquities Discovered in the State of Ohio and Other Western States. *Transactions and Collections of the American Antiquarian Society* 1.

Behm, J. A.
 1980   Do You Have Any Hixton Silicified Sandstone Artifacts? *Wisconsin Archeologist* 61:500–504.
 1997   Prehistoric Technology. *Wisconsin Archeologist* 78:21–47.

Behm, J. A., and A. Faulkner
 1974   Hixton Quartzite: Experiments in Heat Treating. *Wisconsin Archeologist* 55:271–276.

Bleed, P., and M. Meier
 1980   An Objective Test of the Effects of Heat Treatment of Flakeable Stone. *American Antiquity* 45:502–507.

Bond, S. C., Jr.
 1981   Experimental Heat Treatment of Cedar Creek Cherts. *Journal of Alabama Archaeology* 27:1–31.

Bordes, F,
 1969   Traitement thermique du silex au solutréen. *Bulletin de la Société Préhistorique Française* 66(7):197.

Boszhardt, R.

1998a   *An Archaeological Survey of an Orthoquartzite District in West-Central Wiscon-sin.* Newly Discovered Lithic Resources in Western Wisconsin (Omnibus Issue 1996–1999), vol. 306. Mississippi Valley Archaeology Center, University of Wisconsin–LaCrosse, LaCrosse.

1998b   *Hixton Silicified Sandstone: A Unique Lithic Material Used by Prehistoric Cul-tures.* Newly Discovered Lithic Resources in Western Wisconsin (Omnibus Issue 1996–1999), vol. 306. Mississippi Valley Archaeology Center, University of Wisconsin–LaCrosse, LaCrosse.

Carr, D.

2004   The Paleoindian Use of Hixton Silicified Sandstone: Examining the Organiza-tion of Western Great Lakes Paleoindian Lithic Procurement Strategies. Mas-ter's thesis, Department of Archaeology, University of Ontario, New London.

Collins, M. B.

1974   Observations on the Thermal Treatment of Chert in the Solutrean of Laugerie Haute, France. *Proceedings of the Prehistoric Society* 39:461–463.

Collins, M. B., and J. M. Fenwick

1974   Heat Treating of Chert: Methods of Interpretation and Their Application. *Plains Anthropologist* 19:134–145.

Crabtree, D. E., and B. R. Butler

1964   Notes on Experiments in Flint Knapping: 1 Heat Treatment of Silica Materials. *Tebiwa* 7:1–6.

Domanski, M., and J. A. Webb

1992   Effect of Heat Treatment on Siliceous Rocks Used in Prehistoric Lithic Tech-nology. *Journal of Archaeological Science* 19:610–614.

Draper, J. A., and J. J. Flenniken

1984   The Use of the Electron Microscope for the Detection of Heat Treated Lithic Artifacts. *Northwest Anthropological Research Notes* 18:117–123.

Ebright, C. A.

1987   Quartzite Petrography and Its Implications for Archaeological Analysis. *Ar-chaeology of Eastern North America* 15:29–45.

Flenniken, J. J., and E. G. Garrison

1975   Thermally Altered Novaculite and Stone Tool Manufacturing Techniques. *Journal of Field Archaeology* 2:125–131.

Flenniken, J. J., and J. P. White

1983   Heat Treatment of Siliceous Rocks and Its Implications for Australian Prehis-tory. *Australian Aboriginal Studies* 1:43–48.

Gould, R. A.

1976   A Case of Heat Treatment of Lithic Materials in Aboriginal Northwestern California. *Journal of California Anthropology* 3:142–144.

Greber, N., and K. C. Ruhl
   1989   *The Hopewell Site: A Contemporary Analysis Based on the Work of Charles C. Willoughby.* Westview, Boulder.

Gregg, M. L., and R. J. Grybush
   1976   Thermally Altered Siliceous Stone from Prehistoric Contexts: Intentional Versus Unintentional Alteration. *American Antiquity* 41:189–192.

Hatch, J. W., and P. E. Miller
   1985   Procurement, Tool Production, and Sourcing Research at the Vera Cruz Jasper Quarry in Pennsylvania. *Journal of Field Archaeology* 12:219–230.

Hester, T. R.
   1972   Ethnographic Evidence for the Thermal Alteration of Siliceous Stone. *Tebiwa* 12:63–65.

Holmes, W. H.
   1971   *Handbook of Aboriginal American Antiquities Part I: Introductory, the Lithic*
   [1919]   *Industries.* Bulletin 60. Smithsonian Institution Bureau of American Ethnology, Washington, D.C.

Jeske, R. J.
   1987   Efficiency, Economy, and Prehistoric Lithic Assemblages in the American Midwest. PhD dissertation, Department of Anthropology, Northwestern University, Evanston, Ill.
   1989   Economies in Lithic Use Strategies among Prehistoric Hunter-Gatherers. In *Time, Energy, and Stone Tools*, ed. R. Torrence, 34–45. Cambridge University Press, Cambridge.

Jeske, R. J., and R. Lurie
   1993   The Archaeological Visibility of Bipolar Technology: A Blind Test. *Midcontinental Journal of Archaeology* 18(2):131–160.

Johnson, G. M.
   1985   The Use of the Scanning Electron Microscope in Studying the Heat Treatment of Prehistoric Lithic Artifacts from the North Florida Weeden Island Period Mckeithen Site. *Scanning Electron Microscopy* Part 2:651–658.

Joyce, D. J.
   1985   Heat Treatment of Alibates Chalcedony. *Lithic Technology* 14:36–40.

Kowalewski, M., and M. Labarbera
   2004   Actualistic Taphonomy: Death, Decay, and Disintegration in Contemporary Settings *Palaios* 19:423–427.

Lavin, L.
   1983   Heat-Treatment and Its Effects on Chert Color: The Results of Thermal Experimentation on Some Hudson and Delaware Valley Chert Types. *Bulletin and Journal of Archaeology for New York State* 87:1–12.

Luedtke, B. E.
   1992   *An Archaeologist's Guide to Chert and Flint.* Archaeological Research Tools 7. University of California at Los Angeles Institute of Archaeology, Los Angeles.

Lurie, R.

1982   Economic Models of Stone Tool Manufacture and Use. PhD dissertation, Department of Anthropology, Northwestern University, Evanston, Ill.

1989   Lithic Technology and Mobility Strategies: The Koster Middle Archaic. In *Time, Energy, and Stone Tools*, ed. R. Torrence, 46–56. Cambridge University Press, Cambridge.

Mandeville, M. D., and J. J. Flenniken

1974   A Comparison of the Flaking Qualities of Nehawka Chert before and after Thermal Pretreatment. *Plains Anthropologist* 19:146–148.

Morrow, T. A.

1994   A Key to the Identification of Chipped-Stone Raw Materials Found on Archaeological Sites in Iowa. *Journal of the Iowa Archaeological Society* 41:108–129.

Morrow, T. A., and J. A. Behm

1985   Description of Common Lithic Raw Materials Encountered on Wisconsin Archaeological Sites. Paper presented at the Wisconsin Archaeological Survey meeting, Madison.

Olausson, D. S.

1983   Experiments to Investigate the Effects of Heat Treatment on Use-Wear on Flint Tools. *Proceedings of the Prehistoric Society* 49:1–13.

Olausson, D. S., and L. Larsson

1982   Testing for the Presence of Thermal Pretreatment of Flint in the Mesolithic and Neolithic of Sweden. *Journal of Archaeological Science* 9:275–285.

Patterson, L. W.

1984   Comments on Studies of Thermal Alteration of Central Pennsylvania Jasper. *American Antiquity* 49:168–173.

Pavlish, L. A., and P. J. Sheppard

1983   Thermoluminescent Determination of Paleoindian Heat Treatment in Ontario, Canada. *American Antiquity* 48:793–799.

Pond, A. W.

1930   *Primitive Methods of Working Stone, Based on the Experiments of Halvor L. Skavlem.* Logan Museum Bulletin 2(1). Beloit College, Beloit, Wis.

Porter, J.

1961   Hixton Silicified Sandstone: A Unique Lithic Material Used by Prehistoric Cultures. *Wisconsin Archeologist* 42:78–85.

Price, T. D., S. Chappell, and D. J. Ives

1982   Thermal Alteration in Mesolithic Assemblages. *Proceedings of the Prehistoric Society* 48:467–485.

Purdy, B. A.

1974   Investigations Concerning the Thermal Alteration of Silica Minerals: An Archeological Approach. *Tebiwa* 17:37–66.

Purdy, B. A., and H. K. Brooks
   1971   Thermal Alteration of Silica Minerals: An Archaeological Approach. *Science*
             173:322–325.

Rick, J. W.
   1978   *Heat-Altered Cherts of the Lower Illinois Valley: An Experimental Study in Pre-
             historic Technology.* Prehistoric Records 2. Northwestern University Archeo-
             logical Program, Evanston, Ill.

Robins, G. V., N. J. Seeley, D.A.C. McNeil, and M.R.C. Symons
   1978   Identification of Ancient Heat Treatment in Flint Artefacts by ESR Spectros-
             copy. *Nature* 276:703–704.

Schindler, D. L., J. W. Hatch, C. A. Hay, and R. C. Bradt
   1982   Aboriginal Thermal Alteration of a Central Pennsylvania Jasper: Analytical and
             Behavioural Implications. *American Antiquity* 47:526–544.
   1984   Thermal Alteration of a Bald Eagle Jasper: Authors' Reply to Patterson. *Ameri-
             can Antiquity* 49:173–177.

Winkler, D. M., and D. Blodgett
   2004   The Thermal Alteration of Silicified Sandstone from Western Wisconsin. Paper
             presented at the Annual Meeting of the Society for American Archaeology,
             Montreal.

Withrow, R. M.
   1983   An Analysis of Lithic Resource Selection and Processing at the Valley View Site
             (47lc34). Master's thesis, Department of Anthropology, University of Minne-
             sota, Minneapolis.

CHAPTER SEVEN

Understanding Grinding Technology through Experimentation

Jenny L. Adams

○ ○ ○
○ ○ ○
○ ○ ○

Replication studies are enlightening, not only for recognizing the best solution to a technological problem but also for understanding that sometimes the prehistoric agent made unexpected choices or choices that created satisfactory rather than optimal solutions. Experimentation with replicated tools has been a learning technique for over seventy years and is now commonly used for understanding how things worked, especially with tools manufactured through flaking techniques (Amick, Mauldin, and Binford 1989:5–6; Haury 1931; Mathieu 2002; Morris 1939; Semenov 1964; Vaughan 1985:3–6).

Flaked lithic technologists started earlier and have been much more aggressive with experimental research on use-wear, wear rates, and kinetics than have ground stone technologists (e.g., Amick and Mauldin 1989; Hayden 1979; Hayden and Kamminga 1979; Keeley 1980; Mathieu 2002; Odell and Odell-Vereecken 1980; Tringham et al. 1974; Unger-Hamilton 1984; Vaughan 1985). In the 1970s and 1980s, the emphasis of flaked tool experiments was on controlling as many variables as possible, restricting the types of strokes, and counting the number of strokes before certain types of wear became visible on flaked edges or before retouch was needed. Some studies confronted the problem of identifying use-wear specific to different material types (see Vaughan 1985 for a summary of these studies). Tools modified by grinding or impaction (commonly referred to as pecking) or involved in grinding or crushing activities have only recently received much scientific attention. Yet these tools were involved in such daily activities as food processing, pottery manufacture, resource procurement, and others.

Early ground stone experiments in the U.S. Southwest included Emil Haury (1931) drilling tiny stone beads with cactus spines and Earl Morris (1939) cutting down trees with a stone axe. These were quick exploratory events. Systematic experiments were uncommon during the next fifty years, with Sergei Semenov's studies (1964) the best-known exception. Then, beginning in the 1980s, experiments with ground stone tools focused primarily on food-processing activities but also on other processing and manufacturing activities (Adams 1988, 1989a, 1989b). Research goals at this time were to establish baseline patterns for use-wear comparisons with prehistoric tools and to explore manufacturing techniques, wear rates, efficiency, and kinetics. Examples of research on such topics can now be found for contexts in both the New World (see, for example, Adams 1993a, 1993b, 1999, 2002a, 2002b; Kamp 1995; Logan and Fratt 1993; Mauldin 1993; Mills 1993; Rowe 1995; Wright 1993) and the Old World (see, for example, Dubreuil 2001, 2004; Hamon 2008; Menasanch, Risch, and Soldevilla 2002; Procopiou and Treuil 2002; Risch 2002).

Research on grinding food with sets of manos and metates and mortars and pestles in the U.S. West and Southwest is facilitated by fairly detailed ethnographic descriptions of various grinding processes (Bartlett 1933; Doelle 1976; Euler and Dobyns 1983; Hough 1915; Jackson 1991; Parsons 1939; Spier 1933:127; Stephen 1936; Underhill 1979). These descriptions serve as guides for designing experiments that compare and contrast various tools and techniques. Fewer ethnographic examples exist for other items, such as stone beads and axes, and for these we need either imaginative scenarios like those of Haury (1931) or cross-cultural comparisons like those of Peter Mills (1993).

BASIC CONCEPTS

Form and Function

Lithic analysts have repeatedly asked certain questions. Is it reasonable to assume that every item of the same shape was used in the same way? How do we evaluate the range of possible uses for a prehistoric tool? When learning how to analyze artifacts, it is easy to assume that "form equals function." This concept has been evaluated in the context of flaked stone analysis and found not always to be true (see, for example, Hayden 1979:61–62; Hayden and Kamminga 1979:5–6). Clearly, the same form functions in many activities, such as the screwdriver used to open paint cans, and the same function can be performed by tools of different forms—for example, all the configurations devised for bottle and can openers.

The success of determining ground stone function based on form was called into question for me twice during a restoration and research project (1975–1980)

FIGURE 7.1 | Stone bowl identified as an eagle watering bowl by Hopi elders (Adams 1979: plate 5d, 2002a:figure 5.21).

conducted through the Museum of Northern Arizona (MNA) at the Hopi Village of Walpi. The first question came up at meetings where community members of all ages were able to look at and talk about some of the items recovered by the excavations. Two items classified as mortars prompted much conversation in Hopi. Mortars, especially the larger mortars and bedrock mortars, are generally classified by archaeologists as food-processing tools. Historically, they were used for processing mesquite pods in Arizona and acorns in California (Castetter and Bell 1951:96; Doelle 1976; Euler and Dobyns 1983:259; Jackson 1991; Spier 1933:57, 96). The two items on display fit the typical description of mortars by having deep basins in which pestles crushed and stirred foods.

After one of the community meetings, a village elder explained that one of the items was an eagle watering bowl (Figure 7.1). It was used to hold water for eagles tethered on the roof during the ceremonial season. The other item was used to soften meat for elderly people who no longer had teeth for chewing. These two items had basically the same attributes, each with a basin that was manufactured into a large rock, yet the elder easily distinguished between the two.

The second question was raised during a conversation with a Hopi moccasin maker. During the analysis of food-processing tools recovered from Walpi, the manos were all arranged according to size and number of used surfaces, as was standard analytical practice. All of the "one-hand" manos were on one end of the table, and all of the "two-hand" manos were on the other end. Their dimensions and other attributes were being recorded when Willie Coin, a Hopi who worked at MNA, visited the analysis room. He looked at the tools classified as one-hand manos and said he had not seen such tools since he stopped making moccasins. He further explained that tools such as these were used to remove hair and soften the hides before cutting the moccasin pattern. However, making analytical matters even worse, manos were sometimes also used for processing hides, and he could not tell me how to distinguish which were food-processing manos and which were hide-processing handstones. All of the one-hand manos would have made good hide-processing stones, in his estimation.

These two events were reason enough to ask new analytical questions. How is it possible to distinguish mortars from watering bowls and hide-processing hand-stones from food-processing manos? The answers are important for documenting the range of prehistoric behaviors and activities at any given prehistoric settlement. The methods for finding the answers involve recognizing and understanding the techniques and attributes associated with tool design, manufacture, and use.

Both the ethnographic record and experiments provide workable models for plausible answers, but ultimately, use-wear analysis is the primary method for distinguishing food from hide-processing stones (Adams 1988) (Figure 7.2). The distinctive use-wear patterns are the result of stone surfaces being worked against differently textured and durable contact surfaces. The use-wear patterns specific to hide and food processing became recognizable only through controlled experiments, as described later.

Both intentional tool design and use-wear analyses are important for distinguishing mortars from eagle watering bowls (Adams 2002a:135). Eagle watering bowls are designed with flat, stable bases and wide rims to accommodate perching birds. A use-wear analysis of the watering bowl's interior determined that the only damage patterns are impact fractures from basin manufacture. No crushing or abrasions from the motions of a pestle are visible in the basin. In contrast, a functional mortar does not require a flat bottom. Stability can be achieved by holding the mortar on a lap, placing it in a floor depression, or propping it up with trivet rocks. Distinctive use-wear patterns are created in the mortar basin by the crushing and grinding motions of pestles.

The lesson learned from the assessment of Hopi tools is that ground stone form does not always reflect function. Rather, in combination, design attributes and use-wear patterns are prime indicators not just of the activities for which tools were designed but also of those in which they were actually used (Adams 2002a:21–24). The concepts of design and form must be distinguished. Form is a descriptive concept, "the shape and structure of something as distinguished from its material," and design is more a plan or a process "to devise for a specific function or end"

FIGURE 7.2 | Experiments comparing handstones used to process hides and grind corn.

(Webster's 1989, *Ninth New Collegiate Dictionary*). Design theory as applied to ground stone (sensu Horsfall 1987:333), "which focuses on the process of differential selection and modification of raw materials in order to achieve a desired end product, offers the potential for understanding the integration of material and non-material aspects of culture." Applied to archaeological tools, if we deconstruct the design process in combination with use-wear analyses, then we begin to reconstruct interactions between people and their things.

Design Theory

Questions about how design reflects ground stone function are effectively assessed through design theory. Design theory has application in the fields of architecture, engineering, and industry but was introduced into ground stone studies for evaluating metate manufacture and use in the Guatemalan Highlands (Horsfall 1987). As restructured for ground stone analysis, design theory assumes that tools are made to solve problems deriving from functional, economic, or other realms. The designed differences in form are sometimes brought about by sociocultural constraints, such as economy of manufacture; by physical properties of the rock, such as durability; or by perceived efficiency.

Cost of manufacture issues, such as distance to material source and difficulty of manufacture, often dictate choices among design specifications. Furthermore, the prioritization of choices reflects the sociocultural context of the relevant group making the choices (Horsfall 1987:334). To varying degrees, these disparate sociocultural constructs govern such issues as why metates are not always made of the most durable material, why there are various techniques for constructing an angled grinding surface, and why broken tools continue in use as food-grinding tools, among other things. Design theory allows for the uncertainty of knowing the best possible choice and assumes that tool design is often a compromise among choices affecting performance and costs that create satisfactory rather than the best tools for the job at hand (Horsfall 1987:335).

Gayel Horsfall (1987:369) stresses the point that properties inherent in the chosen rock types are probably more closely related to function than is form. Furthermore, multiple morphological solutions are possible for performing similar functions, yet these solutions may be delimited by sociocultural standards met through group-specific technological traditions. For example, in the U.S. Southwest, some Puebloan groups designed flat metates to be anchored in bins, while other groups continued to use freestanding metates with troughs to process their foods (Adams 2002a:120–127).

Design theory contributes to ground stone studies in two important ways: (1) it brings to the foreground the assumption that technological knowledge is behaviorally expressed in object design and manufacture, and (2) it accommodates competing constraints (Horsfall 1987:340–350; Lechtman 1999:223). The first concept is particularly useful because knowledge of the principles that structure technological performance is passed intergenerationally. The older generation passes along to the younger generation the techniques and rules for making and using things (Schiffer and Skibo 1987). Culturally specific traditions are thereby created that continue to be identifiable even as people move from workspace to workspace or settlement to settlement. The second concept is important because it allows for the recognition that people make choices among constraints that might not always be obvious. For example, choices made for economic as opposed to performance reasons may not be apparent without reconstructing the costs of acquiring the range of materials available for manufacture. Ultimately, it becomes clear that people's actions complicate analysis beyond finding simple cause-and-effect relationships.

EXPERIMENTAL SETTINGS

Two basic types of experimental settings have addressed research issues specific to grinding technology: (1) controlled laboratory settings and (2) "natural" settings, which are more typical of prehistoric contexts than of archaeological laboratories. Each experimental setting has its advantages, and choosing a setting should depend on the research question being explored. Is it more important to have the control provided by a laboratory or to recreate the natural, probably dirtier and less stable environment in which the tools were used prehistorically?

Experiments that attempt to replicate prehistoric tool manufacture and use can be further divided into those that employ a native technician who is presumably knowledgeable about specific tool use (see, for example, Mauldin 1993) and those conducted by an analyst who is attempting to replicate a specific pattern of tool manufacture or use recognized on prehistoric tools (see, for example, Adams 1999; Dubreuil 2004; Haury 1931; Kamp 1995; Logan and Fratt 1993; Mathieu and Meyer 2002; Mills 1993; Risch 2002; Rowe 1995; Wright 1993). Replication experiments such as those conducted with axes (Mills 1993; Morris 1939), manos and metates (Adams 1993a, 1999; Wright 1993), cupstones (Rowe 1995), bead manufacture (Haury 1931), and pottery manufacture (Kamp 1995) provide an opportunity for researchers to use the tools themselves and to come to understand kinetics, design differences, and use-wear patterns.

Mona Wright (1993) conducted her grinding experiments in a laboratory setting because she needed careful control over environmental variables. Her concern with wear rates required that she hold constant as many variables as possible to evaluate differences in material type, stroke type, stroke rate, and surface area. Wright (1993:346) proposed to quantify experimental wear rates and to devise a model for prehistoric wear rates, thereby making it possible to determine the life history of recovered tools and evaluate prehistoric discard rates. Traditional Puebloan ethnographies were her model for kinetics and duration of use. Replicated tools mirrored the average size and rock type (Dakota Formation sandstone) of the tools found at Duckfoot, a prehistoric settlement in southwestern Colorado. Mechanical devices were employed to control and measure changes. Wright documented that manos and metates do wear at measurable rates and that manos wear out faster than metates (Wright 1993:table 2). Ultimately, she concluded that determining prehistoric wear rates is virtually impossible because of "the inability to determine the initial weight and thickness of prehistoric manos and metates before they were used to grind maize" (Wright 1993:353). Wright's conclusions do not mean that her experiments failed; rather, they force us to rethink our concept of what is quantifiable and to formulate new strategies for future research.

To answer questions concerning kinetics, one series of experiments replicated the use of stone axes in varying "natural" settings with the intent of replicating the use-wear patterns found on the prehistoric axes recovered from Sand Canyon Pueblo in southwestern Colorado (Mills 1993). Lacking local ethnographic references for axe use, Mills (1993:395) gleaned those from New Guinea and then created source-side criteria for modeling possible axe uses in the U.S. Southwest. He manufactured axe heads, hafted them, and worked with them to chop different species of trees and to grub sagebrush out of the dirt. The cross-cultural models he chose, in conjunction with experiments and use-wear analyses, provide multiple lines of evidence for distinguishing the activities in which the prehistoric axes were used (Mills 1993:408–410). After comparing the experimental patterns with those on the archaeological axes, Mills determined that more of the prehistoric Sand Canyon axes had use-wear patterns similar to the replicated axes used to grub sagebrush than to those that chopped wood (Mills 1993:409–410). He concluded, however, that additional experiments are needed to enhance the insights he gained from his studies (Mills 1993:410). Mills used experimentation and ethnography to develop source-side criteria for model building. His subject-side evaluation produced interesting results, but, in recognition of the complexities, he took the option of hedging his conclusions pending more work.

Experiments conducted by native users bring into play their expertise on technique. One study involved a Bolivian grinder who experimentally replicated possible prehistoric strategies for processing foods (Mauldin 1993). The goal was to understand tool efficiency as it relates to tool form. Raymond Mauldin (1993:319) achieved his goal by directing the woman to grind wheat, maize, and *chenopodium* with four different sizes of manos so he could measure and compare results. The data documented that the woman processed the foods faster on the tools with larger surface areas. Because there was also patterning among the sizes of manos at different types of Bolivian settlements (main houses, pastoral, and agricultural), Mauldin (1993:318–320) decided that mano size is a good predictor of subsistence strategy in Bolivia (but see Designing Experimental Research later in this chapter and Adams [1999] for an alternative perspective). The Bolivian grinder provided the source-side criteria for a model Mauldin (1993) applied to the archaeological record in New Mexico.

No evaluation has yet compared experiments conducted with native participants to those conducted by the analysts. An experienced tool user may produce very different results from those of a novice. Documenting this distinction may have utility as well for evaluating the archaeological record.

These examples are exploratory experiments. They are useful not only for setting a baseline against which others can be compared but also for identifying the problems that have yet to be, and should be, addressed. Additional but differently designed exploratory experiments, as well as confirmatory experiments that test whether the same results are accomplished every time, are needed. Exploratory experiments show us that conceptualizations about how things might work cannot substitute for witnessing behaviors. By actually using the tools, we are forced to frame our questions more precisely.

CREATING EXPERIMENTAL BASELINE DATA

The previously described problem of distinguishing hide-processing tools from manos and mortars from watering bowls pointed to the need for a much larger program of experimentation. Clearly, it is important to understand how distinctive use-wear patterns are formed and what role intermediate substances or surfaces of different durability play in creating these patterns. Toward this end, a series of experiments continues to use replicated tools of sandstone, quartzite, and basalt (Adams 1989b, 1993b, Burton 2007). The purpose of the experiments is to establish baseline use-wear patterns from known contact situations and to create working knowledge of how use-wear is formed. This knowledge can then be used in the evaluation of archaeological surfaces and in the creation of more educated interpretations of prehistoric activities.

In a series of experiments, replicated grooved (Figure 7.3) and flat abraders (Figure 7.4) are used to work sheep medapodials into awls, smooth arrow shafts, shape digging sticks, shape gaming pieces, and make shell beads (Adams 1989b, 1993b). Replicated manos, metates, handstones, netherstones, mortars, and pestles are used to process food and nonfood substances. Through these experiments we have learned that a functional awl can be made in less than half an hour, a digging stick can be made in less than one hour, one olivella shell bead can be readied for stringing in ten minutes, and different amounts of flour are processed in one hour depending on what was ground and the design of the grinding tools (Adams 1989a, 1993b, 1999; Burton, personal communication 2008) (Table 7.1). Some of these experiments have been in progress intermittently since 1987, but other researchers should conduct additional confirmatory experiments to verify that these results are independent of individuals (Adams 1988, 1989a, 1989b, 1993b, 1999). With this caveat in mind, it is possible to discuss damage patterns in general. Jargon specific to the use-wear patterns recognized on ground stone surfaces is defined elsewhere (Adams 2002a).

Stone-against-Stone Contact

The experiments, using new manos and metates, were specifically designed to determine whether it is possible to differentiate damage caused by different inter-

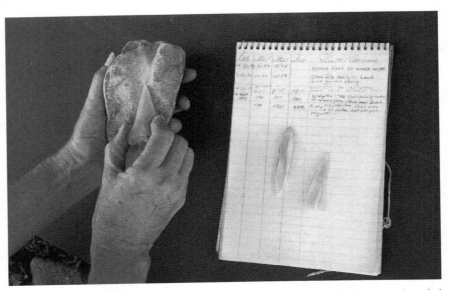

FIGURE 7.3 | Experiment with a grooved abrader. Three portions of a sheep medapodial were worked to points in the grooved abrader. Notes were kept tracking the start and stop times, the name of the experimenter, and any comments specific to the use process.

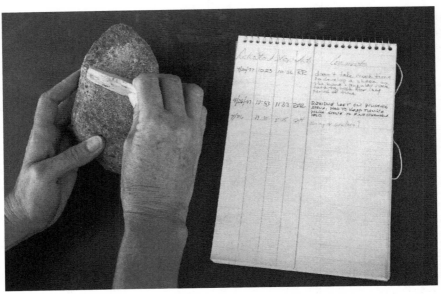

FIGURE 7.4 | Experiment with a flat abrader. One portion of a sheep bone was smoothed against the flat abrader. Notes were kept tracking the start and stop times, the name of the experimenter, and any comments specific to the use process.

Table 7.1. Results of grinding experiments conducted with each mano/metate set.*

Task	Basin Metate Granite	Flat/Concave Metate Sandstone	Trough Metate Vesicular Basalt
Dried kernels Amount/hour Results	1 cup 75% fine flour; 25% coarse meal several rock fragments	3/4 cup 75% coarse meal; 25% fine flour several rock fragments	2 cups 90% fine flour; 10% coarse meal rock dust
Soaked kernels Amount/hour Results	2 cups 75% masa; 25% fine flour few rock fragments	4 cups 75% masa; 25% fine flour no rock fragments	4 cups 90% masa; 10% kernel fragments no dust
Popcorn Amount/hour Results	3/4 cup 75% coarse meal; 25% fine flour several rock fragments	3/4 cup 100% coarse meal several rock fragments	1 cup 75% coarse meal; 25% fine flour rock dust
Sunflower seeds, raw shelled Amount/hour Results	1½ cup 75% paste; 25% seed fragments no rock fragments	2½ cup 75% paste; 25% seed fragments no rock fragments	3 cups 75% paste; 25% seed fragments no rock dust
Amaranth seeds Amount/hour Results	1½ cup 75% fine flour; 25% seed fragments several rock fragments	3/4 cup 50% fine flour; 50% seed fragments several rock fragments	2 cups 75% fine flour; 25% seed fragments rock dust

* Note: Grinding rates should not be considered indicative of prehistoric rates.
Source: Adams 1999:table 2, 2002a:table 3.1.

mediate substances between the stones. The main question is, do maize, sunflower seeds, amaranth seeds, clay, and sherds create different use-wear patterns when worked between two grinding stone surfaces? Other resources and other rock types need to be tested specifically for other archaeological contexts. After six to fifteen hours of grinding each substance, it is possible to make some preliminary observations about the different wear patterns.

The effects of abrasive and fatigue wear mechanisms are the easiest and quickest to observe at a macroscopic or low-power (40×) microscopic level. Crushed grains and striations happen immediately. As grinding proceeds, however, fine powder or meal fills up the interstices or vesicles of the lithic material and appears to slow down the crushing effects of fatigue wear. Essentially, this makes the surface less asperite and reduces the stone's grinding efficiency. Once the surface is cleaned, some roughness is restored, and the efficiency improves.

A comparison of the experimentally used surfaces suggests that no matter what is ground, the stones' surfaces have at least a few striations and impact fractures from abrasive and fatigue wear mechanisms. However, the most distinctive wear pattern is a result of tribochemical mechanisms (a combination of mechanical and chemical interactions [see Adams 2002a]) and is manifest on the surface as sheen. The sheen builds up as a by-product of tribochemical interactions between the oils in the intermediate substances and the mineral properties of the stone, enhanced through frictional heat. Whether the sheen can withstand post-depositional conditions is a question yet to be analyzed.

The tribochemical sheen is most obviously visible with the grinding of sunflower seeds. The sheen accumulates on the highest and lowest topographic elevations on the stone's surface. It does not, however, extend into the microtopographic interstices or vesicles. The sheen on surfaces used to grind amaranth or corn becomes visible only when the reaction products are no longer worn away by abrasive or fatigue wear. In fact, on lightly used surfaces, it is impossible to distinguish those used to grind corn or amaranth from those used to grind clay or sherds. The most appropriate conclusion is that the concomitant operation of wear mechanisms makes it difficult to see distinctive sheen until a point is reached in the wear process at which the tribochemical wear mechanism is more dominant than either the abrasive or the fatigue wear mechanisms (Adams 1993b).

Stone-against-Wood or Bone Contact

The experimental tools used to make arrow shafts, digging sticks, and bone tools provide a baseline for describing the differences in use-wear patterns created between stone and a resilient or a pliable surface (Adams 1989a, 1989b, 1993b). Because they are more pliable, wood and bone push deeper into the topographic lows, vesicles, and interstices than would another stone surface. Furthermore, wood and bone are less asperite than stone, so the gouges and scratches were most likely caused by rock grains loosened from the stone tool or from the general environment. All exposed edges of the grains are much more involved in the wear process than in stone-against-stone wear. The abrasive action of softer material against the grains rounds off their sharp edges. For this reason, it is important to be familiar with the appearance of unused material. Naturally round grains should not be confused with grains rounded through use-wear.

The working of green wood, such as a fresh willow branch, against an abrader leaves a sticky residue over the stone's grains and within the interstices and vesicles. Further rubbing removes the residue from the grains, but the interstices and vesicles become clogged and are hard to clean. Dry wood, such as an old greasewood branch, leaves drier dust on the stone surface that does not interfere with the abrasion process as much as the residue from the green wood does. The resultant wear patterns from green and dry wood are fairly similar, although there has been too little experimentation to determine more specific use-wear patterns.

The abrading of bone, on the other hand—especially green bone—leaves much more distinctive use-wear patterns than those created by wood, either green or dry. The distinctive patterns are most likely the result of oils that remain in the green

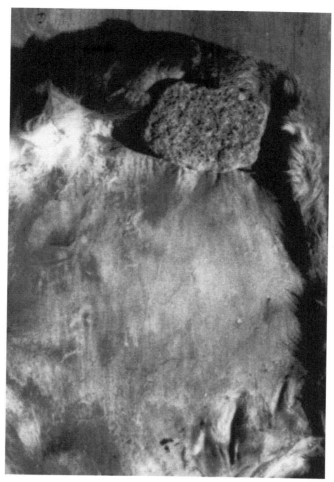

FIGURE 7.5 | Experiment with hide processing. A dried deer hide was worked with a medium-grained quartzite handstone.

bone and tribochemically interact on the stone surface to create sheen. Noticeably more sheen is visible on the surface of the tool used to abrade green bone than on stones used to abrade dry bone or dry wood. The sheen is similar to that created by grinding sunflower seeds (also oil-rich), although the green bone does not level the grains as happens with sunflower seed grinding. It is somewhat discouraging to find very little difference between use-wear patterns produced by abrading dry bone and dry wood. Albeit, this conclusion is based on fewer than ten hours of abrading, and it might be possible to recognize more distinctive use-wear patterns on more extensively used tools.

Stone-against-Hide Contact

An experimental stone used to process a dried deer hide (Figure 7.5) provides the baseline for describing the damage created on a stone used against a soft surface (Adams 1988). When water is worked into the hide with a stone, the hide pushes up against the stone surface, completely filling the topographic lows and the interstices or vesicles. There is nothing intrinsically abrasive in the hide. Abrasive material is available only if a stray grain dislodged from the stone's surface or a particle from the environment is trapped between the hide and the stone.

Pressure, triggering fatigue wear, is a factor only if the user pushes down on the stone as it moves across a hide placed on a hard surface. Adhesive wear and tribological wear are the most dominant mechanisms. Frictional heat, although less obvious than with stone-against-stone contact, helps change the contact environment. The resulting residues build up and become visible as a sheen on the tops of grains, down the sides of the grains, and deep into interstices and vesicles.

The ease with which the handstone moves across the hide depends on the amount of connective tissue and moisture on the hide. Until the connective tissues are removed and the hide is worked to a relatively dry state, the handstone texture becomes clogged and nonabrasive. Washing removes the clogging material and restores abrasiveness, but the extra effort slows the overall process. An abrasive stone can easily work a nap into a dry hide, creating a soft, suede-like surface. A handstone seems much more useful for working a dry hide than a fresh one. The use-wear created by rubbing a hide is unlike anything on the surfaces of tools used to grind food or abrade other items. The wear that results from handling is closest to that of hide working but is generally distinguishable by its location on the tool.

Summary

Each description of a particular contact situation makes it clear that much can be discerned about damage patterns by simply looking at the surface of a ground stone tool without magnification. Striations, crushed grains, impact fractures, leveled areas, and sheen are all macroscopically visible indications of surface wear. The locations of damage patterns are important to note for assessing contact situations. For example, if surface topography is diverse and use-wear patterns are visible only on the highest elevations, then the stone was probably in contact with another stone or some other very rigid surface. If the damage extends into the lower elevations as well, then the contact surface must have been pliable enough to reach into those depths (Adams 1989a, 1989b, 1993b). Macroscopic observations also help us recognize the kinetics of the tool manufacturer or manipulator. The direction of abrasive striations indicates the direction of use. The location of the damage patterns also indicates if the tool was rocked or rotated during manufacture or use.

Clearly, replication experiments often raise more questions than they can answer; however, some very basic principles have been learned. When a stone surface contacts another surface of any type, both surfaces are altered in some way. The manner of contact and the nature of each surface are recognizable by the patterns of alteration. Kinetics and direction of use are also recognizable by these patterns. Experimentation is a process, a basic element of the scientific method. There will always be more factors to vary and more response variables to interpret.

DESIGNING EXPERIMENTAL RESEARCH

There is no "best way" to design scientific experiments that will solve archaeologically derived research questions (see, for example, Mathieu and Meyer 2002). The guidelines in this section are distilled from personal experience and general references on designing experiments for scientists (Diamond 1989; Robinson 2000). The usefulness of the guidelines is illustrated with the description of a set of experiments organized to demonstrate how tool configuration reflects the ways tools were designed and used (Adams 1999:484–487, 1993a:337–340). One goal was to identify use and wear variables specific to tool design that can be compared with those on items in the archaeological record. A second goal was to quantify output amounts to compare the relative efficiency of each design.

With exploratory experiments, it is appropriate to deliberately vary some factors just to see what happens—to identify the response variables (Robinson 2000:30). *Factors* are independent variables, the things that can be varied, such as selecting either coarse-grain or fine-grain material. *Response variables*, as dependent variables, are indicators of a process. For example, the striations or wear facets caused by one surface moving against another are indicators of wear. The objective of an exploratory experiment is to identify a starting point for the next level of experimentation with the recognition of which response variables were created by particular factors. If uncertainty exists about which factors caused which responses, then a series of experiments should be designed that alternately hold all but one factor constant. Ultimately, confirmatory experiments should be run to be certain that the results are replicable and not just random products. The experiments used as an example in the guidelines that follow were exploratory. Many more questions were generated than answered, demonstrating the need for future experimentation.

Guidelines

1. Define the Questions. The first step in designing experimental research is to frame the questions in answerable formats. For these experiments (hereafter referred to as the design experiments), the main question was: what are the differences among three specific mano and metate designs (Figure 7.6a–c)? The intent was to learn about the strokes used with each design, to learn how the different strokes and the different rock types affected the product, and to discover other possible behaviors associated with their use. More specifically, the questions were: (1) are tool

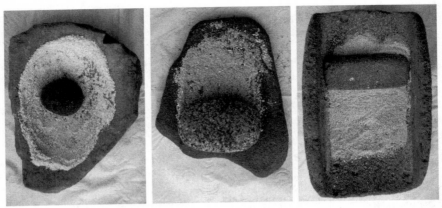

FIGURE 7.6 | Three types of metates used in experiments: (a) basin mano and metate, (b) flat/concave mano and metate, (c) trough mano and metate.

designs and kinetics related in a way that makes one design more comfortable to use than the other two; (2) is one design capable of grinding more product during a set amount of time, making it more efficient than the others; and (3) are certain seeds and kernels easier to grind with one design than the others? These questions were posed because of certain assumptions accepted by many archaeologists without empirical confirmation. The first assumption is that coarse-grain materials were selected for manos and metates that ground maize (considered large grains), and fine-grain materials were selected for those that ground gathered grains and seeds (considered small grains). The second assumption is that trough manos (large) and metates were designed for grinding maize, and basin manos (small) and metates were designed for grinding gathered grains and seeds.

2. Decide on an Experiment Strategy. Have previous experiments been conducted upon which this experiment can build? If so, either select different factors to vary and evaluate those response variables, or replicate the same experiments to confirm or confound the previous results. If no prior experiments exist, then a strategy that includes a series of exploratory experiments is the best way to select relevant factors. Even though other experiments had been conducted with manos and metates (Mauldin 1993; Wright 1993), their problem orientation was different and did not identify factors appropriate to answering questions about tool design. Therefore, the selected strategy for the design experiments was one of exploration.

3. Select Factors and Response Variables. Once the experiments begin, it may become obvious which factors are important and which are inconsequential. Those that are inconsequential can be dropped from further evaluation. For the design experiments, selections included a basin metate made from granite, a flat/concave metate made from sandstone, and a trough metate made from vesicular basalt (Figure 7.6). These are unprovenienced prehistoric tools found in southern Arizona that have been used for educational purposes. The materials to be ground were selected to include a range of large and small sizes, oily and dry textures—amaranth seed, shelled raw sunflower seeds, blue popcorn kernels, dried dent kernels, and soaked white flint kernels (*nixtamal,* which is processed with lime). We decided that efficiency differences in tool design would be evaluated by measuring the amount per hour of processed seeds and kernels. Other observed response variables included the types of use-wear damage on the tool's surfaces and the types of strokes used with each tool design. These responses were not quantified. Rather, qualitative evaluations were made at the end of each experiment run. The experiments were conducted by me and student volunteers.

We hypothesized that the trough set would grind the most efficiently because the surface area between the mano and metate was the largest of the three designs. We further expected that the basin set would be the least efficient because the contact surface area is smallest. These expectations were based on previous experiments such as those reported by Mauldin (1993), who determined that mano size was correlated with relative efficiency. Because the basin mano is worked with only one hand, we expected that it would be the most tiring to use. The trough metate was expected to be the least tiring because it was worked with two hands and assumed to be more efficient. The expectation about material texture was that the coarse-grain material would be the most efficient because it has the roughest surface texture.

4. Design a System for Recording the Data. Pertinent information should include the name of the experimenter, the date and time of the experiment run, what happened during the run, and records of all quantifiable and qualitative observations. For the design experiments, we created tables with columns for the initials of the experimenter, the experiment date, the times at which the experiment run started and stopped, how much seed was worked, and the quantity of processed meal. Additional notes described the type of stroke used with each mano/metate set, including the body positions and different muscles involved in each stroke. Special attention was given to where pressure was exerted on the mano and how that related to the observed use-wear patterns.

5. Perform the Experiment Runs and Record the Data. The design experiments began with the careful measuring of equal quantities of each seed or kernel type into each mano/metate set. The strokes used with the manos and metates imitated those described in the ethnographic literature and those described to me by Hopi grinders. Hopi women who have ground food all their lives emphasize using rhythmic strokes and describe how they put their entire back into the stroke, not just their arms. After an hour of grinding with each set, the nature and quantity of the product were evaluated, and observations about strokes and ease of grinding were recorded. We recognized that a novice grinder may grind differently than an experienced one, and this variable should be subject to future experimentation. The experiments continued for several hours, but the recorded observations use a consistent measure of time to standardize the results.

6. *Evaluate Expectations.* This is the time for reflection on, and consideration of, the initial questions posed, as well as others. Did the results meet expectations? Why, or why not? Was the experiment design faulty? Here, the experiment testing design showed that seed grindability and ease of use varied with each mano/metate design, but not quite as expected. Everything was easily ground with both the basin and trough sets. The same was not true with the flat/concave mano and metate because the dried seeds kept falling off the surface (Table 7.1). No matter what tool was used, it was clearly easier to create fine-textured flour from soaked kernels than it was from dried kernels. However, even while grinding dried kernels, some fine flour was produced with all tools.

The experiments made it possible to observe that grinding with a basin mano/metate set was the most tiring, as expected. Furthermore, even though the trough design was more restrictive to specific motions and thus fatiguing, it was the most efficient for grinding dried foods. Flat/concave and trough manos and metates were perhaps equally efficient for processing soaked kernels and oily seeds. This was not an expected result. Nor was it expected that granular and vesicular materials would be equally efficient in reducing dried seeds and kernels to flour, at least until the granular material was worn smooth when vesicular material was clearly superior. The conclusions suggested by these experiments are that vesicular material is a better choice for grinding dried seeds and kernels because it does not add rock grains to the flour (Adams 1999:487) and that because the motions used with the flat/concave mano were easily varied, this design is the most comfortable to use for an extended period.

7. *Communicate Results.* There is a responsibility to share the results of experiments, even if they are only exploratory results, so that others can build upon them and avoid unnecessary duplication. Experiment methodology should be clearly defined, along with explanations about why one method was chosen over another. The decision-making process should be made clear, especially which variables to hold constant and why. Explain which factors were discovered to be important and which were inconsequential and why. Communicate the answers to the questions posed during the evaluation portion of the experiments. The results of the design experiments were reported in *American Antiquity* (Adams 1999) and through several conference papers and lectures in classes and public forums.

8. Evaluate the Experiment. Probably the most important step in the exploratory process is the evaluation of what went wrong and what went right with the individual experiments and the experiment process as a whole. Were the correct factors chosen for observation? Was the selected unit of measurement the best, and did it actually measure what it was intended to measure? What factors need to be varied next, and what are the expected response variables?

The design experiments discussed here identified many important factors that should be systematically varied in the next series of experiments. Because material texture does seem to be important, it should be evaluated independently from tool morphology. The next series of experiments should involve a set of each design made from the same material. Grinding times should also be extended so efficiency can be evaluated over a longer period. This should bring into play the variables associated with wear management. In a later series of experiments, more than one grinder should run the experiments so comparisons can be made to evaluate the human agent who uses the tools. Is individual stamina or size important, and does experience matter in efficiency? It might also be possible at this time to decide when enough experimentation has occurred. If, after a number of confirmatory runs, the results are always the same, then they can apparently be trusted, and significant relationships among factors have been recognized. If trough manos and metates of vesicular basalt always perform more efficiently than basin manos and metates of the same material, then there is confidence in the conclusions, and it should be possible to apply the observed patterns to the archaeological record.

CONCLUDING THOUGHTS

There continues to be a dearth of research on how ground stone tools were used, how they are classified, and how classification skews interpretations made about human behavior. The class of artifacts typed as "ground stone" is large and varied. Ground stone has been defined elsewhere (Adams 2002a:1) as "any stone item that is primarily manufactured through mechanisms of abrasion, polish, or impaction, or is itself used to grind, abrade, polish, or impact." It is not useful to compare and contrast ground stone and flaked stone for classificatory reasons—they are artificial constructs of archaeologists. After all, hammers and grinding technology (i.e., grinding platforms) are used to make flaked stone tools, ground stone tools are often manufactured by flaking, and flaked drills are used to perforate pendants, beads, and pipes that are shaped by grinding.

The range of activities in which ground stone items were used encompasses almost every activity that was performed in daily life. It is clear that prehistoric technicians understood the differences between smoothing and polishing and selected their materials accordingly. They recognized that appropriately sized and formed food-grinding tools had better performance characteristics than any random rock. Our understanding of how rich and varied prehistoric lifestyles truly were can be enhanced through a better understanding of grinding technology. It is possible to imagine how a tool might have been used or how it functioned in a particular setting. However, reasoned arguments are much stronger if backed by empirical evidence generated directly through experimentation or by documentation of how stone items were used by native people. It may not be possible to know exactly how a prehistoric item was used or functioned, but it is incumbent on us as researchers to outline the range of possibilities and to explore methods that refine our interpretation of the evidence.

REFERENCES CITED

Adams, J. L.
  1979   Groundstone from Walpi. In *Walpi Archaeological Project, Phase 2: Vol. 4. Stone Artifacts from Walpi*, part 2, by J. L. Adams and D. Greenwald, 1–220. Museum of Northern Arizona, Flagstaff.
  1988   Use-Wear Analysis of Handstones Used to Grind Corn and Process Hides. *Journal of Field Archaeology* 15(3):307–315.
  1989a   Experimental Replication of the Use of Ground Stone Tools. *Kiva* 54(3):261–271.
  1989b   Methods for Improving Ground Stone Analysis: Experiments in Mano Wear Patterns. In *Experiments in Lithic Technology*, ed. D. S. Amick and R. P. Mauldin, 259–276. BAR International Series 528. Archaeopress, Oxford.
  1993a   Technological Development of Manos and Metates on the Hopi Mesas. *Kiva* 58(3):331–344.
  1993b   Mechanisms of Wear of Ground Stone Surfaces. *Pacific Coast Archaeological Society Quarterly* 29(4):61–74.
  1999   Refocusing the Role of Food-Grinding Tools as Correlates for Subsistence Strategies in the U.S. Southwest. *American Antiquity* 64(3):475–498.
  2002a   *Ground Stone Analysis: A Technological Approach.* University of Utah Press, Salt Lake City.
  2002b   Mechanisms of Wear on Ground Stone Surfaces. In *Moudre et Broyer*, ed. H. Procopiou and R. Treuil, 57–68. CTHS, Paris.

Amick, D. S., and R. P. Mauldin (editors)
  1989   *Experiments in Lithic Technology.* BAR International Series 528. Archaeopress, Oxford.

Amick, D. S., R. P. Mauldin, and L. R. Binford
  1989   The Potential of Experiments in Lithic Technology. In *Experiments in Lithic Technology*, ed. D. S. Amick and R. P. Mauldin, 1–14. BAR International Series 528. Archaeopress, Oxford.

Bartlett, K.
  1933   *Pueblo Milling Stones of the Flagstaff Region and Their Relation to Others in the Southwest: A Study in Progressive Efficiency.* Bulletin 3. Museum of Northern Arizona, Flagstaff.

Burton, M. M.

2007   Understanding Hunter-Gatherer Grinding Technology through Experimentation, NSF Award 0714727. Manuscript on file at the San Diego Archaeological
Center, Escondido, Calif.

Castetter, E. F., and W. H. Bell

1951   *Yuman Indian Agriculture: Primitive Subsistence on the Lower Colorado and
Gila Rivers*. University of New Mexico Press, Albuquerque.

Diamond, W. J.

1989   *Practical Experiment Designs for Engineers and Scientists,* 2nd ed. Van Nostrand
Reinhold, New York.

Doelle, W. H.

1976   *Desert Resources and Hohokam Subsistence: The Conoco Florence Project*. Archaeological Series 13. Arizona State Museum, University of Arizona, Tucson.

Dubreuil, L.

2001   Functional Studies of Prehistoric Grindingstones: A Methodological Research.
Bulletin du Centre de Recherche Français de Jérusalem 9:73–87.

2004   Long-Term Trends in Natufian Subsistence: A Use-Wear Analysis of Ground
Stone Tools. *Journal of Archaeological Science* 31:1613–1629.

Euler, R. C., and H. F. Dobyns

1983   The Ethnoarchaeology of Pai Milling Stones. In *Collected Papers in Honor of
Charlie Steen, Jr.,* ed. N. L. Fox, 253–267. Papers of the Archaeological Society
of New Mexico 8. Albuquerque Archaeological Society Press, Albuquerque.

Hamon, C.

2008   Functional Analysis of Stone Grinding and Polishing Tools from the Earliest Neolithic of North-Western Europe. *Journal of Archaeological Science* 35:
1502–1520.

Haury, E. W.

1931   Minute Beads from Prehistoric Pueblos. *American Anthropologist* 33:80–87.

Hayden, B. (editor)

1979   *Lithic Use-Wear Analysis: Proceedings of the Conference on Lithic Use-Wear
Analysis, Simon Fraser University, Burnaby (Vancouver), British Columbia,
March 1977*. Academic Press, New York.

Hayden, B., and J. Kamminga

1979   An Introduction to Use-Wear: The First CLUW. In *Lithic Use-Wear Analysis:
Proceedings of the Conference on Lithic Use-Wear Analysis, Simon Fraser Univer-
sity, Burnaby (Vancouver), British Columbia, March 1977,* ed. B. Hayden, 1–13.
Academic Press, New York.

Horsfall, G. A.

1987   Design Theory and Grinding Stones. In *Lithic Studies among the Contemporary Highland Maya,* ed. B. Hayden, 332–377. University of Arizona Press,
Tucson.

Hough, W.

1915   *The Hopi*. Torch Press, Cedar Rapids, Iowa.

Jackson, T. L.
  1991   Pounding Acorn: Women's Production as Social and Economic Focus. In
          Engendering Archaeology: Women and Prehistory, ed. J. M. Gero and M. W.
          Conkey, 301–325. Basil Blackwell, Oxford.

Kamp, K. A.
  1995   A Use-Wear Analysis of the Function of Basalt Cylinders. *Kiva* 61(2):109–
          119.

Keeley, L. H.
  1980   *Experimental Determination of Stone Tools Uses: A Microwear Analysis*. Univer-
          sity of Chicago Press, Chicago.

Lechtman, H.
  1999   Afterword. In *The Social Dynamics of Technology: Practice, Politics, and World
          View*, ed. M. A. Dobres and C. R. Hoffman, 223–232. Smithsonian Institution
          Press, Washington, D.C.

Logan, E. N., and L. Fratt
  1993   Pigment Processing at Homol'ovi III: A Preliminary Study. *Kiva* 58(3):415–
          428.

Mathieu, J. R. (editor)
  2002   *Experimental Archaeology: Replicating Past Objects, Behaviors, and Processes*.
          BAR International Series 1035. Archaeopress, Oxford.

Mathieu, J. R., and D. A. Meyer
  2002   Reconceptualizing Experimental Archaeology: Assessing the Process of Exper-
          imentation. In *Experimental Archaeology: Replicating Past Objects, Behav-
          iors, and Processes*, ed. J. R. Mathieu, 73–82. BAR International Series 1035.
          Archaeopress, Oxford.

Mauldin, R. P.
  1993   The Relationship between Ground Stone and Agricultural Intensification in
          Western New Mexico. *Kiva* 58:317–330.

Menasanch, M., R. Risch, and J. A. Soldevilla
  2002   Las Tecnologías del Procesado de Cereal en le Sudeste de la Peninsula Ibérica
          durante el III y el II milenio A.N.E. In *Moudre et Broyer: l'Interprétation Fonc-
          tionnelle de 'Outilage de Mouture et de Broyage dans la Préhistoire e l'Antiquité*,
          ed. H. Procopiou and R. Treuil, 81–110. CTHS, Paris.

Mills, P. R.
  1993   An Axe to Grind: A Functional Analysis of Anasazi Stone Axes from Sand Can-
          yon Pueblo Ruin (5MT765), Southwestern Colorado. *Kiva* 58(3):393–413.

Morris, E. H.
  1939   *Archaeological Studies in the La Plata District, Southwestern Colorado and
          Northwestern New Mexico*. Carnegie Institution, Washington, D.C.

Odell, G., and F. Odell-Vereecken
  1980   Verifying the Reliability of Lithic Use-Wear Assessments by "Blind Tests": The
          Low Power Approach. *Journal of Field Archaeology* 7:87–120.

Parsons, E. C.
1939   *Pueblo Indian Religion*. University of Chicago Press, Chicago.

Procopiou, H., and R. Treuil (editors)
2002   *Moudre et Broyer*. CTHS, Paris.

Risch, R.
2002   *Recursos naturales, medios de producción y exploración social*. Iberia Archarolog-
        ica Band 3. Deutsches Archaologisches Institut, Madrid.

Robinson, G. K.
2000   *Practical Strategies for Experimenting*. John Wiley and Sons, Chichester, N.Y.

Rowe, R.
1995   Towards Cupstone Classification: An Experimental Approach. *Ohio Archaeolo-
        gist* 45(3):11–17.

Schiffer, M. B., and J. M. Skibo
1987   Theory and Experiment in the Study of Technological Change. *Current Anthro-
        pology* 28:595–622.

Semenov, S. A.
1964   *Prehistoric Technology*. Adams and Dart, Bath.

Spier, L.
1933   *Yuman Tribes of the Gila River*. University of Chicago Press, Chicago.

Stephen, A. M.
1936   *Hopi Journal of Alexander M. Stephen*. Edited by E. Clews Parson. Columbia
        University Contributions to Anthropology 23. Columbia University Press,
        New York.

Tringham, R., G. Cooper, G. Odell, B. Voytek, and A. Whitman
1974   Experimentation in the Formation of Edge Damage: A New Approach to
        Lithic Analysis. *Journal of Field Archaeology* 1:171–196.

Underhill, R. M.
1979   *Social Organization of the Papago Indians*, reprinted. Contributions to Anthro-
[1939] pology 30. Columbia University Press, New York.

Unger-Hamilton, R.
1984   The Formation of Use-Wear Polish on Flint: Beyond the "Deposit versus Abra-
        sion" Controversy. *Journal of Archaeological Science* 11:91–98.

Vaughan, P. C.
1985   *Use-Wear Analysis of Flaked Stone Tools*. University of Arizona Press, Tucson.

Webster's Ninth New Collegiate Dictionary
1989   Mirriam-Webster, Springfield, Mass.

Wright, M. K.
1993   Simulated Use of Experimental Maize Grinding Tools from Southwestern Col-
        orado. *Kiva* 58(3):345–355.

CHAPTER EIGHT

Retrieving the Perishable Past: Experimentation in Fiber Artifact Studies

Edward A. Jolie and Maxine E. McBrinn

○ ○ ○
○ ○ ○
○ ○ ○

Throughout most of humanity's history, perishable objects such as cordage, netting, textiles, and basketry have constituted a large percentage of peoples' material culture. Despite this fact, until recently perishables have been largely ignored in archaeological research because of preservation's bias toward durable objects (e.g., ceramics, bone, stone, antler, and ivory), the historical association of perishable technologies with women's work (Adovasio, Soffer, and Page 2007; Barber 1994; Mason 1899), and a failure to sufficiently account for variation in the archaeological record (Wobst 2001). Yet since the beginning of perishables studies, experimentation has been key to understanding the interrelatedness of material, technique, and form in perishable artifacts.

Professional interest in archaeological perishables has increased dramatically over the past three decades, with substantial growth in the number and sophistication of studies. Yet experimentation continues to be an uncommon and often underreported component of this research, despite being integral to informed interpretation (Clark 2002.) In this chapter we address how experimentation enriches our understanding of perishable technologies and the people who made and used them. By reviewing previous work, suggesting avenues for future study, and offering guidelines for developing experiments, our goal is to take a step toward establishing a body of knowledge that can be drawn on by other archaeologists in the analysis and interpretation of perishable material culture wherever it is encountered.

PERISHABLES, THE PAST, AND EXPERIMENTATION

In the present context the term "perishables" denotes a class of artifacts constructed from organic materials, including diverse but interrelated technologies wherein the primary raw material source is plant or animal tissue. Wherever perishables are recovered archaeologically, the depositional context has retarded decay and microbial growth. Typically, these settings are limited to extremely wet, dry, or cold depositional contexts, although on occasion perishables become mineralized or are preserved through contact with corroding metal as pseudomorphs.

The inherent plasticity of the many fiber sources and techniques employed by different peoples dictates that many types of items can be manufactured using them. The most commonly recognized perishable technologies are additive ones associated with well-known production sequences. These typically include basketry, textiles, cordage, and cordage products such as netting. Objects such as sandals, fish traps, skin bags, moccasins, animal fur robes and blankets, and other miscellaneous constructions are also included, but such technologies typically receive less-focused research attention. This is true because of their considerable technological variability through time and space, as in the case of sandals, or a complete lack of any comprehensive schema for their classification, as with many items of wood, animal fur, feathers, and hide.

As many colleagues have told us, among the most daunting aspects of perishables are the complex analytical and descriptive terminologies associated with them. This is especially true of basketry and textiles, where technical terms and inconsistent uses of those terms abound. Recognizing this, our use of technical terms here is limited. A discussion of terminology in perishables studies is beyond the scope of this chapter, and we refer the reader to the generally accepted treatments of analytical and descriptive terms that exist for basketry (Adovasio 1977; Wendrich 1994), textiles (Emery 1995; Seiler-Baldinger 1994), and cordage and netting (Emery 1995; Hurley 1979). Although less standardized, useful summaries also exist for footwear (Andrews, Adovasio, and Carlisle 1986; Deegan 1993; Goubitz 2007) and, to some extent, wooden artifacts (Adovasio et al. 2002; Dillehay 1997; Sands 1997).

Retrieving the Perishable Past

The substantial increase in perishable studies over the past three decades is in part the result of improved recovery techniques, the maturation of archaeological textiles research, and its wider recognition within the discipline as a viable avenue of anthropological inquiry (Drooker 2001a; Drooker and Webster 2000; Good 2001).

In addition, Accelerator Mass Spectrometry (AMS) radiocarbon dating now allows perishable artifacts to be accurately placed into a temporal framework without sacrificing a significant part of the artifact itself. One of the most important observations to emerge from this has been the recognition that perishable technologies, particularly basketry and textiles, are among the most culturally "sensitive" classes of material culture available for study (e.g., Adovasio 1986a; Baumhoff 1957; King 1975; Pryor and Carr 1995; Webster and Loma'omvaya 2004).

Unlike many other artifact classes, perishables dramatically illustrate each step of the manufacturing process because by being an additive technology, the very acts by which they are made are preserved in the finished product. They are also the results of learned behavior, governed by a set of fixed standards of what is and is not locally "acceptable" (Adovasio and Pedler 1994; Hayden and Cannon 1984; Minar 2000, 2001a; Pryor and Carr 1995). To paraphrase Dorothy Washburn (2001:70), a perishable artifact can be viewed as made up of many "essential features" that embody its particular cultural character, identity, and meaning. Recognizing that individual choices are culturally informed and constrained, the student of perishable technologies is given a rare glimpse into a physical embodiment of individual and group identity that may yield clues to the formation and maintenance of sociocultural boundaries across time and space (e.g., Adovasio 1986a; Adovasio and Gunn 1986; Adovasio and Pedler 1994; Barber 1991; Carr and Maslowski 1995; Kent 1983; Mason 1904; Minar 1999, 2001b; Morris and Burgh 1941; Petersen, Heckenberger, and Wolford 2001; Webster 2007). These observations are even more significant when it is realized that perishables constituted a significant fraction of a given society's material culture, particularly among hunter-gatherers (Adovasio 1986b; Fowler and Dawson 1986; Petersen, Heckenberger, and Wolford 2001). Walter Taylor (1966:73) noted of his excavations in Coahuila, Mexico, that *finished* fiber-based artifacts outnumbered stone tools by a ratio of twenty to one, and other research has reaffirmed this fact (Andrews et al. 2002; Collins 1937; Croes 1997; Kidder and Guernsey 1919).

Perishable technologies hold great promise to inform us about many aspects of past human behavior that are typically inaccessible through more durable material culture. However, the precise role of experimentation in perishable artifact studies remains unclear. What is (or should be) the nature of experimentation in such studies? Why bother experimenting with perishable technologies at all? To address these questions, we must now consider the nature of experimental archaeology and the significance of experimenting with perishables.

The Role of Experimentation

Experimental archaeology, broadly construed, seeks to understand human actions within a scientific framework (Clark 2002). It is fundamentally a scientific process grounded in hypothesis testing. As a consequence, experiments must be replicable and replicated. This is what distinguishes experimentation from exploration (e.g., making a basket and cooking with it) and experience (e.g., living history, reenactment) (Reynolds 1999). A further distinction can be drawn between "archaeological experiments" and "experimental archaeology" (Schiffer et al. 1994). The former are isolated, typically resulting from a specific question about how a tool was made or used. The latter is program-based, denoting a series of repeated experiments whose findings are made meaningful through the accumulation of knowledge, forming a base of data for explaining technological variability and change (Schiffer and Skibo 1987, 1997; see also Clark 2002). In contrast to an archaeological experiment, an experimental program yields richer data that enhance experimental designs and improves our understanding of technical decisions and the technological traditions in which they are embedded. Individual experiments may contribute to a program or supply greater technological insight when they are carried out according to accepted methodologies and consider research questions that pertain to other investigators. A primary archaeological goal is to maximize the information about human behavior that can be retrieved from material remains. Acknowledging this, a program-based approach to experimentation in perishable artifact studies that complements archaeological research offers the best chance of achieving this goal.

Why experiment with perishable technologies? To answer this, we must consider the sources of our information on these technologies and their inherent limitations. The vast majority of our information on raw materials, techniques of manufacture, functions, and contexts of use is derived from the ethnographic literature and historical documents. While these data may be sufficient in many cases, there are often instances where a particular technique or form commonly seen archaeologically lacks an ethnographic analog. A good example comes from recent research on sandal technology. Phil Geib (2000, e-mail communication 2005) has conducted research on regional differences in forager material culture using Archaic period (7500–1800 BP) sandals from the Colorado Plateau of the American Southwest. These sandals come in two varieties, open-twined and warp-faced plainweave, and both lack comparable ethnographic analogs (Figure 8.1). Geib observed that in replicating and wearing pairs of both types on a five-mile-plus hike with a forty-pound pack, open-twined sandals provided greater traction, especially on slick rock (Figure 8.2). These preliminary results provide insight into performance characteristics not discussed in the ethnographic literature and indicate that some sandal construction techniques may have a practical aspect.

Even when a technology is known historically, a researcher may find that specific information relating to manufacture or performance simply does not exist. Take as an example yucca (*Yucca* sp.) fiber cordage production. In the analysis of cordage from prehispanic sites on Wetherill Mesa, Carolyn Osborne (1965) identified three distinct types of yucca fiber cordage on the basis of color and texture. After excluding the effects of post-depositional factors on the specimens, she became interested

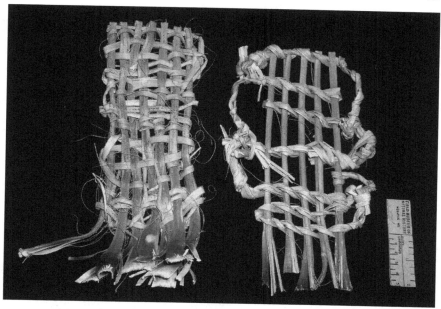

FIGURE 8.1 | Unused replicas of Colorado Plateau Archaic period sandals woven of yucca by Phil Geib. Sandal on left is plaited, and sandal on right is open-twined.

in methods of production that would yield three different forms of the same plant fiber. Noting a paucity of data on yucca fiber in the ethnographic literature, she set out to experiment with fiber preparation. Through a series of experiments and trial and error, she was able to reasonably approximate two of the fiber types and suggest points for future investigation on the third.

Experimentation with perishable technologies yields insights not only into process and product but also on aspects that are difficult to quantify, including information on thought processes, sensory perception (e.g., Hurcombe 2007), social status, worldview, and other aspects of cultural context. For instance, during their analysis of Paracas textiles from Peru, Junius Bird and Louisa Bellinger (1954) found it difficult to appreciate the weaver's skill without having personally worked hands-on with Alpaca hair, the original raw material, and a backstrap loom, the weaving apparatus. Martha Stanley's (personal communication 2005; see also Stanley 1995) experiments reconstructing the magnificent diamond twill tapestry from Grand Gulch, Utah (Kent 1983:plate 10), gave her insight into how one Ancestral Puebloan weaver consciously abstracted weave structure to affect visually stunning and technically complex designs. Patricia Anawalt's (1990, 1993, 2001) examination of Aztec textiles and their visual representations incorporated textile recreation and afforded a new understanding of the geopolitical and mythological foundations of authority in Mesoamerica.

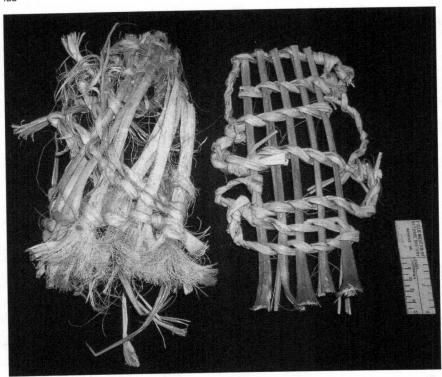

FIGURE 8.2 | Used (*left*) and unused (*right*) open-twined yucca sandals worn by Phil Geib on five-plus-mile hike.

Tangential to these studies, a body of work by Lucy Sibley, Kathryn Jakes, and their colleagues (Deegan 1997; Jakes 1996; Jakes and Ericksen 1997; Sibley and Jakes 1989; Sibley, Jakes, and Larson 1996; Sibley, Jakes, and Swinker 1992) suggests a coherent methodological framework derived from Michael Schiffer and James Skibo's (Schiffer 1972, 1975; Schiffer and Skibo 1997) research on archaeological context and behavior that seeks to infer cultural context from archaeological textiles. Recently, Annette Ericksen and colleagues (2000:70) have expanded this model by detailing potential sources of variability throughout a textile's life cycle to facilitate the identification of behaviorally meaningful archaeological correlates. The model allows the researcher to focus on individual aspects of textile production and consumption with the aim of explaining the "social, technological, and economic variability of a textile at all levels of construction and use, and to examine the relationship of this variability to a cultural system" (Ericksen, Jakes, and Wimberley 2000:70). Complementary research by Jenna Kuttruff (1988, 1991, 1993) has resulted in the Textile Production Complexity Index, a production-step measure analogous to those used in ceramic studies that formalizes a ranking process to differentiate the complexity and production costs of preindustrial textiles to identify patterns in social status differentiation. Notably, both of these frameworks view experimental work as crucial to their proper application, requiring the acquisition of quantifiable data on labor investments.

While experimentation affords the researcher an opportunity to supplement or revise existing archaeological and historical lines of perishable evidence, it can also inform on broader issues of anthropological interest, ranging from technological change and economy to aspects of sociopolitics and worldview. We also urge archaeologists to note that experimentation, whether in perishable artifact studies or archaeology in general, is not just a powerful research method but also an effective educational tool and a valuable medium for public outreach. Because both children and adults enjoy the opportunity to do things as they were done in the past, experimentation as a form of public outreach offers archaeologists a unique opportunity to interact with and educate the public. If the required skill level is kept low, public participation can even contribute to the collection of additional data. Simultaneously, experimentation allows us to engage the public while performing practical research grounded in solid archaeological theory. Experimental archaeology, then, should not just be about retrieving the past, perishable or otherwise, but about sharing it with others, too.

PREVIOUS RESEARCH

Some of the earliest focused research on perishable artifacts in the Americas dates to the late nineteenth century. Conducted by William Holmes (1884, 1896, 1901), this research was geared toward the identification of textile and basketry impressions preserved in fired ceramics. Notably, this research also included the first example of directed experimentation when Holmes (1901) replicated woven structures and experimentally impressed them in clay pots to help identify the source of some of the archaeological impressions he encountered. Although the corpus of experimental research involving perishable artifacts that has accumulated since this early research is considerable, it is not yet so large as to be on the impressive scale of work conducted with ceramic or lithic technologies. For the most part, previous research has been restricted to archaeological experiments (Schiffer et al. 1994) involving cordage, basketry, and textile manufacture—likely because these technologies have structural configurations that are evident in even the smallest preserved fragments of the original artifact. Such is not usually the case with objects manufactured primarily from wood, animal fur, feathers, or hide, as it is less likely that the archaeologist can ascertain the entire production sequence from small fragments of these constructions (e.g., Koerper 1998). As a consequence, little experimental work has been geared toward a better understanding of members of these classes of perishable material culture.

While a detailed review of the existing literature is not possible here, our aim is to provide a brief overview of previous studies. For ease, we have organized previous research into four thematic categories that capture major trends in research, although there is some overlap between the categories. Categories include Technological Studies, Performance Studies, Contextual Studies, and Ethnoarchaeological and Enculturative Studies. Geographic focus is necessarily broad to reflect the past and present scope of experimentation, but the literature is still biased toward the North American work with which we are most familiar. General references containing exploratory and experimental research of value to those interested in experimenting with fiber perishables include the *Bulletin of Primitive Technology* and *Wilderness Way Magazine*, journals primarily designed for people interested in avocational reenactments of past lifeways and organizations committed to broad-scheme experimental programs, such as the European Association for the Advancement of Archaeology by Experiment. Table 8.1 provides a guide to experimental research involving perishables by technology, geographic region, and category of study, although this compilation is far from exhaustive. In a final section we briefly consider the limitations of existing work and suggest future directions for experimental inquiry.

Technological Studies

Technological studies make up the vast majority of published experimental work. Herein, technology is understood to constitute the raw materials and techniques employed during the manufacture of an object. As a unit, these studies are concerned with aspects of a specific technology or related technologies. A primary goal of these studies is to elucidate the construction process and technique, either to identify or clarify individual technical choices for the purposes of analysis and documentation. Attendant goals are to understand assemblage variability, infer possible form and function, infer cultural context, and estimate labor costs. It is often the case that technological studies focused on one or more of these goals will also complement larger experiments geared toward the investigation of performance, social learning, or some aspect of archaeological context.

While technological studies all share a general focus on artifact design, raw material preparation, and the process or technique of manufacture, the pathway to understand some facet of a particular item or technique may vary. *Replication, reconstruction,* and *recreation* are three related approaches used to illuminate decision-making processes and obtain information about production costs, raw materials, and technological performance (Barber 2003). These three experimental approaches are not mutually exclusive, however, and a research program may incorporate one or more of them. Unfortunately, the use of this terminology in the literature has been alarmingly inconsistent and interchangeable. We must be explicit about distinguishing among them because all three approaches have dis-

Table 8.1. Experimental research involving perishables by technology, country/geographic region, and category of study.

Technology	Country/Geographic Region[a]	References[a]
TECHNOLOGICAL STUDIES		
Cordage and spinning	Canada, Egypt, northeastern United States, southeastern United States, western United States	Cooke and El Gamal 1990; Cooke, El Gamal, and Brennan 1991; Deegan 1997; Drooker 1992, 2001b; Gordon 1997; Haas 2001, 2006; Jones 1948; Jones and Fonner 1954; King and Gardner 1981; Morris and Burgh 1954; Osborne 1965; Salls 1985; Teague 1998; Tiedemann 2001; Tiedemann and Jakes 2006; Wilson 1996; Woltz 1998
Netting	Southwestern United States	Andrews and Adovasio 1980
Basketry	Canada, central United States, northeastern United States, southwestern United States, western United States	Gordon 1993, 1997; Hamilton 2001; Harding 1998; James 1970; Morris and Burgh 1941; Tulloch and Polanich 1999; Woltz 1998
Matting	Canada, central United States, northeastern United States, northwestern United States, western United States	Croes 1995; Fowler, Hattori, and Dansie 2000; Gordon 1995; Jones 1948; Schultz 2002a, 2002b
Textiles, production implements, and dress	Egypt, Europe, Guatemala, Mexico, Peru, southeastern United States, southwestern United States	Anawalt 1990, 1993, 2001; Andrews et al. 2002; Barber 1991, 1994; Batzer and Dokkedal 1992; Bird 1985; Bird and Bellinger 1954; Desrosiers 1985; Emery 1995; Gaustad 2005; Gilbert 2005; Hald 1980; Jones 2000; Jørgensen 1994; Kemp and Vogelsgang-Eastwood 2001; Knudsen 1998; Kuttruff, Standifer, and DeHart 2004; Munksgaard 1991; O'Neale 1945; Owen 2005; Sibley, Swinker, and Jakes 1991; Siewertsz van Reesema 1926; Stanley 1995
Footwear	Northeastern United States, southeastern United States, southwestern United States	Geib 2000; Kidder 1926; Kuttruff, Standifer, and DeHart 2004; Miller 1988; Talge 1995; Thompson 1958; Willey 1974
Slings	Western United States	Heizer and Johnson 1952; O'Neale 1947
Fishing gear	Northwestern United States, western United States	Croes 1995, 1997; Salls 1989
Fiber perishable impressions	Caribbean, Ecuador, Europe, Japan, northeastern United States, southeastern United States	Drooker 1992; Holmes 1901; Hurley 1979; Hutcheson 2001; Oppelt 1999; Quimby 1961; Sosna 1999, 2000; Strothert et al. 1991
Dyes and dyeing	Northeastern United States, South America (Andes), southwestern United States	Baldia 2005, 2006; Cassman 1990; Dean 2005; Kent 1957, 1983; Thompson and Jakes 2002

continued on next page

Table 8.1—*continued*

Technology	Country/Geographic Region[a]	References[a]
PERFORMANCE STUDIES		
Cordage	Northwestern United States, southeastern United States, southwestern United States, western United States	Botkin and Shires 1944; Botkin, Shires, and Smith 1943; Croes 1995, 1997; Loud and Harrington 1929; Nyerges 1999; Roberts 2004; Salls 1989; Tiedemann 2001; Tiedemann and Jakes 2006
Basketry	Western United States	Barlow, Henriksen, and Metcalfe 1993
Footwear	Europe, southwestern United States	Geib 2000; Holden 2003
Robes	Western United States	Yoder, Blood, and Mason 2005
Fishing gear	Northwestern United States, western United States	Croes 1995, 1997; Salls 1989
CONTEXTUAL STUDIES		
Basketry	Europe	Hurcombe 1994, 2008a, 2008b
Cordage	Europe, northeastern United States, southeastern United States, southwestern United States	Chen, Jakes, and Foreman 1998; Hurcombe 2008a, 2008b; Jakes 1996; Jakes, Sibley, and Yerkes 1994; McBrinn and Smith 2006; Song, Jakes, and Yerkes 1996; Srinivasan and Jakes 1997; Tiedemann 2001
Tanned leather	Egypt	van Driel-Murray 2002
ETHNOARCHAEOLOGICAL AND ENCULTURATIVE STUDIES		
Cordage and spinning	Brazil, Chile, Mexico, Middle East, New Guinea, southeastern United States, southwestern United States	Belcher 1994; Haas 2006; MacKenzie 1991; Minar 1999, 2000, 2001a, 2001b; Neff 1996; Oakland 1982; Parsons 1972; Parsons and Parsons 1990; Petersen, Heckenberger, and Wolford 2001
Basketry	Canada, Egypt, Iraq, northwestern United States, Philippines, western United States	Ochsenschlager 2004; O'Neale 1932; Pryor 1988; Pryor and Carr 1995; Silvestre 1994, 2000; Weber 1986; Wendrich 1999
Netting	Mexico, Middle East, New Guinea	Belcher 1994; MacKenzie 1991; Parsons 2006
Textiles	Europe, Iraq, Mesoamerica, Peru, Southeast Asia (U.S. Loatian immigrants)	Franquemont 1979, 1986, 1988; Franquemont and Franquemont 1987; Greenfield 2004; Hayden and Cannon 1984; Hoffmann 1964; Ochsenschlager 2004; Washburn and Petitto 1993

[a] Entries have been alphabetized.

tinct operating assumptions and implications for what we can reasonably infer about the past.

Replication connotes the production of an exact replica or copy, based on a complete or almost complete original. The aim of replicative studies is accuracy, to the end of copying the original in all details by using identical raw materials and techniques. *Reconstruction* refers to taking a fragmentary artifact and mending it or extrapolating from it to create a complete or nearly complete artifact. *Recreation* is, at best, an approximation of the original based on a combination of iconographic imagery, written documents, sculpture, or some other visual representation of the object of interest. An object that has been recreated has no guarantee of accuracy and may only vaguely mirror an intact original. The differences among the three approaches are subtle, then, and ultimately demonstrated by the accuracy or "correctness" of their final products relative to the data available in the beginning. While all three approaches have been integral to perishable artifact studies, attempts to replicate, recreate, or do both with perishable artifacts constitute the vast bulk of the published material on experimentation and have long been recognized for their ability to educate participants about the mechanics of construction and technical decisions (Smith 1909).

Performance Studies

The goal of performance studies is to test hypotheses about function and use, as well as quantify particular performance characteristics such as durability or longevity. They can be viewed as a subset of technological studies, as they often require the accurate replication or recreation of individual artifacts—although this is not always the case because actual artifacts can be used (e.g., Loud and Harrington 1929). The most prominent of these studies have looked at the tensile strength of ancient cordage or cordage made from indigenous fiber sources (Roberts 2004).

Contextual Studies

Contextual studies examine factors that affect the location and condition of perishable artifacts, in situations of both their use and discard. Controlled contextual experiments have the potential to shed light on the physical and chemical processes that affect processed fibers and the factors that determine perishability. Contextual experiments are by their nature multidisciplinary, incorporating insights obtained from chemistry, geology, and pedology, among other fields.

Ethnoarchaeological and Enculturative Studies

As a strategy complimentary to, and sometimes subsumed under, experimental archaeology, ethnoarchaeology emphasizes the incorporation of ethnographic fieldwork into research on archaeological problems. Enculturative studies, like ethnoarchaeological ones, rely heavily on ethnographic fieldwork and data to generate insights and questions about the ways particular perishable technologies were learned and taught in the past, but they may also incorporate perspectives from research on learning theory, cognition, and developmental psychology. Enculturative studies have a decided focus on what might also be thought of as socialization, but the term "enculturative" is used here because socialization is often associated only with children.

Ethnoarchaeological work on perishable technologies has accelerated in recent years, and although ethnoarchaeological observations are sometimes incorporated into broader discussions of archaeological data, focused studies are much fewer in number. Research that may be considered enculturative is also on the rise, but some of the earliest studies to incorporate this avenue of research had only minor interest in archaeological questions (e.g., O'Neale 1932). Taken together, ethnoarchaeological and enculturative studies yield insights into the social context of perishable production and use by affording more controlled situations in which particular technological or social actions and their effects can be studied.

Past and Future Directions

Early research was crucial for establishing baseline data to build upon but was confined to isolated archaeological experiments. Technological studies subsume the vast majority of past and present experimental work because data derived from archaeological contexts and experiments are more easily applied to questions about technological choice (Schiffer and Skibo 1987, 1997). The recent swell of studies that move beyond technology to consider aspects of performance and enculturation indicates new research that complements changing analytical interests. Undoubtedly, artifact perishability and the small number of researchers who actively study archaeological perishables aided the initially slow pace of this process.

Future researchers should make it a goal to develop a thorough experimental program that investigates one or more perishable technologies and incorporates features of technological, performance, contextual, ethnoarchaeological, and enculturative studies. The field sorely needs a program of comparative experiments that develops rigorous and detailed understanding of the materials, manufacture, and use of perishables, rather than a continuing proliferation of uncoordinated tests, many of which are simply designed to test a limited hypothesis. A commitment to adequate recording and reporting of experimental studies will help carry this experimentation forward. Important technological studies on dyeing and contextual research on fibers by Jakes and her students (e.g., Baldia 2003, 2005; Chen, Jakes, and Foreman 1998; Jakes 1996; Jakes, Sibley, and Yerkes 1994; Srinivasan and Jakes 1997; Thompson and Jakes 2002; Tiedemann and Jakes 2006) have come the closest to a focused experimental program.

Aside from continuing along already established lines of inquiry, several areas are worth exploring in greater depth in the future. Performance studies, very common in ceramic and lithic experimentation, are uncommon in perishables studies. This is unfortunate because these types of studies stand to contribute vastly to our understanding of perishable artifacts' life histories or "behavioral chains" (Schiffer and Skibo 1997). Data on use-wear that may inform discussion of the form and function of many perishable artifacts would be particularly valuable. Performance studies also allow a vastly improved understanding of the costs and benefits of different construction and material choices. For example, something that at first appears to be a costly item based on production time or rarity of materials may have a significantly longer use-life. Performance studies may also facilitate more informed speculation about "nonfunctional" reasons new technologies were adopted. Similarly, ethnoarchaeological and enculturative studies yield unparalleled insights into the social context of perishable artifact production and use, but they, too, remain uncommon.

THEORETICAL AND EPISTEMIC CONSIDERATIONS

Experimentation with perishable technology can be extremely rewarding, but, as with any anthropological endeavor, it is not free from interpretive dilemmas. Theory directs us on which data to gather and guides us from data to interpretation, while epistemic concerns ensure that we are aware of the potentials and perils inherent in the process of experimental inquiry. In particular, several interrelated theoretical and epistemic concerns affect the conclusions we ultimately draw from archaeological data. Some of these are broadly applicable to all archaeological interpretation, while others are more specific to the study of perishable artifacts.

Paramount among theoretical and epistemic concerns are the nature, quality, and quantity of our source data. Typically, researchers working with perishables rely heavily on ethnographic data, supplemented when possible by historical documents and archaeological and ethnoarchaeological evidence. Readers are undoubtedly aware of many of the general and specific criticisms to which each of these lines of evidence may be subjected, but several points about ethnographic data germane to perishable studies bear reiteration.

Several scholars (e.g., Costin 1996; Wobst 1978) remind us that reliance on ethnographic analogy is fraught with the danger of replicating historically contingent phenomena. So it is necessary to continually evaluate individual data sources with a critical eye, in the context of both the larger body of literature on the subject and complementary lines of evidence. Invariably, errors, inconsistencies, or gaps in the literature bias experiment design and the interpretation of results. As mentioned previously, early work by Holmes (1884, 1896, 1901) used secondary evidence of textiles and basketry, in the form of negative impressions left in ceramics, to recreate ancient weaving traditions. During his analyses, Holmes (1884) speculated on the devices that may have been used to weave several of the structures he identified. Unfortunately, as Penelope Drooker (2001a:180–181) notes, Holmes fell prey to the danger of making assumptions about a past technology without testing them. Holmes's error was not in misidentifying the structure preserved by the impression but rather in developing a highly improbable theoretical process for producing twined fabric. Yet even if a researcher adequately surveys the available literature, there is never a guarantee that good ethnographic information exists on a particular craft, as was shown earlier with Osborne's (1965) experimental work replicating yucca fiber processing.

Even when substantial ethnographic data do exist for a specific perishable technology, it does not preclude the possibility that a technology may have no analog or that available information may be misused in the interpretation of archaeological data. Consider this example: spindle whorl weight is a prominent variable that influences the way yarns used in textiles are spun, but it can vary considerably and does not always affect the finished yarn. There is no simple correspondence between whorl weight and the type of fiber spun or between whorl weight and the fineness of the produced thread. Very broadly, heavier whorls seem to be preferred for longer and coarser fibers, while lighter whorls (or no whorl at all) are used for shorter, more slippery fibers, although this is not always the case. Heavier whorls can also be used for plying (twisting together) two separate yarns to make a thicker-diameter yarn. The opaque relationship between whorl size/weight and fiber type has long been a point of confusion. Lynn Teague (1998:45) points out an error made by Elizabeth Brumfiel (1996) when she applied Mary Parsons's (1972; Parsons and Parsons 1990) work to her own sample of Mesoamerican spindle whorls. Brumfiel inferred intentional cultural meaning from the differences in yarn sizes that would result from minor changes in the formal attributes of spindle whorls. While the differences in mean whorl weight and diameter were significant statistically—1 g and 2 mm, respectively—they would not have been perceptible to handspinners and would not have produced different yarns as a consequence.

In short, these cases illustrate not only the importance of attentiveness to larger bodies of literature on a particular perishable technology but also the value of practical technological experience when applying data derived from ethnoarchaeological and experimental work. Skill with materials and methods is a major factor that has bearing on both the way an experiment is conducted and the results it produces. It is noteworthy, then, that many contributions to understanding archaeological textiles and other perishables have been made by archaeologists who experimented or who were already spinners and weavers themselves and could draw on personal experience (e.g., Barber 1991; Ciszuk 2007; Drooker 1992; Fowler, Hattori, and Dansie 2000; Teague 1998). Of course, the other side to bringing prior technological knowledge and assumptions to experiments is that doing so may influence the way an experiment is conducted and described and encourage experimenters to eliminate valid hypotheses on the basis of invalid assumptions. Indeed, a variety of non-technological factors (e.g., social, ideological) must be considered, and Schiffer and Skibo (1987) remind us that despite whatever knowledge and assumptions we bring to the study of a technology, we have no guarantee that the ancient or more recent makers of these artifacts were aware of every consequence of their actions.

These points underscore the importance of specifying research goals and assumptions beforehand and also raise several important epistemic issues relating to how we measure and evaluate the experiments we conduct. Precision and accuracy are two complementary concepts that allow us to evaluate forms of measurement in archaeological research (Ramenofsky and Steffen 1998). Taken individually, precision refers to the consistency of repeated measurements, while accuracy describes the closeness of measurements to their absolute or true value. High precision is the result of an experimental apparatus and process that does not add random errors, while high accuracy shows a conformance to the true value. While both precision and accuracy are desired, accuracy is more important for theoretical interpretation and the more critical concern for a science still in its infancy, as is experimentation on perishables. In an oft-used example, measurements made from a stopped clock may be very precise, but a clock that always runs five minutes slow is much more accurate. Chemical and physical experimental apparatuses use a known standard to evaluate both precision and accuracy, but determining these values is much harder for archaeological experimentation, where there are no acknowledged "standards." Taken together, precision and accuracy determine reliability, which refers to both the consistency and replicability of measurements. In contrast, the idea of experimental validity makes us think about the appropriate scale of measurement and the experiment's relevance to research goals. Using an earlier example, Teague (1998) questioned the validity of Brumfiel's (1996) conclusions, even though the reliability of Brumfiel's results was high. Consideration of reliability and validity when experimenting with perishables has implications for how we collect and, in turn, interpret data.

To ensure accuracy, we want a high degree of similarity between experimental conditions and those of the moment in the past we are studying. This requires that we conduct experiments in "natural" or "field" settings designed to mimic the original production sequence and environment as closely as possible. Unfortunately, this type of experimental environment makes it difficult to control individual variables of interest (Schiffer et al. 1994). Human repetition of a given action will vary more than mechanical repetition will. Craftspeople may apply different stress to the weft in loom weaving, for example, depending on their alertness, fitness, skill, and so on, thereby introducing uncontrolled variables. The alternative is to conduct laboratory-based experiments in which as many variables as possible are controlled but at the expense of some accuracy. The obvious solution to this dilemma is to conduct multiple experiments, some in which one controls for multiple variables and others in which the experimenter relinquishes some control to better approximate "natural" conditions. The added benefit to conducting experiments in both "natural" and laboratory settings is that the experimenter can avoid the fallacy of taking the results from a single experiment and applying them to other situations, since the results of one trial may not necessarily reflect original manufacture and use or be entirely accurate. Employing multiple trials or experiments also enhances statistical significance, making it easier to argue that the results are valid.

GUIDELINES FOR DEVELOPING EXPERIMENTS

The diversity of available raw materials and the inherent plasticity of many of the construction techniques employed in a given perishable technology necessarily mean there are a number of ways to arrive at a desired end product. As a consequence, there is no single definitive or best way to conduct an experiment, and even successful experiments may not produce definitive results about techniques used in the past. The goal of this section is simply to enumerate a set of generalized guidelines drawn from the published literature, our personal experience, and conversations with knowledgeable individuals that will help the reader design and execute a variety of experimental studies involving perishable technology. Emphasis is placed on technological-, performance-, and context-themed experiments.

1. Goals and Assumptions. The first step in designing experimental research is to identify, in explicit terms, the project's goals and operating assumptions. Several questions should be considered initially. What problems or questions are being investigated? What kind of knowledge is sought through the experimental process (Figure 8.3)? What prior knowledge does the researcher bring to the experiment, and how might that knowledge inform, bias, or otherwise affect the experiment? Is the desire to facilitate an object's identification and analysis or to understand the logic of particular technical decisions? Is an artifact being replicated to establish the amount of time and labor involved? Or is the replication part of a larger study examining an individual or suite of performance characteristics, such as durability or permeability? Perhaps the study seeks to investigate a combination of technical action, performance characteristics, and contextual problems? Does the artifact(s) have auxiliary treatments, such as decorative embellishment and function-related enhancements (e.g., handles, reinforcing elements, or mends), that require advance planning to integrate into the structure? It is important to remember that although one may replicate, reconstruct, or recreate an archaeological perishable, there is no guarantee that the original manufacturing sequence or "recipe for action" (Schiffer and Skibo 1987) is followed precisely; equifinality is always an issue to consider.

In addition, an experiment that tries to examine too many variables at once is poorly conceived. Each new variable requires additional controlled tests that may quickly make the entire undertaking unwieldy and time-consuming. Multiple variables are also likely to make it difficult to produce a meaningful and valid conclusion. Most successful experiments are tightly focused, examining the effect of changing a single independent variable and thus understanding the role that part alone played in the larger puzzle. If the final purpose of the research is to

FIGURE 8.3 | Cordage manufacturing trial to enhance skill with materials and methods. Here, retted and soaked yucca leaves are beaten to remove pulp and separate individual fibers.

examine the interplay of several variables, a series of linked experiments should be planned.

Once these preliminary questions have been answered, it is necessary to conduct a thorough review of the literature, surveying relevant lines of archaeological and ethnohistorical evidence for information on raw materials, techniques, forms, and use contexts that will inform the present study. The researcher should ascertain whether any comparable experiments exist that might be helpful. The researcher may also want to evaluate the level of detail required to replicate an item and execute the experiment. In light of the information, or lack thereof, available on a given topic, it may be necessary to revise the experiment's original goals. Next, the researcher needs to consider what setting, "natural" or laboratory, will best accommodate the research questions. What variables must, can, and will be controlled during the experiment? Is it possible to conduct a series of experiments in both settings?

With all these questions addressed, the researcher can move on to consider other aspects of the research design.

2. Data Collection. The types of data collected are dependent upon the technology being addressed, the nature of the research question, and the available recording technology. At a basic level, some qualitative and metric data should be recorded specimen-by-specimen. The character of the experiment will determine if these data should be collected both before the experiment begins and after it has been executed. This information generally entails descriptive analytic data on structural technique, including shape, starting and finishing methods, auxiliary or supplemental structures (e.g., repairs, decoration), and constituent materials. Metric data that should be recorded often include specimen dimensions, individual element dimensions, and woven structure element density. The presence of design features specific to individual perishable technologies requires that data be recorded in accordance with standard published references for identification and analysis (see the Perishables, the Past, and Experimentation section earlier in this chapter). For example, nets may be produced with cordage that has its own design attributes to document, including fiber type and preparation, construction technique (e.g., twisted or braided), spin and ply (or plies) of elements, diameter of elements, angle of twist, twists per centimeter, and splices. Nets themselves may be described in terms of construction technique, method of starting and finishing, splicing, mesh size, and mesh patterning (if present). Terminology is always a problem with perishables, so it is useful to specify the source of descriptive terms employed and, when possible, provide synonyms.

Other data that should be documented during all stages of experimentation are time and effort expenditures. These data are particularly important when conducting preliminary trials and test runs, as they can inform the researchers about skill as they establish confidence with materials and methods. Time and energy data applicable to the archaeological record, however, are best taken from experimenters who have achieved a measure of skill comparable to the ancient craftsperson. If an attempt has been made to replicate or reproduce a copy of an item, then details about the quantity, sources, and time used to acquire and process raw materials should be noted, including actual manufacturing time. Additional data may be collected that are specific to the experiment, such as tabulated observations for tensile strength tests. Regardless of the type of experiment, it is crucial that the researcher's technical choices be accounted for during each phase of the experiment. Nothing should be assumed, and it is safer to over-record rather than under-record. Recording the experiment's materials and methods in detail facilitates replicability and may help isolate problems later if trouble should occur.

3. Materials. The experiment's research goals will dictate the minimal level of accuracy necessary to conduct the experiment. With this knowledge, the researcher can contemplate what types or combinations of materials will be sufficient for the goals of the experiment. Yet, several practical issues are worth considering regarding the procurement of plant and animal fiber sources to be used for experimentation. A significant problem stems from fiber and colorant (dye or other pigment) identifications made during the initial analysis of an artifact. For example, it is conceivable that a single length of cordage may be composed of several different types of plant fibers, or, more simply, that some classes of materials are very similar to others in their class. Modern experimenters may help with future identifications by ruling out some materials, establishing what materials look like when they are processed, and so on. Cultural modifications (e.g., use-wear, raw material preparation) and an artifact's depositional context may further hinder identification and analysis. As a result, accurate identifications are notoriously difficult to acquire, and there is no guarantee that a specialist (e.g., botanist, chemist, zoologist) consulted will have the necessary tools and experience to make them (King 1978).

Certain raw materials—such as wool (*Ovis* sp.), cotton (*Gossypium* sp.), flax (*Linum* sp.), and willow (*Salix* sp.), among others—can be purchased from weaving supply stores. Potential differences between modern materials or modern preparation of materials and those of the past should be considered before using these ready-made materials. Fiber staple length in wool and cotton, for example, has varied over time and place. Store-bought spinning materials have already been cleaned and combed, perhaps in ways that might affect their experimental use. Other fibers may be very difficult to procure in sufficient quantities or at all, depending on the time of year. Willow, for instance, is often gathered for basketry during the spring when young shoots are still pliable and have not yet put on new growth. Some factors influencing availability may be out of the researcher's control, however. Changes over time in regional climate, vegetation distributions, the introduction of invasive species, and human modifications to the landscape (e.g., farming, irrigation, draining marsh areas, discontinuation of deliberate burning practices) have in many places reshaped plant and animal communities, making materials procurement difficult. Researchers who live outside the region under study may have to make a special collecting trip or have materials gathered by proxy. If raw material procurement from a "natural" setting is not practical for these reasons, researchers may wish to explore the feasibility of growing the plant(s) themselves. Another solution, if using the same raw material is not crucial to the experiment, is to substitute the "correct" raw materials for readily available raw materials with physical or chemical properties that approximate the unavailable material. Varieties of juniper bark (*Juniperus* sp.), for example, are well-known throughout western North America as fiber sources for cordage, matting, sandals, and bags, among other products. If juniper bark were unavailable or too costly to acquire for experimentation, other fibers such as sagebrush (*Artemisia* sp.) or cliff rose (*Cowania* sp.) bark may suffice. Any substitution, however, must be justified explicitly by the experimenter.

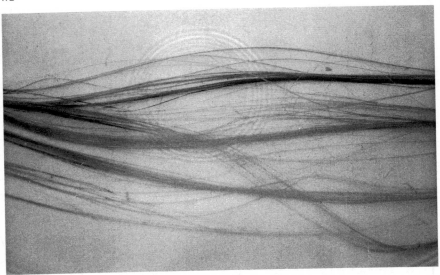

FIGURE 8.4 | Close-up view of separated yucca fiber bundles soaking in water prior to thigh-spinning. The water improves fiber pliability and also prevents the fibers from tangling.

Although problems with raw material availability can lead to compromises in experiment accuracy, in some instances archaeological or ethnographic specimens themselves may be available for experiments. Llewellyn Loud and M. R. Harrington (1929) used archaeological cordage specimens made from Indian hemp (*Apocynum* sp.) to run tests on tensile strength, unfortunately breaking many specimens in the process. Modern collection conservation ethics would probably prohibit this kind of experiment today. Aside from risking damage to an artifact, however, the researcher may be unable to interpret the experiment's results properly if the artifact's exact function or use is not known and if appropriate technical data for the specimens are not recorded (e.g., for cordage, diameter, spin and ply sequence, and tightness of spin may all affect tensile strength). More simply, materials used in this way may no longer present a valid test of the quality being examined as a result of the aging process. Further, too few archaeological specimens may exist to make the results statistically significant.

4. Materials Preparation. With raw materials in hand, the researcher is faced with the question of how to prepare them. Not unexpectedly, wide arrays of fiber-processing techniques exist, all with the ultimate goal of improving fiber workability. Fibers used to make cordage for nets and textiles may be retted, beaten, scraped, masticated, or some combination thereof (see Figure 8.3). Basketry fibers may have their bark removed (decorticated) or left intact, and they can be used whole or split longitudinally into two or more rods. Soaking plant fiber in water is a virtually universal method for improving fiber plasticity prior to and during manufacture (Figure 8.4). Hides may be tanned or untanned, then pulled, stretched, or chewed to soften them. Sometimes, though, fibers require only minimal processing. Tule (*Schoenoplectus* sp.) stems and yucca leaves can be used whole or cut longitudinally with minimal soaking, while animal skins can simply be removed, cut into long strips, and then plied together to make cordage. The method of preparation will vary greatly depending on the specific fiber source and the part of the plant or animal being used, as some fibers require more processing than others. This is especially true when dyeing fiber, which may require multiple plant parts and additional components (e.g., wood ash, urine) that will act as "dye assistants" (mordants) to help fix the dyes (Thompson and Jakes 2002).

In short, there are numerous ways to process fibers. Unfortunately, no easy way exists to determine precisely the entire process of fiber preparation for a given artifact. A thorough review of regional ethnographic literature and an examination of individual fibers under magnification for clues to processing are the best approaches. It is inadvisable to go into experimental fiber processing blindly, as the possibility exists of causing oneself bodily injury. Masticating plant fibers is one way to separate individual fibers and remove pulp, but it is not wise to use this technique on all plant fibers, since accidentally ingesting the juices of some plants will make a person ill. Similarly, several varieties of nettle (*Urtica* sp.) used for cordage have small, hollow hairs that contain irritating substances. Wild bear grass (*Xeryophyllum tenax*), a plant commonly used as a decorative element in basketry in western North America, has a sharp spine on the underside of its blades that must first be removed to protect fingers and improve flexibility. Care should be taken, then, not only in properly identifying fiber sources but also in processing them.

5. Executing Experiments. In the context of carrying out experiments, several factors warrant consideration. Similar to the difficulty of raw material identification, it is important to have accurate structural identifications before initiating replicative work with perishable artifacts. While cultural modifications (e.g., use-wear, raw material preparation) and the artifact's depositional context may inhibit identification and analysis of a specimen's structure, knowledge of structure is crucial to understanding how an object was produced and determining alternative production sequences. For instance, several structures cannot be positively identified without selvages (finished edges) or access to both sides of the artifact. Further, when working with impressions, coiled basketry, pairs of twining elements, and plied cordage may all be mistaken for each other if certain design features (e.g., warp elements, splices) are not clearly registered (King 1978.)

Skill is another major factor that affects the manipulation of raw materials and construction techniques (Figure 8.5). Initially, it can be useful to work as an apprentice with someone more experienced. In some regions, classes on spinning, loom weaving, basket weaving, and many other technologies are available. Lucky

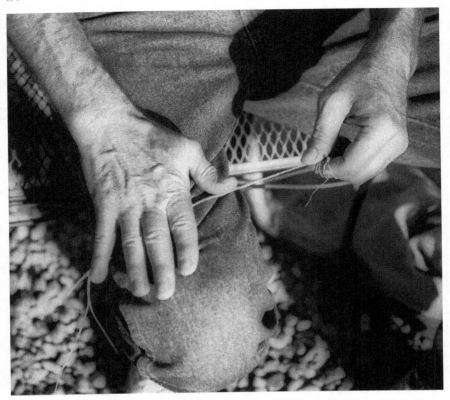

FIGURE 8.5 | Thigh-spinning yucca fibers to improve skill and confidence.

researchers may be able to take these classes from native practitioners who may use techniques similar to those used in the past. This will help the researcher learn both the necessary motor habits and tactile clues that accompany certain manufacturing techniques. Some experiments may not require complete expertise from the researcher, but others will. Preliminary trials or test runs using different materials or models may be practical to ensure that the researcher is confident with the materials and methods before conducting actual experiments. Models can be made in numerous ways, but easily assembled frames of dowel rods and pipe elbows can function as mock weaving setups for a number of woven and non-woven flexible structures (Figure 8.6). The advantage of these frame models is that using them highlights some of the technical decisions that may be encountered and enables the researcher to quickly and easily obtain experience using different techniques.

In some cases, the act of fabricating the desired replica or recreation will amount to executing the experiment. However, as demonstrated by the recent increase in experiments, future work will likely move beyond production to include

FIGURE 8.6 | A model weaving frame (28 cm²) for technical replication made from wooden dowel rods and plastic pipe elbows (*top*). An in-progress close, simple, and diagonal twined fabric is illustrated (*bottom*).

more performance- and context-themed studies. The question that arises is how to choose appropriate test methods. Some experiments, such as those for the tensile strength of cordage, are straightforward. A dry poundage test measures the amount of weight a piece of cordage can support before breaking. Given that so few performance and contextual experiments have been conducted on fiber perishables to date, the researcher interested in developing new experiments to test these characteristics is aided only by existing studies (see the Previous Research section earlier in this chapter) and apparently is limited only by imagination. Regardless of the method ultimately selected, the researcher should always plan on performing multiple runs to ensure confidence with the materials and methods and help reduce mistakes and mitigate random error.

6. Evaluation and Communication. After the experiment has been completed, it is necessary to reflect on the research design and ask what worked and what did not. The researcher should consider whether the experiment was reliable and valid. Experience and knowledge obtained from an experiment should be used to revise the research design for the next series of experiments. Based on these findings, the researcher may decide to relax control over some variables or increase it over others.

Finally, as with all archaeological research, the researcher has a professional ethical responsibility to report the project's findings in a timely manner. The reasoning behind the decisions made and any limitations to the study should be explicitly stated, as should any questions or problems that arose during the experiment. This analysis of the experimentation process should also include all sources of experimental error the researcher identified. Doing so helps establish an experimental program in fiber studies by contributing common knowledge to the subject and affording archaeologists working in other areas the opportunity to draw useful comparisons.

Experimentation with fiber perishable technologies contributes knowledge and insight that frame the way we ask questions about the patterns we see archaeologically and what we may want to ask about them next. Experimental research cannot be employed as a singular means of interpreting archaeological data, however. Although it enables us to enhance our resolution of the past in ways that are meaningful to questions we have, experimental research should always be viewed as complementary to other archaeological research.

CONCLUDING THOUGHTS

After more than a century of archaeological investigation, research on fiber technologies finally appears to be coming into its own. Increasingly, high-quality experimental research has become a critical component of perishables studies. Recognizing these facts, our aim in this chapter has been threefold: (1) to explore how experimentation enriches our understanding of perishable technologies and the people who made and used them, (2) to summarize dominant research themes in previous work and identify directions for future study, and (3) to elucidate the broad range of variables that affect experimentation with perishables to help guide research.

We have argued that although experimentation has been, and continues to be, integral to research on archaeological fiber perishables, it has never been standardized. Much existing work consists largely of isolated archaeological experiments and, by itself, is insufficient to confidently answer many of the complex questions about human behavior we would like to address through perishable data. Our intent is not to detract from the importance or high quality of this body of work but instead to suggest that we are reaching a new phase in the development of fiber perishables studies. What the field requires now to advance our knowledge of the past is an explicit program of experimental archaeology in perishables studies that involves the evaluation of a series of experiments, each designed in light of the results of earlier experiments. This is essential to the development of a robust research program in perishables studies that will produce a corpus of knowledge other archaeologists can draw from to better analyze and interpret perishable material culture wherever it is encountered.

This is vital because programmatic experimentation allows us to develop alternative explanations for archaeological phenomena and, based on the evidence available, to discriminate between them. Experimental archaeology assumes a critical role in bridging the gap between "classic" experimental sciences, such as chemistry, and historical sciences, such as archaeology, that seek to explain existing phenomena in the context of the past. Although "classic" experimental sciences often test and retest hypotheses in laboratory settings, historical sciences operate by critically evaluating hypotheses that explain specific past events (Cleland 2002). The salient distinction is that archaeology, as a historical science, cannot test many of its hypotheses as controlled experiments but instead must collect as much empirical evidence as possible to support or refute them. Importantly, experimental archaeology provides a means by which we can directly test many of our hypotheses. Future research involving experimentation will ensure that fiber artifact studies continue to evolve, remaining an important avenue of anthropological inquiry.

ACKNOWLEDGMENTS

This chapter would not have been written without the assistance of many friends and colleagues. Their contributions greatly enhanced the final product, but we alone are responsible for any errors in fact or interpretation. For helpful discussions, constructive criticism, and bibliographic input, we thank Eric Blinman, Glenna Dean, Penelope Ballard Drooker, Catherine S. Fowler, Phil R. Geib, David Goldstein, William Randall Haas Jr., Ken Howard, Linda Hurcombe, Kathryn A. Jakes, Ruth B. Jolie, Judith K. Polanich, Elizabeth Schultz, Barabara Sloan, Marvin

T. Smith, Martha Stanley, Lynn Teague, Ian Thompson, and John Peter Wild. The final version of this chapter benefited from reviews by Jeffrey R. Ferguson, Michael B. Schiffer, John C. Whittaker, and an anonymous reviewer.

REFERENCES CITED

Adovasio, J. M.
    1977   *Basketry Technology: A Guide to Identification and Analysis*. Aldine, Chicago.
    1986a   Artifacts and Ethnicity: Basketry as an Indicator of Territoriality and Population Movements in the Prehistoric Great Basin. In *Anthropology of the Desert West: Essays in Honor of Jesse D. Jennings*, ed. C. J. Condie and D. D. Fowler, 43–89. University of Utah Anthropological Papers 110. University of Utah Press, Salt Lake City.
    1986b   Prehistoric Basketry. In *Handbook of North American Indians*, vol. 11: *Great Basin*, ed. W. L. d'Azevedo, 194–205. W. C. Sturtevant, general editor. Smithsonian Institution, Washington, D.C.

Adovasio, J. M., and J. Gunn
    1986   The Antelope House Basketry Industry. In *Archaeological Investigations at Antelope House*, ed. D. P. Morris, 306–397. National Park Service, U.S. Department of the Interior, Washington, D.C.

Adovasio, J. M., D. C. Hyland, R. L. Andrews, J. S. Illingworth, R. B. Burgett, A. R. Berkowitz, D. E. Strong, and D. A. Schmidt
    2002   Wooden Artifacts. In *Windover: Multidisciplinary Investigations of an Early Archaic Florida Cemetery*, ed. G. H. Doran, 166–190. University Press of Florida, Gainesville.

Adovasio, J. M., and D. R. Pedler
    1994   A Tisket, a Tasket: Looking at Numic Speakers through the "Lens" of a Basket. In *Across the West: Human Population Movement and the Expansion of the Numa*, ed. D. B. Madsen and D. H. Rhode, 114–123. University of Utah Press, Salt Lake City.

Adovasio, J. M., O. Soffer, and J. Page
    2007   *The Invisible Sex: Understanding the True Roles of Women in Prehistory*. Smithsonian Books, New York.

Anawalt, P. R.
    1990   The Emperor's Cloak: Aztec Pomp, Toltec Circumstances. *American Antiquity* 55(2):291–307.
    1993   Riddle of the Emperor's Cloak. *Archaeology* 46(3):30–36.
    2001   Perished but Not Beyond Recall: Aztec Textile Reconstruction via Word, Image, and Replica. In *Fleeting Identities: Perishable Material Culture in Archaeological Research*, ed. P. B. Drooker, 187–209. Occasional Paper 28. Center for Archaeological Investigations, Southern Illinois University, Carbondale.

Andrews, R. L., and J. M. Adovasio
    1980   *Perishable Industries from Hinds Cave, Val Verde County, Texas*. Ethnology Monographs 5. Department of Anthropology, University of Pittsburgh, Pittsburgh.

Andrews, R. L., J. M. Adovasio, and R. C. Carlisle
1986   *Perishable Industries from Dirty Shame Rockshelter, Malheur County, Oregon.* University of Oregon Anthropological Papers 34, issued jointly as Ethnology Monographs 9. Department of Anthropology, University of Pittsburgh, Pittsburgh.

Andrews, R. L., J. M. Adovasio, B. Humphrey, D. C. Hyland, J. S. Gardner, D. G. Harding, J. S. Illingworth, and D. E. Strong
2002   Conservation and Analysis of Textile and Related Perishable Artifacts. In *Windover: Multidisciplinary Investigations of an Early Archaic Florida Cemetery*, ed. G. H. Doran, 121–165. University Press of Florida, Gainesville.

Baldia, C. M.
2003   Prehistoric Textile Materials: Technology of Dyeing with Bloodroot. Master's thesis, Department of Anthropology, Ohio State University, Columbus.
2005   Development of a Protocol to Detect and Classify Colorants in Archaeological Textiles and Its Application to Selected Prehistoric Textiles from Seip Mound in Ohio. PhD dissertation, Department of Anthropology, Ohio State University, Columbus.

Barber, E.J.W.
1991   *Prehistoric Textiles: The Development of Cloth in the Neolithic and Bronze Ages with Special Reference to the Aegean.* Princeton University Press, Princeton, N.J.
1994   *Women's Work, the First 20,000 Years: Women, Cloth, and Society in Early Times.* W. W. Norton, New York.
2003   Archaeology by Experiment and Reproduction. In *Metron: Measuring the Aegean Bronze Age, Proceedings of the 9th International Aegean Conference, 18–21 April 2002*, ed. K. P. Foster and R. Laffineur, 193–195. Aegaeum 24. Université de Liège, Liège.

Barlow, K. R., P. R. Henriksen, and D. Metcalfe
1993   Estimating Load Size in the Great Basin: Data from Conical Burden Baskets. *Utah Archaeology* 6(1):27–37.

Batzer, A., and L. Dokkedal
1992   The Warp-Weighted Loom: Some Experimental Notes. In *Archaeological Textiles in Northern Europe*, ed. L. B. Jørgensen and E. Munksgaard, 231–234. Tidens Tand 5. Textilmuseum Neumünster, Neumünster, Germany.

Baumhoff, M. A.
1957   Preface. In *Basketry: A Proposed Classification*, by Hèléne Balfét, 1–21. Reports of the University of California Archaeological Survey 38. University of California, Berkeley.

Belcher, W. R.
1994   Multiple Approaches towards Reconstruction of Fishing Technology: Net-Making and the Indus Valley Tradition. In *From Sumer to Meluhha: Contributions to the Archaeology of South and West Asia in Memory of George F. Dales*, ed. J. M. Kenoyer, 129–141. Wisconsin Archaeological Reports 3. University of Wisconsin, Madison.

Bird, J. B.
   1985   *The Preceramic Excavations at the Huaca Prieta, Chicama Valley, Peru.* Anthro-
            pological Papers of the American Museum of Natural History 62, Part I. Amer-
            ican Museum of Natural History, New York.

Bird, J. B., and L. Bellinger
   1954   *Paracas Fabrics and Nazca Needlework, 3rd Century B.C.—3rd Century A.D.*
            The Textile Museum Catalogue Raisonné. National Publishing Company,
            Washington, D.C.

Botkin, C. W., and L. B. Shires
   1944   *Tensile Strength of Yucca Fibers.* Bulletin 316. Agricultural Experiment Station
            of the New Mexico College of Agriculture and Mechanic Arts, State College,
            New Mexico.

Botkin, C. W., L. B. Shires, and E. C. Smith
   1943   *Fiber of Native Plants in New Mexico.* Bulletin 300. Agricultural Experiment
            Station of the New Mexico College of Agriculture and Mechanic Arts, State
            College, New Mexico.

Brumfiel, E. M.
   1996   The Quality of Tribute Cloth: The Place of Evidence in Archaeological Argu-
            ment. *American Antiquity* 61(3):453–462.

Carr, C., and R. F. Maslowski
   1995   Cordage and Fabrics: Relating Form, Technology, and Social Processes. In
            Style, Society, and Person: Archaeological and Ethnological Perspectives, ed. C.
            Carr and J. E. Neitzel, 297–343. Plenum, New York.

Cassman, V.
   1990   Natural Dye Research in the South Central Andes. *WAAC Newsletter* 12(2):
            2–3.

Chen, H. L., K. A. Jakes, and D. W. Foreman
   1998   Preservation of Archaeological Textiles through Fibre Mineralization. *Journal
            of Archaeological Science* 25(10):1015–1021.

Ciszuk, M.
   2007   The Academic Craftsman—A Discussion on Knowledge of Craft in Textile
            Research. In *Ancient Textiles: Production, Craft and Society*, ed. C. Gillis and
            M.-L. B. Nosch, 13–15. Oxbow Books, Oxford.

Clark, J. E.
   2002   Ancient Technology, Justifiable Knowledge, and Replication Experiments:
            Resolving the Inferential Impasse. In *Traditions, Transitions, and Technologies:
            Themes in Southwestern Archaeology*, ed. S. H. Schlanger, 259–271. University
            Press of Colorado, Boulder.

Cleland, C. E.
   2002   Methodological and Epistemic Differences between Historical Science and
            Experimental Science. *Philosophy of Science* 69(3):474–496.

Collins, H. B., Jr.
1937   *Archaeology of St. Lawrence Island, Alaska.* Smithsonian Miscellaneous Collections 196. Smithsonian Institution, Washington, D.C.

Cooke, W. D., and M. El-Gamal
1990   Ancient Textile Technology: The Hand Spinning of Ultra-Fine Yarns. *Bulletin du CIETA* 68:69–74.

Cooke, W. D., M. El-Gamal, and A. Brennan
1991   The Hand Spinning of Ultra-Fine Yarns, Part 2: The Spinning of Flax. *Bulletin du CIETA* 69:17–23.

Costin, C. L.
1996   Exploring the Relationship between Gender and Craft in Complex Societies: Methodological and Theoretical Issues of Gender Attribution. In *Gender and Archaeology*, ed. R. P. Wright, 111–142. University of Pennsylvania Press, Philadelphia.

Croes, D. R.
1995   *The Hoko River Archaeological Site Complex: The Wet/Dry Site (45CA213), 3000–1700 B.P.* Washington State University Press, Pullman.
1997   The North-Central Cultural Dichotomy on the Northwest Coast of North America: Its Evolution Suggested by Wet-Site Basketry and Wooden Fish Hooks. *Antiquity* 71(273):594–615.

Dean, G.
2005   In Hot Water: Experiments with Natural Springs and Vegetable Dyes. *Spin-Off* 29(4):74–77.

Deegan, A. C.
1993   Anasazi Fibrous Sandal Terminology. *Kiva* 59(1):49–64.
1997   Anasazi Sandals of Tseyi-Hatsosi Canyon, Arizona: Attributes and Cultural Context. *Clothing and Textile Research Journal* 15(1):12–19.

Desrosiers, S.
1985   Experience de technologie: La reconstruction d'une ceinture Precolombienne a partir d'un texte code du XVIIe siecle/An Experiment in Technology: The Reconstruction of a Pre-Columbian Belt from an Encoded XVII Century Text. *Techniques and Culture* 6:111–144.

Dillehay, T. D.
1997   Archaeological and Taphonomical Analyses of the Wood Assemblage. In *Monte Verde, a Late Pleistocene Settlement in Chile*, vol. 2: *Archaeological Context and Interpretation*, ed. T. D. Dillehay, 507–648. Smithsonian Institution Press, Washington, D.C.

Drooker, P. B.
1992   *Mississippian Village Textiles at Wickliffe.* University of Alabama Press, Tuscaloosa.
2001a   Leaving No Stone Unturned: Making the Most of Secondary Evidence for Perishable Material Culture. In *Fleeting Identities: Perishable Material Culture in*

       Archaeological Research, ed. P. B. Drooker, 170–186. Center for Archaeological
       Investigations, Southern Illinois University, Carbondale.

Drooker, P. B. (editor)
    2001b   *Fleeting Identities: Perishable Material Culture in Archaeological Research.* Center
             for Archaeological Investigations, Southern Illinois University, Carbondale.

Drooker, P. B., and L. D. Webster (editors)
    2000   *Beyond Cloth and Cordage: Archaeological Textile Research in the Americas.* Uni-
            versity of Utah Press, Salt Lake City.

Emery, I.
    1995   *The Primary Structures of Fabrics: An Illustrated Classification.* The Textile Mu-
    [1980] seum, Washington, D.C. Reprinted by Watson-Guptil Publications, the Whit-
            ney Library of Design, and the Textile Museum, Washington, D.C.

Ericksen, A. G., K. A. Jakes, and V. S. Wimberley
    2000   Prehistoric Textiles: Production, Function, Semiotics. In *Beyond Cloth and
            Cordage: Archaeological Textile Research in the Americas*, ed. P. B. Drooker and
            L. D. Webster, 69–83. University of Utah Press, Salt Lake City.

Fowler, C. S., and L. E. Dawson
    1986   Ethnographic Basketry. In *Handbook of North American Indians*, vol. 11: *Great
            Basin*, ed. W. L. d'Azevedo, 705–737. W. C. Sturtevant, general editor. Smith-
            sonian Institution, Washington, D.C.

Fowler, C. S., E. M. Hattori, and A. J. Dansie
    2000   Ancient Matting from Spirit Cave, Nevada: Technical Implications. In *Beyond
            Cloth and Cordage: Archaeological Textile Research in the Americas*, ed. P. B.
            Drooker and L. D. Webster, 119–139. University of Utah Press, Salt Lake
            City.

Franquemont, C. R.
    1979   Watching, Watching, Counting, Counting. *Human Nature* 2(3):82–84.
    1986   Chinchero Pallays: An Ethnic Code. In *The Second Junius B. Bird Conference on
            Andean Textiles*, ed. A. P. Rowe, 331–338. The Textile Museum, Washington,
            D.C.
    1988   Chinchero Plant Categories: An Andean Logic of Observation. PhD disserta-
            tion, Department of Anthropology, Cornell University, Ithaca, N.Y.

Franquemont, E. M., and C. R. Franquemont
    1987   Learning to Weave in Chinchero. *Textile Museum Journal* 26:56–79.

Gaustad, S.
    2005   Time Warp: Confessions of a Museum Weaver. *Spin-Off* 29(2):40–43.

Geib, P. R.
    2000   Sandal Types and Archaic Prehistory on the Colorado Plateau. *American Antiq-
            uity* 65(3):509–524.

Gilbert, R.
    2005   Decisions Taken in Planning a Replica Artefact. *Archaeological Textiles Newslet-
            ter* 40:18–19.

Good, I. L.
  2001   Archaeological Textiles: A Review of Current Research. *Annual Review of Anthropology* 30:209–226.

Gordon, J.
  1993   *Construction and Reconstruction of a Mi'kmaq Sixteenth-Century Cedar-Bark Bag.* Curatorial Report 76. Nova Scotia Museum, Halifax.
  1995   *Mi'kmaq Textiles: Sewn Cattail Matting, BkCp-1 Site, Pictou, Nova Scotia.* Curatorial Report 80. Nova Scotia Museum, Halifax.
  1997   *Mi'kmaq Textiles: Twining Rush and Other Fibers, BkCp-1 Site, Pictou, Nova Scotia.* Curatorial Report 82. Nova Scotia Museum, Halifax.

Goubitz, O.
  2007   *Stepping through Time: Archaeological Footwear from Prehistoric Times Until 1800.* SPA Uitgevers, Zwolle, The Netherlands.

Greenfield, P. M.
  2004   *Weaving Generations Together: Evolving Creativity in the Maya of Chiapas.* School of American Research Press, Santa Fe.

Haas, W. R., Jr.
  2001   The Basketmaker II Fiber Industry of Boomerang Shelter, Southeastern Utah: A Synthesis of Cordage Morphology Analysis and Experimentation. *Kiva* 67:167–185.
  2006   The Social Implications of Basketmaker II Cordage Design Distribution. *Kiva* 71(3):275–298.

Hald, M.
  1980   *Ancient Danish Textiles from Bogs and Burials: A Comparative Study of Costume and Iron Age Textiles.* Publications of the National Museum Archaeological Historical Series 21. National Museum of Denmark, Copenhagen.

Hamilton, D. L.
  2001   *Prehistory of the Rustler Hills: Granado Cave.* University of Texas Press, Austin.

Harding, D. G.
  1998   Cheyenne-Style Coiled Willow Gaming Basket. *Bulletin of Primitive Technology* 15:75–76.

Hayden, B., and A. Cannon
  1984   Interaction Inferences in Archaeology and Learning Frameworks of the Maya. *Journal of Anthropological Archaeology* 3:325–367.

Heizer, R. F., and I. W. Johnson
  1952   A Prehistoric Sling from Lovelock Cave, Nevada. *American Antiquity* 18(2):139–147.

Hoffmann, M.
  1964   *The Warp-Weighted Loom: Studies in the History and Technology of an Ancient Implement.* Hestholms Boktrykkeri, Oslo, Norway.

Holden, C.
  2003   Hay Beats Gore-tex. *Science* 301(5629):43.

Holmes, W. H.
  1884   Prehistoric Textile Fabrics of the United States, Derived from Impressions on
            Pottery. In *Third Annual Report of the Bureau of Ethnology to the Secretary of
            the Smithsonian Institution, 1881–'82*, by J. W. Powell, 397–425. Government
            Printing Office, Washington, D.C.
  1896   Prehistoric Textile Art of the Eastern United States. In *Thirteenth Annual
            Report of the Bureau of Ethnology to the Secretary of the Smithsonian Institution,
            1891–'92*, by J. W. Powell, 9–46. Government Printing Office, Washington,
            D.C.
  1901   Use of Textiles in Pottery Making and Embellishment. *American Anthropologist*
            3(3):397–403.

Hurcombe, L. M.
  1994   Plant-Working and Craft Activities as a Potential Source of Wear Variation.
            Helinium 34(2):201–209.
  2007   A Sense of Materials and Sensory Perception in Concepts of Materiality. *World
            Archaeology* 39:532–545.
  2008a   Organics from Inorganics: Using Experimental Archaeology as a Research Tool
            for Studying Perishable Material Culture. *World Archaeology* 40:83–115.
  2008b   Looking for Prehistoric Basketry and Cordage Using Inorganic Remains: The
            Evidence from Stone Tools. In *Prehistoric Technology 40 Years Later: Functional
            Studies and the Russian Legacy*, ed. L. Longo and N. Skakun, 205–216. British
            Archaeological Reports International Series. Archaeopress, Oxford.

Hurley, W. M.
  1979   *Prehistoric Cordage: Identification of Impressions on Pottery*. Aldine, Chicago.

Hutcheson, C. D.
  2001   Re-Weaving the Strands: Continued Exploration into the Basketry Technol-
            ogy of Prehistoric Bahamians. In *Proceedings of the 18th International Con-
            gress for Caribbean Archaeology*, vol. 1, ed. G. Richard, 185–198. l'Association
            Internationale d'Archéologie de la Caraibe, Région Guadeloupe, Mission
            Archéologique, Guadeloupe.

Jakes, K. A.
  1996   Clues to the Past: Further Development of the Comparative Plant Fiber Col-
            lection. In *Archaeological Chemistry: Organic, Inorganic, and Biochemical Anal-
            ysis*, ed. M. V. Orna, 202–222. American Chemical Society Symposium Series
            625. American Chemical Society, Washington, D.C.

Jakes, K. A., and A. G. Ericksen
  1997   Socioeconomic Implications of Prehistoric Textile Production in the Eastern
            Woodlands. In *Materials Issues in Art and Archaeology V*, ed. P. Vandiver, J.
            Druzik, J. F. Merkel, and J. Stewart, 281–286. Materials Research Society Sym-
            posium Proceedings 462. Materials Research Society, Pittsburgh.

Jakes, K. A., L. R. Sibley, and R. Yerkes
1994   A Comparative Collection for the Study of Fibers Used in Prehistoric Textiles from Eastern North America. *Journal of Archaeological Science* 21(5):641–650.

James, G. W.
1970   *Indian Basketry and How to Make Indian Baskets.* Rio Grande Press, Glorieta, N.M.

Jones, B. R.
2000   Revealing Minoan Fashions. *Archaeology* 53(3):36–41.

Jones, V. H.
1948   Notes on the Manufacture of Cedar-Bark Mats by the Chippewa Indians. *Michigan Academy of Science Arts and Letters Papers* 32:341–363.

Jones, V. H., and R. L. Fonner
1954   Appendix C: Plant Materials from Sites in the Durango and La Plata Areas, Colorado. In *Basket Maker II Sites Near Durango, Colorado,* by E. H. Morris and R. F. Burgh, 93–122. Carnegie Institution of Washington Publication 604. Carnegie Institution of Washington, Washington, D.C.

Jørgensen, L. B.
1994   Ancient Costumes Reconstructed: A New Field of Research. In *Textilsymposium Neumünster: Archäologische Textilfunde—Archaeological Textiles,* ed. G. Jaacks and K. Tidow, 109–113. Textilmuseum Neumünster, Neumünster, Germany.

Kemp, B. J., and G. Vogelsang-Eastwood
2001   *Ancient Textile Industry at Amarna.* Excavation Memoirs 68. Egypt Exploration Society, London.

Kent, K. P.
1957   *The Cultivation and Weaving of Cotton in the Prehistoric Southwestern United States.* Transactions of the American Philosophical Society 47, part 5. American Philosophical Society, Philadelphia.
1983   *Prehistoric Textiles of the Southwest.* School of American Research, Santa Fe.

Kidder, A. V.
1926   A Sandal from Northeastern Arizona. *American Anthropologist* 28(4):618–632.

Kidder, A. V., and S. J. Guernsey
1919   *Archaeological Explorations in Northeastern Arizona.* Bureau of American Ethnology Bulletin 65. Government Printing Office, Washington, D.C.

King, M. E.
1975   Archaeological Textiles. In *Irene Emery Roundtable on Museum Textiles 1974 Proceedings: Archaeological Textiles,* ed. P. L. Fiske, 9–16. The Textile Museum, Washington, D.C.
1978   Analytical Methods and Prehistoric Textiles. *American Antiquity* 43(1):89–96.

King, M. E., and J. S. Gardner
  1981   The Analysis of Textiles from Spiro Mound, Oklahoma. In *The Research Potential of Anthropological Museum Collections*, ed. A. E. Cantwell, J. B. Griffin, and N. A. Rothschild, 123–139. Annals of the New York Academy of Sciences 376. New York Academy of Sciences, New York.

Knudsen, L. R.
  1998   An Iron Age Cloak with Tablet-Woven Borders: A New Interpretation of the Method of Production. In *Textiles in European Archaeology*, ed. L. B. Jørgensen and C. Rinaldo, 79–84. GOTARC Series A, vol. 1. Göteborg University Department of Archaeology, Göteborg, Sweden.

Koerper, H. C.
  1998   A Game String and Rabbit Stick Cache from Borrego Valley, San Diego County. *Journal of California and Great Basin Anthropology* 20(2):252–270.

Kuttruff, J. T.
  1988   Textile Attributes and Production Complexity as Indicators of Caddoan Status Differentiation in the Arkansas Valley and Southern Ozark Regions. PhD dissertation, Department of Textiles and Clothing, Ohio State University, Columbus.
  1991   Interpretation of Textile Production and Use by High and Low Status Caddoan Groups. In *Materials Issues in Art and Archaeology II*, ed. P. B. Vandiver, J. Druzik, and G. Wheeler, 777–783. Materials Research Society, Pittsburgh.
  1993   Mississippian Period Status Differentiation through Textile Analysis: A Caddoan Example. *American Antiquity* 58(1):125–145.

Kuttruff, J. T., M. S. Standifer, and S. G. DeHart
  2004   Replication of Prehistoric Footwear and Bags. *Louisiana Agriculture* 47(1): 20–22.

Loud, L. L., and M. R. Harrington
  1929   *Lovelock Cave*. University of California Publications in American Archaeology and Ethnology 25(1). University of California Press, Berkeley.

MacKenzie, M. A.
  1991   *Androgynous Objects: String Bags and Gender in Central New Guinea*. Harwood Academic Publishers, Amsterdam.

Mason, O. T.
  1899   *Woman's Share in Primitive Culture*. D. Appleton, New York.
  1904   Aboriginal American Basketry: Studies in a Textile Art without Machinery. In *Annual Report of the U.S. National Museum for 1901–1902*, 171–548. Government Printing Office, Washington, D.C.

McBrinn, M. E., and C. P. Smith
  2006   A New Spin on Cordage: The Effects of Material and Culture. *Kiva* 71(3): 265–274.

Miller, J.
  1988   Experimental Replication of Early Woodland Vegetal Fiber Slippers. *Southeastern Archaeology* 7(2):132–137.

Minar, C. J.
  1999   Impression Analysis of Cord-Marked Pottery, Learning Theory, and the Origins of the Alachua. PhD dissertation, Department of Anthropology, University of California, Riverside.
  2000   Spinning and Plying: Anthropological Directions. In *Beyond Cloth and Cordage: Archaeological Textile Research in the Americas*, ed. P. B. Drooker and L. D. Webster, 85–99. University of Utah Press, Salt Lake City.
  2001a   Motor Skills and the Learning Process: The Conservation of Cordage Final Twist Direction in Communities of Practice. *Journal of Anthropological Research* 57(4):381–405.
  2001b   Material Culture and the Identification of Prehistoric Cultural Groups. In *Fleeting Identities: Perishable Material Culture in Archaeological Research*, ed. P. B. Drooker, 94–113. Occasional Paper 28. Center for Archaeological Investigations, Southern Illinois University, Carbondale.

Morris, E. H., and R. F. Burgh
  1941   *Anasazi Basketry: Basket Maker II through Pueblo III: A Study Based on Specimens from the San Juan River Country*. Carnegie Institution of Washington Publication 533. Carnegie Institution of Washington, Washington, D.C.
  1954   *Basket Maker II Sites Near Durango, Colorado*. Carnegie Institution of Washington Publication 604. Carnegie Institution of Washington, Washington, D.C.

Munksgaard, E.
  1991   Kopien af drakten fra Mammengraven. In *Mammen: Grav, Kunst og Samfund I Vikingetid*, ed,. M. Iversen, 151–153. Aarhus University Press, Aarhus, Denmark.

Neff, L. S.
  1996   Ancient Pueblo Spinning Traditions in the Northern Southwest. Master's thesis, Department of Anthropology, Northern Arizona University, Flagstaff.

Nyerges, C.
  1999   The World Is Tied Together with Fiber: The Value of Fiber in Primitive Cultures. *Bulletin of Primitive Technology* 17:12–14.

Oakland, A. S.
  1982   Pre-Columbian Spinning and *Lloq'e* yarn: An Ethnographic Analogy. *Andean Perspectives Newsletter* 4:25–30.

Ochsenschlager, E. L.
  2004   *Iraq's Marsh Arabs: In the Garden of Eden*. University of Pennsylvania Museum of Archaeology and Anthropology, Philadelphia.

O'Neale, L. M.
  1932   Yurok-Karok Basket Weavers. *University of California Publications in American Archaeology and Ethnology* 32(1):1–184.
  1945   *Textiles of Highland Guatemala*. Carnegie Institution of Washington Publication 567. Carnegie Institution of Washington, Washington, D.C.
  1947   Note on an Apocynum Fabric. *American Antiquity* 13(2):179–180.

Oppelt, N. T.
  1999   Basket-Impressed Anasazi Pottery in the Northern San Juan. *Southwestern Lore*
           65(4):4–21.

Osborne, C. M.
  1965   The Preparation of Yucca Fibers: An Experimental Study. *American Antiquity*
           31(2:2):45–50.

Owen, L. R.
  2005   *Distorting the Past: Gender and the Division of Labor in the European Upper
           Paleolithic.* Kerns Verlag, Tübingen, Germany.

Parsons, J. R.
  2006   *The Last Pescadores of Chimalhuacán, Mexico: An Archaeological Ethnography.*
           Museum of Anthropology Anthropological Papers 96. Museum of Anthropol-
           ogy, University of Michigan, Ann Arbor.

Parsons, J. R., and M. H. Parsons
  1990   *Maguey Utilization in Highland Central Mexico: An Archaeological Ethnogra-
           phy.* Museum of Anthropology Anthropological Papers 82. Museum of Anthro-
           pology, University of Michigan, Ann Arbor.

Parsons, M. H.
  1972   Spindle Whorls from the Teotihuacán Valley, Mexico. In *Miscellaneous Stud-
           ies in Mexican Prehistory*, by M. W. Spence, J. R. Parsons, and M. H. Parsons,
           45–79. Museum of Anthropology Anthropological Papers 45. Museum of
           Anthropology, University of Michigan, Ann Arbor.

Petersen, J. B., M. J. Heckenberger, and J. A. Wolford
  2001   Spin, Twist, and Twine: An Ethnoarchaeological Examination of Group Iden-
           tity in Native Fiber Industries from Greater Amazonia. In *Fleeting Identities:
           Perishable Material Culture in Archaeological Research*, ed. P. B. Drooker, 226–
           253. Occasional Paper 28. Center for Archaeological Investigations, Southern
           Illinois University, Carbondale.

Pryor, J. H.
  1988   Temporal and Spatial Stylistic Patterns of Northern California Indian Baskets.
           PhD dissertation, Department of Anthropology, State University of New York
           at Binghamton, Binghamton.

Pryor, J. H., and C. Carr
  1995   Basketry of Northern California Indians: Interpreting Style Hierarchies. In
           Style, Society, and Person: Archaeological and Ethnological Perspectives, ed. C.
           Carr and J. E. Neitzel, 259–296. Plenum, New York.

Quimby, G. I.
  1961   Cord Marking Versus Fabric Impressing of Woodland Pottery. *American An-
           tiquity* 26(3):426–428.

Ramenofsky, A. F., and A. Steffen
1998   Units as Tools of Measurement. In *Unit Issues in Archaeology: Measuring Time, Space, and Material*, ed. A. F. Ramenofsky and A. Steffen, 3–17. University of Utah Press, Salt Lake City.

Reynolds, P. J.
1999   The Nature of Experiment in Archaeology. In *Experiment and Design: Archaeological Studies in Honour of John Coles*, ed. A. F. Harding, 156–162. Oxbow Books, Oxford.

Roberts, D.
2004   Unraveling a Mystery: Did the Anasazi Use Ropes to Reach Cliffside Homes? *National Geographic* 206(3):Geographica.

Salls, R. A.
1985   The Scraper Plane: A Functional Interpretation. *Journal of Field Archaeology* 12:99–106.
1989   To Catch a Fish: Some Limitations on Prehistoric Fishing in Southern California with Special Reference to Native Plant Fiber Fishing Line. *Journal of Ethnobiology* 9(2):173–199.

Sands, R.
1997   *Prehistoric Woodworking: The Analysis and Interpretation of Bronze and Iron Age Tool Marks*. UCL Institute of Archaeology, London.

Schiffer, M. B.
1972   Archaeological Context and Systemic Context. *American Antiquity* 37(2):156–165.
1975   Behavioral Chain Analysis: Activities, Organization, and the Use of Space. In *Chapters in the Prehistory of Eastern Arizona*, vol. 4, ed. P. S. Martin, W. A. Longacre, and J. N. Hill III, 103–119. Fieldiana Anthropology, vol. 65. Field Museum of Natural History, Chicago.

Schiffer, M. B., and J. M. Skibo
1987   Theory and Experiment in the Study of Technological Change. *Current Anthropology* 28(5):595–622.
1997   The Explanation of Artifact Variability. *American Antiquity* 62(1):27–50.

Schiffer, M. B., J. M. Skibo, T. Boerlke, M. Neupert, and M. Aronson
1994   New Perspectives on Experimental Archaeology: Surface Treatments and Thermal Response of the Clay Cooking Pot. *American Antiquity* 59(2):197–217.

Schultz, E.
2002a   A Study of Sewn Cattail Mats. B.A. thesis, Department of Sociology and Archaeology, University of Wisconsin, La Crosse. Manuscript in author's possession.
2002b   Sewn Cattail Mats. Electronic document, http://www.uwlax.edu/sociology/Archaeology/students/schultz/, accessed August 10, 2008.

Seiler-Baldinger, A.
1994   *Textiles: A Classification of Techniques*. Smithsonian Institution Press, Washington, D.C.

Sibley, L. R., and K. A. Jakes
  1989   Etowah Textile Remains and Cultural Context. *Clothing and Textiles Research Journal* 7(2):37–45.

Sibley, L. R., K. A. Jakes, and L. H. Larson
  1996   Inferring Behavior and Function from an Etowah Fabric Incorporating Feathers. In *A Most Indispensable Art: Native Fiber Industries from Eastern North America*, ed. J. B. Petersen, 73–87. University of Tennessee Press, Knoxville.

Sibley, L. R., K. A. Jakes, and M. E. Swinker
  1992   Etowah Feather Remains from Burial 57: Identification and Context. *Clothing and Textile Research Journal* 10(3):21–28.

Sibley, L. R., M. E. Swinker, and K. A. Jakes
  1991   The Use of Pattern Reproduction in Reconstructing Etowah Textile Remains. *Ars Textrina* 15:179–202.

Siewertsz van Reesema, E.
  1926   *Contribution to the Early History of Textile Technics*. Edited by E. Nierstrasz. Afdeeling Letterkunde Nieuwe Reeks, Deel 26, no. 2. Uitgave van de Koninklijke Akademie van Wetenschappen te Amsterdam.

Silvestre, R.E.J.
  1994   The Ethnoarchaeology of Kalinga Basketry: A Preliminary Investigation. In *Kalinga Ethnoarchaeology: Expanding Archaeological Method and Theory*, ed. W. A. Longacre and J. M. Skibo, 199–207. Smithsonian Institution Press, Washington, D.C.
  2000   The Ethnoarchaeology of Kalinga Basketry: When Men Weave Baskets and Women Make Pots. PhD dissertation, Department of Anthropology, University of Arizona, Tucson.

Smith, H. I.
  1909   Primitive Industries as a Normal College Course. In *Putnam Anniversary Volume Anthropological Essays: Presented to Frederic Ward Putnam in Honor of his Seventieth Birthday, April 16, 1909*, ed. F. Boas, R. B. Dixon, A. L. Kroeber, F. W. Hodge, and H. I. Smith, 487–520. G. E. Stechert, New York.

Song, C. A., K. A. Jakes, and R. W. Yerkes
  1996   Seip Hopewell Textile Analysis and Cultural Implications. *Midcontinental Journal of Archaeology* 21(2):247–265.

Sosna, D.
  1999   Experimental Proof of Textile Production during the Upper Paleolithic. *Archeologické rozhledy* 51(1):95–103.
  2000   The Origin of the Textile Industry. Master's thesis, Department of Anthropology, Masaryk University, Brno, Czech Republic.

Srinivasan, R., and K. A. Jakes
  1997   Optical and Scanning Electron Microscope Study of the Effects of Charring on Indian Hemp (*Apocynum cannabinum* L.) Fibers. *Journal of Archaeological Science* 24(6):517–527.

Stanley, M.
1995   Cloth of the Anasazi. *Handwoven* September-October:44–46.

Stothert, K. E., K. A. Epstein, T. R. Cummins, and M. Freire
1991   Reconstructing Prehistoric Textile and Ceramic Technology from Impressions in Cloth in Figurines from Ecuador. In *Materials Issues in Art and Archaeology II*, ed. P. B. Vandiver, J. Druzik, and G. Wheeler, 767–776. Materials Research Society, Pittsburgh.

Talge, J. R.
1995   Replication of Ancient Puebloan Sandal-Toe Constructions: Comparisons of Complexity. Master's thesis, Department of Human Environments, Utah State University, Logan.

Taylor, W. W.
1966   Archaic Cultures Adjacent to the Northeastern Frontiers of Mesoamerica. In *Handbook of Middle American Indians*, vol. 4: *Archaeological Frontiers and External Connections*, ed. G. F. Ekholm and G. R. Willey, 59–94. R. Wauchope, general editor. University of Texas Press, Austin.

Teague, L. S.
1998   *Textiles in Southwestern Prehistory*. University of New Mexico Press, Albuquerque.

Thompson, A. J., and K. A. Jakes
2002   Replication of Textile Dyeing with Sumac and Bedstraw. *Southeastern Archaeology* 21(2):252–256.

Thompson, G. M.
1958   An Analysis of Prehistoric Woven Materials from Eastern Colorado. Unpublished manuscript on file at the Department of Anthropology, University of Denver, Denver, Colo.

Tiedemann, E. J.
2001   Characterization of Prehistoric Spinning Technology: Toward the Determination of Spinning Practices Employed in Mississippian Textiles. PhD dissertation, Department of Anthropology, Ohio State University, Columbus.

Tiedemann, E. J., and K. A. Jakes
2006   An Exploration of Prehistoric Spinning Technology: Spinning Efficiency and Technology Transition. *Archaeometry* 48(2):297–307.

Tulloch, A., and J. K. Polanich
1999   U'kuyus Basketry of Central California. *Bulletin of Primitive Technology* 17: 43–47.

van Driel-Murray, C.
2002   Practical Evaluation of a Field Test for the Identification of Ancient Vegetable Tanned Leathers. *Journal of Archaeological Science* 29(1):17–21.

Washburn, D. K.
2001   Remembering Things Seen: Experimental Approaches to the Process of Information Transmittal. *Journal of Archaeological Method and Theory* 8(1):67–99.

Washburn, D. K., and A. Petitto
   1993   An Ethnoarchaeological Perspective on Textile Categories of Identification and
             Function. *Journal of Anthropological Archaeology* 12(2):150–172.

Weber, R. L.
   1986   *Emmons's Notes on Field Museum's Collection of Northwest Coast Basketry:
             Edited with an Ethnoarchaeological Analysis.* Fieldiana Anthropology, New
             Series 9. Field Museum of Natural History, Chicago.

Webster, L. D.
   2007   Mogollon and Zuni Perishable Traditions and the Question of Zuni Origins.
             In *Zuni Origins: Toward a New Synthesis of Southwestern Archaeology*, ed. D. A.
             Gregory and D. R. Wilcox, 270–317. University of Arizona Press, Tucson.

Webster, L. D., and M. Loma'omvaya
   2004   Textiles, Baskets, and Hopi Cultural Identity. In *Identity, Feasting, and the
             Archaeology of the Greater Southwest: Proceedings of the 2002 Southwest Sympo-
             sium*, ed. Barbara J. Mills, 74–92. University Press of Colorado, Boulder.

Wendrich, W.
   1994   *Who Is Afraid of Basketry: A Guide to Recording Basketry and Cordage for Archae-
             ologists and Ethnographers.* CNWS Publications 6. Research School, Centre for
             Non-Western Studies, Leiden University, Leiden, The Netherlands.
   1999   *The World According to Basketry: An Ethno-Archaeological Interpretation of Bas-
             ketry Production in Egypt.* CNWS Publications 83. Research School, Centre
             for Non-Western Studies, Leiden University, Leiden, The Netherlands.

Willey, L. M.
   1974   Functional Analysis of Perishable Artifacts during the Late Woodland Period in
             the Northeastern United States. Master's thesis, Department of Anthropology,
             Pennsylvania State University, State College.

Wilson, S. R.
   1996   Spinning (Bunny) Tails: An Adventure in Experimental Archaeology. *Illinois
             Antiquity* 31(3–4):4–5.

Wobst, H. M.
   1978   The Archaeo-Ethnology of Hunter-Gatherers, or the Tyranny of the Ethno-
             graphic Record in Archaeology. *American Antiquity* 43(2):303–309.
   2001   Matter over Mind: Perishables and the Glorification of Materiality in Archae-
             ology. In *Fleeting Identities: Perishable Material Culture in Archaeological
             Research*, ed. P. B. Drooker, 43–57. Center for Archaeological Investigations,
             Southern Illinois University, Carbondale.

Woltz, B. V., Jr.
   1998   The Use of Agave, Sotol and Yucca at Hinds Cave, Val Verde County, Texas:
             Reconstructing Methods of Processing through the Formation of Behavioral
             Chains. Master's thesis, Department of Anthropology, Texas A&M University,
             College Station.

Yoder, D., J. Blood, and R. Mason
2005   How Warm *Were* They? Thermal Properties of Rabbit Skin Robes and Blankets. *Journal of California and Great Basin Anthropology* 25(1):55–68.

CHAPTER NINE

Weapon Trials: The Atlatl and Experiments in Hunting Technology

John Whittaker

○ ○ ○
○ ○ ○
○ ○ ○

One of my favorite bits of archaeological jargon is the description of stone projectile points as a part of "complex projectile delivery systems" (Christenson 1986:109). While I am amused at the formality of the words and the image of a little man in blue ringing one's doorbell with an arrowhead, the point behind the verbiage is important. Most archaeological analyses of hunting technology work with orts and morts, remainders and dead bits of complicated composite tools and living systems. The most common survivors are imperishable stone components. Meanwhile, many anthropologists have had a consistent fascination with hunting as a dramatic and "manly" occupation that carries considerable symbolic baggage in our own culture. One complication with the archaeological study of hunting is that modern hunting technology is often far removed from that of the past. Most modern hunters find prehistoric technology rather alien, and to understand the functioning and capabilities of past hunting gear, experiments with preindustrial weaponry have been fairly common (Knecht 1997).

In this chapter I focus on the atlatl or spearthrower with a historical slant, as it is important to show how experimentation responds to the archaeological problems of its time. The atlatl is essentially a stick with a hook or socket to engage the spear on one end and a grip for the hand on the other end (Figure 9.1). It allows an

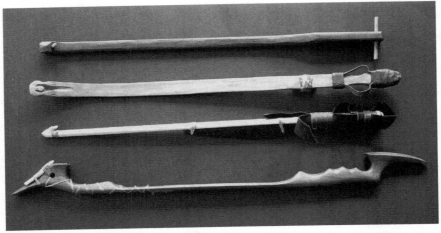

FIGURE 9.1 | Four modern atlatls. *Top to bottom*: Simple "five-minute" model; Basketmaker-inspired form by John Whittaker; modern commercial Great Basin–inspired form by Bob Perkins, BPS Engineering; modern commercial "Wyalusing" model by Bob Berg, Thunderbird Atlatls.

individual to throw a spear considerably harder and farther than can be achieved by hand alone. This projectile technology was common throughout prehistory, antedating the bow and arrow. It is well-known ethnographically and, like archery, is experiencing a revival in the form of recreational sport. The archaeological evidence shows some of the same sampling and interpretation problems visible in the archaeology of all hunting. Because the historical record and tradition of atlatls is much sparser than that for bows and there were fewer ethnographic examples, experimentation arguably played an even larger part in the archaeology of the atlatl, and experiments with atlatls illustrate both the potentials and the difficulties of all experimental archaeology.

ETHNOGRAPHIC BEGINNINGS

In the nineteenth century, ethnographers became aware of a projectile system fairly different from the bow and arrow. Early explorers in the Arctic and Australia observed spears cast with the aid of a "throwing stick," "spearthrower," or "throwing board." A typical account is that of Charles Darwin, traveling on the *Beagle* in 1836, near Bathhurst, Australia.

> At sunset a party of a score of the black aborigines passed by, each carrying, in their accustomed manner, a bundle of spears and other weapons. By giving the leading man a shilling, they were easily detained, and threw their spears for my amusement. . . . In their own arts they are admirable. A cap being fixed at thirty

FIGURE 9.2 | Ethnographic Australian atlatls, showing the variety of forms.

yards distance, they transfixed it with a spear, delivered by the throwing-stick
with the rapidity of an arrow from the bow of a practiced archer. (Darwin
1909:457)

Casual observation soon led to more focused scholarly interest. In the Arctic,
Otis Mason (1885) was one of the first to describe Eskimo throwing sticks and
the distribution of different types of these sticks. He explained their use alongside
bows and arrows by citing the difficulty of using a bow in a kayak when the thrower
had wet and greasy hands. John Murdoch (1892) described in more detail the
hand board or throwing board and the spears used in one area near Point Barrow
in northern Alaska and correctly explained the motion. Edward William Nelson
(1899:152) reported in similar detail on the gear used in western Alaska and was
impressed by the "considerable accuracy and force from 30–50 yards" with which
seal spears were thrown.

In Australia, spearthrowers were described more or less briefly by many ethnographers (e.g., Haddon 1912; Roth 1909; Spencer and Gillen 1938). D. S. Davidson
(1936) classified forms and examined their distribution (Figure 9.2). F. Krause (1905)
included Australian material in a survey of spear slings used around the world.

EARLY ARCHAEOLOGY

According to Jean Pierre Lansac (2001, 2004), French archaeologists Edouard
Lartet and Henry Christy made the first archaeological finds of spearthrowers at

Laugerie-Basse in 1862, although it was not until 1891 that Adrien de Mortillet recognized the carved antler pieces as parts of spearthrowers through analogy to Australian specimens. In the Americas, archaeological interest in spearthrowers seems to have begun with Zelia Nuttall (1891), who surveyed the Mesoamerican codices, sculpture, Spanish historical records, and three extant specimens to describe the Mesoamerican atlatl. She was particularly interested in iconographic and linguistic evidence for spearthrowers and their symbolism. Otis Mason (1893) was the first to claim an archaeological specimen in the New World, recognizing that a southwestern "Cliff Dweller" (Basketmaker) artifact collected by the Wetherills and displayed at the World Columbian Exhibition was equivalent to the atlatls described by Nuttall and also to Mexican ethnographic specimens. Nuttall and Mason popularized the Nahuatl (Aztec) word *atlatl* and are apparently responsible for the dominance of that term used for spearthrowers in American archaeology. The eccentric genius Frank Cushing (1895) quickly became interested and worked various forms of atlatl and other, less plausible devices into an evolutionary scheme that led to bows and arrows. He claimed that his reproduction of the Cliff Dweller atlatl worked, which may make him the first atlatl experimenter on record. He soon recognized other atlatl forms among the wooden artifacts he found during excavations in the Florida Keys (Cushing 1897; Gilliland 1975).

The archaeological problems that still influence atlatl studies developed early, and they all led to experimentation. They can be grouped under three headings: (1) the relationship of spearthrowers to the bow and arrow; (2) the recognition of atlatls in the archaeological record, from projectile point evidence and from atlatl parts themselves, especially stone weights or bannerstones; and (3) the function and capabilities of atlatls.

THE RELATIONSHIP OF SPEARTHROWERS TO THE BOW AND ARROW

In the early days of professional anthropology and archaeology, theoretical attention was focused on issues of technological chronology and the distribution of cultural traits. The question of whether the atlatl was earlier than the bow was primarily one of archaeological chronology, obscured somewhat by the observation that atlatls and bows were used contemporaneously among at least some Mesoamerican and Arctic cultures.

Cushing (1895) immediately accepted that the atlatl was earlier than the bow, apparently because it suited his evolutionary ideas. He proposed a sequence that started with various weakly documented devices derived from classical accounts of augmenting javelin throws with cordage. The flexible atlatl of the Basketmakers followed and led to two hybrids that he called the "spear-crook, or flinging bow" and the "bow-crotch." The former is a speculation based on Zuni prayer sticks: the addition of a string across the crook of some prayer sticks yielded a device that might have been used as an atlatl, with the added springing action of the bowlike part. The

bow-crotch seems even more far-fetched. However, Cushing felt these hypothetical artifacts could logically lead to the bow proper. Perhaps I should not ridicule
the spear-crook or the unfortunately named bow-crotch, as neither has had a fair
experimental trial,[1] but Cushing's entire scheme was based on the mistaken assumption that it was the flex of the atlatl that supplied the power and inspired further
inventions that ultimately led to the bow.

Others who accepted the primacy of the spearthrower over the bow may have
done so simply because it seemed a simpler invention (J. A. Mason 1928) or on the
basis of very limited evidence that atlatls were found in contexts that lacked bows
and therefore appeared to be earlier, as in the southwestern United States (Pepper
1905). However, the southwestern chronological evidence was not securely documented for many years (Baker and Kidder 1937; Fenenga and Wheat 1940; Kidder
and Guernsey 1919). Similarly, in Paleolithic Europe, the carved antler objects
eventually recognized as spearthrowers were seen to appear earlier than any evidence of the bow and arrow (Garrod 1955; J. A. Mason 1928), and in Australia,
considered isolated and primitive by early anthropologists, the bow and arrow never
supplanted the spearthrower.

Any evolutionary relationship between the atlatl and the bow remains specula-
tive and, to my mind, unlikely. As we shall see, atlatls and bows work on completely
different principles, not through a common use of the power of a flexing spring—
although many people still make that mistake in trying to explain the sequence of
inventions (e.g., Farmer 1994; Kjelgaard 1951; Lyons 2004; Perkins 2000b). Nearly
everyone now agrees that the atlatl was earlier than the bow. However, the timing of
the introduction of the bow remains a controversy, both in the Old World (Lansac
2004) and especially in the Americas, largely because the hard evidence for both
atlatl and bow is sparse.

ARCHAEOLOGICAL RECOGNITION

Atlatls and bows are made mostly of perishable materials, and it is remarkable
that we have as many prehistoric specimens as we do. Once archaeologists recognized the existence and basic form of spearthrowing devices, dry contexts in the
American West produced a number of good specimens, Cushing's wet finds in
Florida yielded a few more, and a number were found in frozen Arctic deposits
(Diters 1977). Spearthrowers are older and less well preserved in the Old World,
but cave sites in France yielded bone and antler objects eventually recognized as
spearthrowers or, more correctly, as parts of spearthrowers (Garrod 1955; Stodiek
1992, 1993).

I have found references to more than 120 partial and complete atlatls from
North America, not counting hooks and weights in which all wooden parts have
perished. (For extensive atlatl bibliographies, consult Bruchert 2000; Whittaker
2008a). More than 60 of these cases are from the U.S. Southwest (Turnbow and

Fields 2004). There are likely many more Arctic specimens than I have found in publications (Diters 1977). There are at least a dozen extant atlatls from late prehistoric and contact period Mesoamerica (Saville 1925) and many from South America, less well documented. Pascal Chauvaux (2003), Dorothy Garrod (1955), and Ulrich Stodiek (1993) have information on around 66 specimens from Europe. These are mostly the antler or bone hook portion, which is sometimes elaborately decorated and is a familiar part of the corpus of Upper Paleolithic "art." Lansac (2001), following Pierre Cattelain (1988), lists 118 specimens. I have been unable to find documented archaeological atlatls from the rest of the world. One might expect that Australia, with its dry climate and long prehistoric record, would have produced examples, but the prehistory of hunting equipment there is known mostly from rock art (Morwood 2002:164). The basis for reconstruction and experimentation with spearthrowers is thus archaeological specimens from Europe, mostly France, and the New World, mostly North America, augmented by ethnographic and ethnohistoric examples from the Arctic, Australia, Mexico, New Guinea, South America, and elsewhere.

Early archaeologists interested in the chronology and distribution of atlatls in the Americas were hampered by their fragility, and to this day the difficulty of recognizing either bows or atlatls by fragments or associated artifacts continues to stir up disagreement. Projectile points are the most common evidence cited in attempts to date the arrival of the bow and arrow and to recognize the presence of different types of projectile weapons. The usual expectation was proposed long ago (e.g., Baker and Kidder 1937; Kidder 1938), most explicitly by Franklin Fenenga (1953). The bow propels a lighter projectile than the spearthrower, so the heads of arrows should be much lighter than those on darts used with spearthrowers or on spears thrown by hand. Some early experiments were performed to address this idea. Jim Browne (1938, 1940) tested both bows and atlatls and argued that large points worked perfectly well on arrows. He contended that W. E. Baker and Alfred Kidder should not have concluded that the bow was late; in fact, Folsom points were perfect arrowheads. Browne's words make it clear, though, that his atlatl gear or his skill with that gear was not effective enough to make this evaluation. "Any close degree of accuracy is impossible with atlatl and spear," he said, admitting that after six months of practice he still could not "hit a buffalo once out of 10 shots at 30 yards" (1940:211). To a modern atlatlist this seems laughable; to a prehistoric hunter it would have been pitiable.

Whatever the deficiencies of Browne's experiments, his argument that a wide range of variation in point size is allowable with both bows and atlatls is supported by other experiments (e.g., Couch, Stropes, and Schroth 1999). Ironically, while most archaeologists believe that Folsom and Clovis points were probably used with spearthrowers (Ahler and Geib 2000; Frison 1989; Tankersley 2002), hard evidence for early Paleoindian atlatls has been difficult to find. W. Karl Hutchings (1997) argues that some Clovis point fractures show high-velocity impact, implying atlatl use, and C. Andrew Hemmings (2004; Whittaker 2007a) identifies ivory hooks from Florida rivers as Clovis atlatl parts. Similarly, although no one doubts that small late points tipped arrows, and large early points should have armed atlatl darts, it is still risky to use point size to identify the early arrival of bows (Bachechi, Fabbri, and Mallegni 1997; Bettinger and Eerkens 1999; Geib and Bungart 1989; Hughes 1998; Nassaney and Pyle 1999; Sliva 1999; Webster 1980) or the late retention of atlatls (Lorentzen 1993; Vanpool 2006; Whittaker 2007b). Numerous attempts have been made to clarify the differences between arrow and dart points by examining ethnographic and archaeological material (Corliss 1980; Shott 1993, 1997; Thomas 1978), and most of the articles cited use more sophisticated arguments than point size alone, but the basic difficulty of recognition remains. The situation is similar in Europe (Lansac 2004).

Even recent work with artifacts from melting ice patches in the Yukon and Alaska, where more or less complete projectiles can be examined, is not without difficulties. The Yukon material suggests a fairly clear-cut transition date, with bows replacing atlatls around AD 700 (Dold 2004; Gotthardt et al. 1999; Hare et al. 2004); but in Alaska, arrows seem to have arrived about 200 years earlier, and atlatl darts continued in use much longer (Dixon, Manley, and Lee 2005). Both areas, however, contain some surprisingly ambiguous artifacts whose form or dates do not fit well with the other evidence.

It would seem that parts of actual spearthrowers would be less controversial than the points, which are only indirectly connected as parts of the "complex projectile delivery system," but this is not the case. Finds in the southeastern United States ignited arguments that continue to this day (Whittaker 2008b). Clarence Moore (1916), reporting on a series of excavations along the Green River in Kentucky, led off his monograph with a discussion of the problem of "bannerstones." The class of artifacts known as bannerstones was familiar enough to need no definition by Moore. They are stone objects—drilled lengthwise—with a variety of forms that range from tubular to triangular in cross-section, sometimes with "wings" or other elaboration and often finely made of hard and colorful stone. The name used by collectors and archaeologists reflected a general belief that these objects had no "practical" use and were simply used in rituals or for display.

Moore (1916) noted that at the Archaic shell mound of Indian Knoll, bannerstones were often found associated in graves with antler objects of similarly tubular form and with antler tine hooks. He argued that the hooks were for making netting, with the bannerstones used as sizers to gauge the mesh, and he cited some ethnographic parallels. However, Moore noted that Charles Willoughby, associated with the Harvard Peabody Museum, had suggested that the hooks might be the distal end of throwing sticks. This suggestion had enough force that Moore spent a page refuting it on the grounds that (1) there was no evidence of throwing sticks from that region; (2) throwing sticks are usually one-piece artifacts for reasons of strength; (3) small points of antler or flint were not associated with the bannerstones and hooks; (4) some of the hooks were too crooked for atlatls, and some had holes too small to allow them to be attached firmly; and (5) even if the hooks were atlatl parts, the stone and antler objects that accompanied them remained unexplained. Points one and two seem quaint today because of their assumption of complete archaeological and ethnological knowledge and their disregard for the problems of preservation. Number three seems odd since Moore reported plentiful "arrow" points at his sites, including some that pierced bones. He probably meant that while hooks and sizers were commonly found together, points had not been found in the same graves. As Dianna Doucette (2001) has noted, his burial excavations did not necessarily encompass the furthest edges of the graves, where points on shafts might have been found. However, points four and five finally get to the realm of experiment, since even in Moore's day experiments to determine the function and capabilities of artifacts were common. In fact, Moore had his steamboat captain make a section of net using wooden models of a hook and a sizer and concluded that this was the likeliest function of the sets from graves (Moore 1916: 433). It was left to William Webb (1946, 1957) and others to carry the argument into the modern era of experimentation, demonstrating that hooks and bannerstones do work as atlatl parts, with the bannerstones serving as weights. Currently, most would agree that the antler hooks and similar items elsewhere were atlatl parts, although some atlatl hooks may be less readily recognized.

The issue of bannerstones is far from resolved, although most archaeologists consider them atlatl weights. Webb's experiments were initially aimed at archaeological recognition of atlatls at Indian Knoll; they were intended to show that bannerstones worked as atlatl parts. However, the experiments soon led him to more complex issues, so I will return to bannerstones when I discuss the different goals and results of experimentation with atlatls.

FUNCTION AND CAPABILITIES OF ATLATLS

The bulk of spearthrower experimentation has been directed at understanding the capabilities of atlatls and how they function. This connects to some of the earlier issues involving archaeological recognition.

How Does an Atlatl Work?

Our knowledge of how to throw a light spear with an atlatl, both theoretical and practical, comes from ethnographic observation and practical experience. There are three main models, which typically arose almost as soon as archaeologists began to try to understand spearthrowers. We can refer to these as the lever action, extended force, and flexing spring models. Some of these models are based more on physics theory than on physical experiment. I will concentrate on experiments to resolve the questions of physics.

FIGURE 9.3 | Sequential photos showing throwing motion. Photographs by Jeff Lindow.

1. Lever Action. The atlatl is most correctly described as a lever or, rather, a complex series of levers. The sequence of motions visible on slow-motion film (Whittaker and Hilton 2003) and described by others (Cundy 1989; VanderHoek 1998) is described here (Figure 9.3). With the dart raised level to the ground and aimed at the target, the atlatlist begins by stepping forward, bringing body, arm, and dart forward. As the step is completed, the torso rotates and the throwing arm flexes at the shoulder, bringing the hand and atlatl forward. The atlatl stays level and the dart remains pointed at the target throughout this motion. To complete the throw the wrist flexes violently, swinging the atlatl up to vertical and flicking the dart away. Finally, the arm and body follow through as the dart flies toward the target. The motion is essentially the same as that used in throwing a rock or a baseball, the difference being the atlatl. By flexing the wrist rapidly a small distance, the distal end of the atlatl moves a much greater distance, acting as a lever to impart energy to the dart (Baugh 2003). B. J. Cundy (1989) analyzed 1970 ethnographic films to arrive at the same sequence and notes that this sequence of motions allows slow, powerful muscles to act first, followed by less powerful but faster actions, thereby producing a smooth and efficient acceleration. Most of the gain in velocity is from the wrist and atlatl motion in the last tenth of a second of the throw (Cundy 1989; see also Hutchings and Bruchert 1997). Most atlatl experimenters agree that the lever model is the correct one (Butler 1975), as did some early observers (Murdoch 1892).

2. Extended Force. Calvin Howard (1974) gives the most extensive discussion of how an atlatl might function by extending the time during which force is applied to the dart, although the idea was not new with him (e.g., Krause 1905; Mason 1885). As Howard describes it, "[T]he atlatl is not a catapult or flipping device. During a proper throw, the spur reaches no greater elevation than that of the handle" (1974:102). He believed the hook on a level atlatl simply remains in contact with the dart and delivers thrust longer than does a hand throwing the same spear with a similar motion. Moreover, flipping the dart with a lever action of the atlatl will not work because "hooking [in which the butt end of the dart is pulled down] results when the thrower fails to keep the atlatl level during the thrust" (1974:103) and because the atlatl hook would break off under the stress of a dart rotating on it (1976).

It surprises me that this model received any credence, since numerous ethnographic photos show atlatls swung up to vertical as the spear departs, as do increasing numbers of photos of modern experimentation and sport use (Whittaker and Hilton 2003; Whittaker and Maginniss 2006). Any atlatlist who expects to throw with force for any distance knows that the flipping motion is important. However, a number of authorities apparently still adhere to at least parts of this model (e.g., Raymond 1986; VanderHoek 1998), and experiments and personal experience suggest a reason why. Keeping the atlatl level throughout the throw will work for short throws (VanderHoek 1998). However, it is very poor form with most light darts, and in my own training I found it was a bad habit I had to overcome before I could throw effectively at any distance. Also, the hand can remain at about the same height for most of the throw, dropping down at the end as the atlatl is flipped. I would also guess that with heavy, relatively inflexible darts, such as some Arctic harpoons, keeping the atlatl level may be the proper way to throw them. Specific experimentation and reporting on this issue are needed, however.

3. Flexing Springs. What about the flex of the atlatl, mentioned earlier, and the flex of the dart, which is dramatically visible in many photos? A number of atlatlists, most vocally Bob Perkins (Perkins 1995, 2000a, 2000b; Perkins and Leininger 1989; see also Hayes 1994; Ratzat 1992), argue that as the atlatl pushes against the rear of the dart, both dart and atlatl flex, storing energy that then springs the dart forth from the atlatl, thereby contributing a large part of its velocity. Richard Baugh's (1998; 2003) mathematical modeling suggests that gains of 7–12 percent might be possible with a flexible atlatl. Webb (1957) proposed a somewhat more complex version. He believed the flex of the atlatl, combined with a "bannerstone" weight that through time was placed closer and closer to the hook end of the atlatl, served to "transfer momentum" to the projectile, just as the elasticity of a ball and bat transfers energy to the ball.

A number of arguments can be made against the flexing spring model. First, the majority of ethnographic spearthrowers are rigid or nearly so, so flexibility of the atlatl is clearly not necessary. Webb, Baugh, and the others admit this, but they argue that a flexing atlatl is more efficient than a less flexible one. Most important, high-speed photography shows that the atlatl does flex during a throw but that it is still flexed after the dart has departed, having no time to spring back and add to the dart's velocity (Whittaker and Maginniss 2006). The spring issue is complicated by the fact that the projectile unquestionably flexes—sometimes a great deal—and inflexible darts are almost completely unusable, but that is not because the springing action stores useful energy. As the atlatl is raised at the end of the throw while the dart is kept aimed at the target, the nock end of the dart must rise with the atlatl, thereby flexing the dart. This does store a certain amount of energy, but most of it is released as latitudinal oscillations of the dart (Baugh 1998; Cundy 1989). Finally, Webb's model of "transferring momentum" to the dart is incorrect. The atlatl increases dart velocity, as explained in the lever action model. Adding weight to the end of the atlatl near the hook slows the throw and requires more force in flexing the wrist. A number of atlatlists have tried atlatls with bannerstones near the hook, and some swear by them (Lyons 2002). I find them extremely clumsy and slow, and physical principles show that they decrease the efficiency of the throw (Baugh 2003; Cundy 1989).

Atlatl Motion Experiments

While the lever action model is clearly the most useful for understanding normal atlatls, the others may apply at least in part to some spearthrowers. A few ethnographic spearthrowers from Australia are very long and whippy, as are some of the versions used for modern distance throwing. In these examples, the springing action may be relevant. Similarly, the extended force model promoted by Howard may apply to rigid projectiles like some Arctic harpoons. Further experimentation is needed.

Many descriptions of how an atlatl works come from observations of ethnographic atlatl users (Cundy 1989) or from modern experiments done for other purposes, and they often rely heavily on a theoretical model from physics (Butler 1975; Cotterell and Kamminga 1990). Stop-action, or slow-motion, photography has only begun to be exploited (Cundy 1989; Hutchings and Bruchert 1997; Stodiek 1993; Whittaker and Hilton 2003; Whittaker and Maginniss 2006). It is now possible to do much more sophisticated motion studies, so this is an area in which future experimentation will soon improve our understanding of the physics and human motion and allow better control of variables in controlled experiments.

Experiments with Weights

The issues of bannerstones and the role of weights on spearthrowers have produced more experimentation than any other part of atlatl studies, although such artifacts are limited to parts of North America. As usual, there are several theories about the use of weights on atlatls, some irreconcilable and others allowing a degree of overlap. Most experiments with weighted atlatls have attempted to measure changes in efficiency, or at least maximum throwing distance. As we shall see, this is the easiest variable to measure, but accuracy at short range was probably more important to prehistoric hunters.

The oldest idea is that bannerstones had no practical use. Many early writers agreed with Warren Moorehead (1910:410), who stated: "It has always seemed to me ridiculous to claim that the prehistoric peoples made use of objects, on which a great deal of time and hard labor were spent, for ordinary purposes." Like John Baer (1921) and others, they assumed that fragile, exotic, and unsharpened objects could only have been mounted on handles for ceremonial use or hung around the neck as ornaments. Supporting this position are finds of some bannerstones that do indeed appear to be too heavy for use or that show wear from use or reuse as pendants and other ornaments (Hranicky 2003; Knoblock 1939).

The supposed fragility of bannerstones bothers many people, but it is easily testable. My experience and that of many others, including Webb (1957), is that most are strong enough to serve as atlatl weights. Orville Peets (1959) even used the edge of a winged bannerstone as the hook on his atlatl. Similarly, successful atlatls can be constructed of multiple pieces, including wooden shafts thin enough to pass through the drilled hole in most bannerstones, so the doubts of Clarence Moore (1916) and others (Hothem 1998) on that matter can be laid to rest. Even now, the dominant view among those interested in bannerstones rather than atlatls favors the idea that bannerstones were largely decorative or ceremonial, even if they were sometimes attached to atlatls (Knoblock 1939), or that they may even have originated as atlatl weights (Lutz 2000). From the opposite perspective, as Mary Kwas (1982) and others (Mau 1963; Precourt 1973; Webb 1957; Winters 1968) have pointed out, it should not be surprising that functional objects attached to important weapons might have high intrinsic and symbolic value. The consistent association of stone objects with complete atlatls in the American Southwest and with hooks, handles, or both in the Southeast makes a solid contextual argument for the weight theory (Doucette 2001; Drass and Brooks 1984; Webb 1946, 1957; Whittaker 2008b).

But why would anyone want to attach a weight to an atlatl? The concept of stone atlatl weights originated with the southwestern finds of relatively small stones attached to some Basketmaker atlatls, although Cushing (1895) and others (Guernsey 1931) emphasized their importance as charms. Webb seems to have been the most vehement proponent of the atlatl weight theory. He felt the weight transferred momentum to the projectile, increasing the force and distance of the throw—a theory that makes no physical sense. A number of experiments have attempted to test the effect of adding weights to atlatls. A summary of a few of these efforts shows the diversity of opinions and also some problems with experimental design and comparability that will be emphasized later.

Webb (1957) theorized a great deal, and his reconstruction drawings imply that he tested some of his theories, but nowhere does he report experimental results.

Malcolm Hill (1948) tried two different atlatls with and without small weights near the handle, throwing three different spears with arched and flat throws. He measured distance for six throws for each of the resulting twelve trials and concluded that the weights were negative or useless. Clayton Mau (1963), without expressing a theory as to how weights work, reported that a moderate weight close to the handle of the atlatl increased the distance of his throws by 15–25 percent. However, although his experiments were interesting, he tested several variables and reported in insufficient detail to determine whether his results have statistical significance. John Palter (1976) believed that weight would augment the flex of an atlatl but noted that tests were contradictory; his own showed that distance decreased as more weight was added. Details of his experiments were not given, but his graph shows ten throws with each of five weights (0–450 g) attached at an unstated distance from the atlatl grip—hardly a large sample. Peets (1960) found no significant difference between weighted and unweighted atlatls, but he never stated what weight he used or how many throws he made. He did note that his angle of 40 degrees elevation for distance throws was probably not consistent. Howard (1974) also found no benefit from weights based on a sample of eighteen throws, presumably using the atlatl incorrectly, as described earlier.

Like Palter (1976), Virgil Hayes (1994) and Bob Perkins (1993) believe that adding a weight to an atlatl influences the flex. Perkins reports that the weight acts as resistance, like the projectile itself, to flex the atlatl and store energy; Hayes argues that it is necessary to "tune" the flex of the atlatl to the flex of the dart. As far as I know, no one has experimented systematically with atlatl flex or the effects of weights on it, but, as mentioned earlier, atlatl flex does not affect dart velocity, at least not through spring action (Whittaker and Maginniss 2006).

Another popular theory is that the weight on a spearthrower serves as a balance to steady the spear when it is aimed or at rest (Cundy 1989; Elliott 1989; Peets 1960). Horace Hobbs (1963) attempted to get the best of both worlds by designing a bizarre atlatl that incorporated a bannerstone that slid along a central rod so that it provided balance at rest but during a throw slid out to the end of the atlatl, apparently following Webb's model of increasing momentum. He concluded from his experiments (details not reported) that any atlatl provided twice the throwing distance of a spear thrown by hand, and his "super atlatl" did even better, up to fifty-five yards. I have not tried such an apparatus, but I suspect the sliding weight would make it clumsy and inefficient.

Physical principles (Baugh 2003; Cundy 1989) show that a weight on an atlatl will usually slow it down, increasingly so as the weight is moved nearer the tip. Cundy (1989), VanderHoek (1998), and others argue, however, that a weight can provide steadying inertia, reducing the tendency to sway the atlatl out of line during a throw. Weighting would then be intended to improve accuracy rather than distance. Accuracy is probably the variable of greatest interest to prehistoric atlatl users, but I know of no experiments along these lines.

William Perkins (1993) believes that not only does a weight affect atlatl flex but that some winged bannerstones act as "silencers" to reduce the swishing noise of a throw. He claims that sound recordings of experimental throws support this theory.

Others have suggested functions for bannerstones that are tangentially or not at all related to atlatls. They could be spindles on a drill (Parker 1917) or spindles for spinning cordage (Bruchert 1996). Robert Berg (2005; also Leeth 2004) explains the association of bannerstones with atlatl parts in burials by suggesting that the bannerstone was part of a set that included the atlatl, darts, and a spindle needed to make cordage for hafting. He demonstrates experimentally that bannerstones do work as spindle whorls. Net weaving has also been mentioned, and again, experiments have shown that it is possible to weave a net with antler hooks and bannerstone sizers. Arthur Parker (1917) suggested that a bannerstone could work as fletching on a spear, and George Cole (1972) also put the bannerstone on the spear. He argued that it would have no effect on the atlatl, but on a spear a bannerstone could serve as a balancing weight that would slide down the shaft at impact, hammering the spear deeper. Both ideas are totally implausible.

WEAPON TRIALS:
PROBLEMS WITH EXPERIMENTAL EVALUATIONS OF ATLATLS

Obviously, to understand prehistoric weapons, we must evaluate their efficiency and utility for different tasks. A number of experiments have shown that atlatl-thrown projectiles can be deadly. Most notably, George Frison (1989) experimented with the carcasses of culled elephants to demonstrate that a Clovis point on a spear hurled with the aid of an atlatl could make a fatal wound in even the largest animals. Other archaeologists have also shot dead elephants (Butler 1980; Callahan 1994) or smaller animals or carcasses (Cattelain 1997; Flenniken 1985), and there are many other unpublished experiments of varying quality. Bruce Bradley (personal communication 2003) has told me that he and others killed a bison with atlatls, and François Bordes (personal communication 1973) once told me that as a boy he "threw a spear right through" his neighbor's dog after it had killed his cat. The legal and social complications of this last anecdote make it a poor model. Although atlatls are not currently legal for hunting in most states, except in private game parks and for taking some "nuisance" game, there are numerous reports from the sport atlatl community of deer, boar, and fish (Figure 9.4) having been killed with atlatls (Becker 1992, 2001; Berg 1996, 2002, 2003; Fogelman and Berg 1998; Hutchings and Bruchert 1997).

None of this should be surprising. After all, atlatls were used worldwide for thousands of years, so they must have worked well. The real problems for modern experimental archaeology are deciding how well they worked in comparison to other weapons and comparing the different forms of atlatls. Comparisons are

FIGURE 9.4 | Carp harpooned in knee-deep water, range of a few meters, using unfletched dart and bone harpoon point. Photograph by Mark Bro.

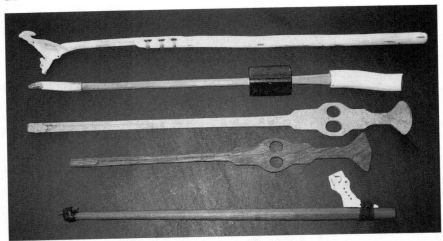

FIGURE 9.5 | Reconstructions of archaeological atlatls. *Top to bottom*: French Paleolithic by Pascal Chauvaux, Indian Knoll reconstruction, two interpretations of Cushing's Key Marco finds, and a replica of coastal Peruvian atlatl 3743 in the University of Pennsylvania Museum, all made by John Whittaker.

difficult to make, though, in the absence of any standard. Which prehistoric atlatl is being compared to what? Does the replica or reconstruction of a prehistoric atlatl reliably replicate the important features of the prehistoric model? It is fairly simple to use the correct materials and to copy the weight, dimensions, and flex of complete specimens, such as those from the prehistoric Southwest or Australian ethnographic examples, but forms that have been only partially preserved—such as the finds from Indian Knoll and Key Marco—are open to some interpretation (Figure 9.5). A combination of practical experience and experimentation with the archaeological evidence can get us fairly close, but the atlatl itself is no more a complete "projectile delivery system" than is the stone point. With the possible exception of some burial sets from South America, I know of no archaeological cases where both the atlatl and the darts to be used with it have been preserved. Ethnographic sets do exist, but even they are rare.

That said, we should be able to provide some quantification, some objective observations, on atlatl function. However, we immediately face the question of what should be measured to determine atlatl efficiency. The damage inflicted by projectiles at different weights and velocities could be considered (Hrdlicka 2002, 2003). Some experimenters have measured dart velocity (Bergman, McEwen, and Miller 1988; Hutchings and Bruchert 1997; Raymond 1986; Tolley and Barnes 1979; Whittaker and Kamp 2007), but accuracy and distance are the two most commonly used measures of a successful throw. Both present problems for experimental design.

Distance is easy to measure, and so most experimenters have used the distance of throws to measure the effect of variations in atlatl design. For instance, recent experimenters have argued that variations in point size (Couch, Stropes, and Schroth 1999), the addition of weights (Bird 1985; Peets 1960; Tolley and Barnes 1979), and the flex of the atlatl have little effect on the distance attainable in a sample of throws. However, other experimenters, also using distance as a measure, have reached the contrary conclusions that the addition of weights to an atlatl increases (Mau 1963; Raymond 1986) or decreases (Hill 1948; Palter 1976) distance and that flex and point weight are also important variables (Perkins 2000b).

Such inconclusive or contradictory results, while having the benefit of allowing observers to hold fast to their own biases, make it difficult to evaluate some aspects of atlatl design and use. Experimental design is to blame in many cases. First, there are many potential variables to manipulate in the equipment itself. It is possible to make atlatls and spears that are closely similar except for one attribute, such as the position of the weight on the atlatl. However, handmade gear is sometimes idiosyncratic, and one suspects that a great deal of noise is present in some experiments. Moreover, it is not safe to assume that the addition of a weight to a long, flexible atlatl has the same effect as the same weight on a short, rigid thrower, so generalizing statements are often difficult to make. Furthermore, in my experience, even the best scholarly institutions are reluctant to allow experiments with projectile weapons to be conducted in the gymnasium, and most atlatl experiments—especially distance throws—are necessarily performed outdoors, where inconstant conditions such as wind also introduce stochastic variation.

The worst problem, of course, is human variation. No one has yet designed a mechanical atlatl device that eliminates the human thrower. As modern sport atlatling demonstrates, each thrower has a slightly different motion, and every throw by the same individual is subject to small uncontrolled variations as well. This is the case because the motion of throwing is complex; it involves the whole body, with several joints and limb segments acting as different lever systems in different parts of the throw. It is impossible to expect the consistency of a gun, a crossbow, or a bow and arrow. Large samples of throws are necessary to compensate for this variation, but, as exemplified earlier, most experiments have used relatively small samples. This alone makes their conclusions suspect, especially when the effects of relatively significant human error might be expected to overwhelm relatively small variations in the equipment, such as a few grams of point weight (e.g., Couch, Stropes, and Schroth 1999). In some experiments, several individuals have used the same equipment. Although using multiple throwers efficiently increases the dataset of throws, it also increases the human variation. However, if the goal is to understand a specific piece of equipment, we do need to see how different thrower physiques and styles affect performance.

The same problems apply to measuring accuracy, which has been done by relatively few experimenters—although as VanderHoek (1998) and others note, this is probably the variable most of interest to prehistoric hunters. Within a single experiment, a standardized target and a large sample of throws could make accuracy a useful measure, but even more human variation exists in how consistently a thrower can hit a target than is present in the distance he or she can throw when trying for a maximum distance. Accuracy is even more difficult to evaluate across different experiments. The atlatl is difficult to master, and modern atlatlists find it a challenging sport, in part because even the most expert thrower is subject to occasional inaccuracy or unexpected wild throws. However, one of the basic premises of experiments with prehistoric technology is that the experimenter should be competent enough in using a tool to give it a fair trial.

SPORT AND SCIENCE

The articles I cite in this chapter include a fair number from recreational atlatlists. Along with traditional archery, flintknapping, and other "primitive skills," the atlatl has experienced a surge of popular interest in recent years. Recreational atlatlists are as devoted and opinionated as enthusiasts in any sport and have developed a body of practical experience and a considerable literature. All this is not as new as many think, and a number of important early studies also came from atlatlists who had little other connection to archaeology. Following the World Open Atlatl Contest, started in 1981 (Laird 1984), the World Atlatl Association was founded in 1988; and a number of state, regional, and European groups have also formed. These organizations' various newsletters publicize some archaeologically relevant material. Because atlatls are fairly easy to make and to use at an elementary level, even if difficult to master, they are ideal for teaching experimental archaeology and for instilling in students and the public a respect for, and interest in, preindustrial technology (Whittaker and Mertz 2002).

As the sporting use of atlatls has grown, a number of people are now making standardized atlatls to sell. Few of these are reproductions of specific prehistoric or ethnographic types, but those can be purchased from skilled makers by experimenters who do not wish to make the equipment themselves. More important, the sporting world of atlatlists not only involves some archaeologists such as myself but also includes a relatively large body of experienced people—some actively experimenting and publishing, others capable of cooperating with experimenters. Much of the experimentation is unsystematic or undocumented (a problem not confined to amateurs), but even that work produces subjective experience that is useful in judging archaeological atlatls. The sporting records that are developing are also more useful than most participants might think.

The International Standard Accuracy Contest (ISAC) was developed in 1996 by Lloyd Pine and is now used as a part of most competitive atlatl events, with scores recorded and publicized by the World Atlatl Association. The contest consists of five throws at 15 m and five at 20 m at a standardized bull's-eye target modeled after those used in archery. The rings are 108 cm, 80 cm, 56 cm, 40 cm, 24 cm, and 10 cm, scoring 6, 7, 8, 9, 10, and X (tie-breaking 10) points, respectively, for a possible high score of 100 with 10 X (WAA 2005).

Although the ISAC was created by and for atlatl sports so there would be one standard of comparison among atlatlists worldwide, it can serve more serious research purposes as well. It is already apparent, for instance, that as sporting interest in atlatls grows, so, too, does skill. More people practice to develop their skill, the top ISAC scores have risen, and the number of people achieving higher scores has increased dramatically. European events using the same targets and distances for bows and atlatls show that proficiency with the atlatl is much harder to attain than is the case with the bow and arrow (Cattelain 1997). As of 2008, the highest score yet achieved in an ISAC competition was Mark Bracken's 2003 score of 98XXXXX. To put this in context, it means that Bracken hit a 10-cm target nine times and missed it once by a few centimeters at distances of 15 and 20 m. The normal range for ethnographic hunters, no matter what weapons they use, is 10 to 30 m (Cattelain 1997; Cundy 1989; Hutchings and Bruchert 1997; Ohtsuka 1989; Stodiek 1993). ISAC scores in the 70s are considered competent but not exceptional, and better scores are comparable to what ethnographic hunters achieve with bows and arrows (Hill and Hawkes 1983; Hutchings and Bruchert 1997; Walker et al. 2002) or atlatls (Tindale 1928). A detailed analysis of the 13,500 scores recorded between 1996 and 2003 (Whittaker and Kamp 2005, 2006) shows that although some new records will probably be set, the top atlatlists have reached a consistent peak. Furthermore, high scores and individual peaks are usually reached after only two or three years of practice. ISAC competition includes people of all ages and skill levels, and the top teenagers and women are now achieving scores close to those of the men. What this means to archaeologists is that although none of us grew up using an atlatl daily or has been able to collect data on habitual subsistence hunters using atlatls, we probably have a pretty good understanding of what ordinary people can consistently achieve with an atlatl.

One of the pleasures of the sport is making and trying out new gear. Score sheets record whether competitors' equipment is "primitive" (no modern material allowed except for glues and fake sinew) or "open." Atlatls and darts used in modern events include a few archaeologically supported replicas, but most are inspired by prehistoric gear and were made using modern tools and a wide range of natural materials. Some atlatls are fully modern innovations that use space-age materials, and fiberglass and aluminum dart shafts are common, as is milled wood. In the ISAC data, scores with primitive equipment averaged slightly higher than scores for modern equipment, probably because some of the most adept and frequent competitors prefer "traditional" gear. (For practical tips on atlatl manufacture, see *The Atlatl*, bulletin of the World Atlatl Association, at http://www.worldatlatl.org/, and references in Whittaker 2008a).

Modern sporting use of atlatls is varied and eccentric and was never intended to be scientific. However, the principles of atlatl use can be studied even using atlatls that would shock an ancient. Moreover, the ISAC serves as a standard against which some early experiments and ethnographic accounts can be gauged. Modern ISAC and other results allow me to say with confidence that if Browne (1940:212) concluded that "any close degree of accuracy is impossible with atlatl and spear" and Peets (1959) was unable to hit a human-sized target at twenty–forty yards, they were doing something wrong. One could use the ISAC as a measure of accuracy in testing atlatl designs or to calibrate experimenters.

Modern distance records with the atlatl are also useful. David Engvall holds the world record of 848' 6⅝" (258.64 m) for an atlatl throw using modern materials and designs (Engvall 1995; Tate 1995). Using primitive materials, Wayne Brian's record is 581' 4" (177.19 m; Clubb 1994). The world record for a modern aerodynamically designed javelin throw is around 98 m. These modern standards suggest that when J. Edge-Partington (1903:38) recorded Australians throwing light reed spears 300 yards with a woomera and heavy wooden spears "accurately to a distance of 120 yards" by hand, we should wonder if these accounts are not exaggerated.

CONCLUDING THOUGHTS

Atlatl experiments have morals applicable to all experimental archaeology. The need for experiments grows out of archaeological problems of the day, but it is noteworthy that many old issues may be ignored for a time and later revived. The two primary reasons for this development are the difficulty of designing effective experiments and the inconclusive or ambiguous nature of most archaeological experimentation. Even a simple technology may have many parts that can be treated as variables, and the element of human error, skill, knowledge, and experience in using any technology is often a major complicating factor. We cannot live as our prehistoric subjects did, and we cannot think their thoughts; to experiment realistically with their technology, therefore, we must become fairly proficient with it, and to compensate for the obscuring effects of random errors and variation in each act, we must create large samples of experimental trials. The recreational use of primitive technology helps in this because more people become experienced users.

Even if we feel we are skillfully recreating the use of a tool, techniques or functions may exist that our imagination and experiments have not encompassed. The fundamental weakness of replicative experiments is that they create only analogies to prehistoric tool use, a body of hypothetical functions that we know work and ones that we are fairly sure do not. Experiments do not quite substitute for actual observations of a tool in use in its living culture. The case of the Indian Knoll artifacts is a perfect illustration. Netting hook and sizer or atlatl hook and weight? Experiments show that they work for either function, and only by examining other evidence—especially archaeological context—can we build a convincing argument. However, the strength of replicative experiments is that they allow us to make much more realistic interpretations of the archaeological evidence and inspire more imaginative ideas that can be tested against further experiments and the evidence provided by the artifacts.

NOTE

1. Richard Lyons has made working models after Cushing's drawings. They do work, as any stick with a hook of the right proportions will, but there is no advantage to the supposed "bowlike" action, as we will see.

REFERENCES CITED

Ahler, S. A., and P. R. Geib
   2000   Why Flute? Folsom Point Design and Adaptation. *Journal of Archaeological Science* 27:799–820.

Bachechi, L., P.-F. Fabbri, and F. Mallegni
   1997   An Arrow-Caused Lesion in a Late Upper Paleolithic Human Pelvis. *Current Anthropology* 38(1):135–140.

Baer, J. L.
   1921   A Preliminary Report on the So-Called "Bannerstones." *American Anthropologist* n.s. 23(4):445–459.

Baker, W. E., and A. V. Kidder
   1937   A Spear Thrower from Oklahoma. *American Antiquity* 3(1):51–52.

Baugh, R. A.
   1998   Atlatl Dynamics. *Lithic Technology* 23(1):31–41.
   2003   Dynamics of Spear Throwing. *American Journal of Physics* 71(4):345–350.

Becker, L.
   1992   Atlatl Boar Hunt. *The Atlatl* 5(3):1–5.
   2001   Hunting Rough Fish with the Ancient Atlatl. *The Atlatl* 14(2):12–13.

Berg, R. S.
   1996   A Wild Boar Hunt at Cold Brook: A Stone Age Adventure. *The Atlatl* 9(1):1–2.
   2002   Atlatl Long Shots and Primal Instinct. *The Atlatl* 15(1):8.
   2003   Fishing with Atlatls and Harpoons. *The Cast,* Spring 2003:15.
   2005   Bannerstones and How They Relate to the Atlatl. Electronic document, http://www.thunderbirdatlatl.com/newspost/arc5-2005.html, accessed January 20, 2008.

Bergman, C. A., E. McEwen, and R. Miller
   1988   Experimental Archery: Projectile Velocities and Comparison of Bow Performances. *Antiquity* 62(237):658–670.

Bettinger, R. L., and J. Eerkens
   1999   Point Typologies, Cultural Transmission, and the Spread of Bow-and-Arrow Technology in the Prehistoric Great Basin. *American Antiquity* 64(2):231–242.

Bird, G.
    1985   The Atl-atl or Spear Throwing Stick. *Artifact* 23(3):7–18. El Paso Archaeologi-
              cal Society.

Browne, J.
    1938   Antiquity of the Bow. *American Antiquity* 3(4):358–359.
    1940   Projectile Points. *American Antiquity* 5(3):209–213.

Bruchert, L. W.
    1996   The Bannerstone: A Continuing Enigma. *The Atlatl* 9(2):1–3.
    2000   *Old and New World Dart-Throwers and Related Topics: An Annotated Bibliogra-
              phy*. World Atlatl Association, Aurora, Colo.

Butler, W. B.
    1975   The Atlatl: The Physics of Function and Performance. *Plains Anthropologist*
              20(68):105–110.
    1980   Penetrating Elephant Hides with Wood Atlatl Darts. *Plains Anthropologist*
              25(90):353–356.

Callahan, E.
    1994   A Mammoth Undertaking. *Bulletin of Primitive Technology* 1(7):23–39.

Cattelain, P.
    1988   *Fiches typologiques de l'industrie osseuse préhistorique, cahier II: Propulseurs.*
              Publications de l'Université de Provence, Aix en Provence.
    1997   Hunting during the Upper Paleolithic: Bow, Spearthrower, or Both? In *Projec-
              tile Technology*, ed. Heidi Knecht, 213–240. Plenum, New York.

Chauvaux, P.
    2003   European Prehistoric Atlatls Inventory Trial. *The Cast,* Spring 2003:12.

Christenson, A. L.
    1986   Projectile Point Size and Projectile Aerodynamics—an Exploratory Study.
              Plains Anthropologist 31(112):109–128.

Clubb, L.
    1994   Untitled. *The Atlatl* 7(3):14.

Cole, G. S.
    1972   The Bannerstone as a Spear Weight. *Michigan Archaeologist* 18(1):1–7.

Corliss, D. W.
    1980   Arrowpoint or Dart Point: An Uninteresting Answer to a Tiresome Question.
              American Antiquity 45(2):351–352.

Cotterell, B., and J. Kamminga
    1990   *The Mechanics of Pre-Industrial Technology*. Cambridge University Press,
              Cambridge.

Couch, J. S., T. A. Stropes, and A. B. Schroth
    1999   The Effect of Projectile Point Size on Atlatl Dart Efficiency. *Lithic Technology*
              24(1):27–37.

Cundy, B. J.
    1989   *Formal Variation in Australian Spear and Spearthrower Technology*. BAR International Series 546. Archaeopress, Oxford.

Cushing, F. H.
    1895   The Arrow. *American Anthropologist* 8(4):307–349.
    1897   Explorations of Ancient Key Dwellers' Remains on the Gulf Coast of Florida. *Proceedings of the American Philosophical Society* 35(153):329–448.

Darwin, C.
    1909   *Voyage of the Beagle*. Harvard Classics. P. F. Collier and Son, New York.

Davidson, D. S.
    1936   The Spearthrower in Australia. *Proceedings of the American Philosophical Society* 76(4):445–483.

de Mortillet, A.
    1891   Les propulseurs à crochet : Modernes et préhistoriques. *Revue de l'École d'Anthropologie de Paris* 1:241–248.

Diters, C. E.
    1977   Norsaq: The Throwing Board, Regional Variation in One Element of Eskimo Material Culture. MA thesis, Department of Anthropology, Brown University, Providence, R.I.

Dixon, J. E., W. F. Manley, and C. M. Lee
    2005   The Emerging Archaeology of Glaciers and Ice Patches: Examples from Alaska's Wrangell-St. Elias National Park and Preserve. *American Antiquity* 70(1): 129–143.

Dold, C.
    2004   Prehistory Defrosted. *American Archaeology* 8(3):20–26.

Doucette, D. L.
    2001   Decoding the Gender Bias: Inferences of Atlatls in Female Mortuary Contexts. In *Gender and the Archaeology of Death*, ed. B. Arnold and N. L. Wicker, 159–177. AltaMira,Walnut Creek, Calif.

Drass, R., and R. Brooke
    1984   A Boatstone and Atlatl Hook from Central Oklahoma. *Newsletter of the Oklahoma Anthropological Society* 32(2):7–10.

Edge-Partington, J.
    1903   Notes on the weapons of the Dalleburra tribe, Queensland, lately presented to the British Museum by Mr. Robert Christison. *Man* 3(19):37–38.

Elliott, D.
    1989   Bannerstones of Missouri. *Missouri Archaeological Society Quarterly* 6(1):8–13, 18–23.

Engvall, D. P.
    1995   The Dynamics of the Off-Axis-Forward-Nock Spear vs. the On-Axis-Aft-Nock Spear as Thrown with an Atlatl Spear Thrower. *The Atlatl* 8(4):4–5.

Farmer, M. F.
1994   The Origins of Weapons Systems. *Current Anthropology* 35(5):679–681.

Fenenga, F.
1953   Weights of Chipped Stone Points: A Clue to Their Functions. *Southwestern Journal of Anthropology* 9(3):309–323.

Fenenga, F., and J. B. Wheat
1940   An Atlatl from the Baylor Rock Shelter, Culberson County, Texas. *American Antiquity* 5(3):221–223.

Flenniken, J. J.
1985   Stone Tool Reduction Techniques as Cultural Markers. In *Stone Tool Analysis: Essays in Honor of Don E. Crabtree,* ed. M. G. Plew, J. C. Woods, and M. G. Pavesic, 265–276. University of New Mexico Press, Albuquerque.

Fogelman, G., and B. Berg
1998   Second Chance Boar. *Indian Artifact Magazine* 17(1):30–31, 69.

Frison, G. C.
1989   Experimental Use of Clovis Weaponry and Tools on African Elephants. *American Antiquity* 54(4):766–783.

Garrod, D.A.E.
1955   Palaeolithic Spear-Throwers. *Proceedings of the Prehistoric Society* 21:21–35.

Geib, P. R., and P. W. Bungart
1989   Implications of Early Bow Use in Glen Canyon. *Utah Archaeology* 2(1):32–47.

Gilliland, M. S.
1975   *The Material Culture of Key Marco, Florida.* University Presses of Florida, Gainesville.

Gotthardt, R., G. W. Kuzyk, D. E. Russell, R. S. Farnell, P. G. Hare, and E. Blake
1999   In Pursuit of Prehistoric Caribou on Thandlat, Southern Yukon. *Arctic* 52(2): 214–219.

Guernsey, S. J.
1931   *Explorations in Northeastern Arizona.* Papers of the Peabody Museum of American Archaeology and Ethnology 12(1). Harvard University, Cambridge.

Haddon, A. C.
1912   *Reports of the Cambridge Anthropological Expedition to Torres Straits, vol. 4: Arts and Crafts.* Cambridge University Press, Cambridge.

Hare, P. G., S. Greer, R. Gotthardt, R. Farnell, V. Bowyer, C. Sweger, and D. Strand
2004   Ethnographic and Archaeological Investigations of Alpine Ice Patches in Southwest Yukon, Canada. *Arctic* 57(3):260–272.

Hayes, V.
1994   Tuning Weights. *The Atlatl* 7(3):1–4.

Hemmings, C. A.
2004   The Organic Clovis: A Single Continent-Wide Cultural Adaptation. PhD dissertation, Department of Anthropology, University of Florida, Gainesville.

Hill, K., and K. Hawkes
  1983   Neotropical Hunting among the Ache of Eastern Paraguay. In *Adaptive Responses of Native Amazonians*, ed. R. Hames and W. Vickers, 139–188. Academic Press, New York.

Hill, M.
  1948   The Atlatl, or Throwing Stick: A Recent Study of Atlatls in Use with Darts of Various Sizes. *Tennessee Archaeologist* 4:37–44.

Hobbs, H. P.
  1963   The Mystery of the Bannerstones and a Possible Solution. *Archaeological Society of Virginia Quarterly Bulletin* 18:2–7.

Hothem, L.
  1998   Chlorite Pick Bannerstones. *Prehistoric Antiquities Quarterly* 18(3):70–72.

Howard, C. D.
  1974   The Atlatl: Function and Performance. *American Antiquity* 39(1):102–104.
  1976   Atlatl Function: A Reply to Butler. *Plains Anthropologist* 21(74):313–314.

Hranicky, W. J.
  2003   Bannerstones: A Study on Their Holes. *Quarterly Bulletin of the Archaeological Society of Virginia* 58(1):35–46.

Hrdlicka, D.
  2002   How Hard Does It Hit? *The Atlatl* 15(4):16–18.
  2003   How Hard Does It Hit? A Revised Study of Atlatl and Dart Ballistics. *The Atlatl* 16(2):15–18.

Hughes, S. S.
  1998   Getting to the Point: Evolutionary Change in Prehistoric Weaponry. *Journal of Archaeological Method and Theory* 5(4):345–408.

Hutchings, W. K.
  1997   The Paleoindian Fluted Point: Dart or Spear Armature? The Identification of Paleoindian Delivery Technology through the Analysis of Lithic Fracture Velocity. PhD dissertation, Department of Anthropology, Simon Fraser University, Vancouver, B.C.

Hutchings, W. K., and L. W. Bruchert
  1997   Spearthrower Performance: Ethnographic and Experimental Research. *Antiquity* 71(274):890–897.

Kidder, A. V.
  1938   Arrow-Heads or Dart Points. *American Antiquity* 4(2):156–157.

Kidder, A. V., and S. J. Guernsey
  1919   *Archeological Explorations in Northeastern Arizona*. Smithsonian Institution Bureau of American Ethnology Bulletin 65. Smithsonian Institution, Washington, D.C.

Kjelgaard, J.
  1951   *Fire Hunter*. Scholastic Book Services, New York.

Knecht, H.
1997   The History and Development of Projectile Technology Research. In *Projectile Technology*, ed. H. Knecht, 3–36. Plenum, New York.

Knoblock, B. W.
1939   *Bannerstones of the North American Indian*. Published by the author, LaGrange, Ill. Reprinted 2008, Gustav's Library Reprints, Davenport, Iowa.

Krause, F.
1905   Sling Contrivances for Projectile Weapons. *Annual Report of the Smithsonian Institution, 1904*, 619–638. Smithsonian Institution Press, Washington, D.C.

Kwas, M.
1982   Bannerstones: A Historical Overview. *Journal of Alabama Archaeology* 28(2): 155–178.

Laird, R. D.
1984   *How to Make and Use the Atlatl: Ancient Weapon of the Ice Age Hunters*. Saratoga Museum Papers 1. Saratoga Historical and Cultural Association Atlatl Press, Saratoga, N.Y.

Lansac, J. P.
2001   Discussion d'un cadre chronologique pour l'utilization du propulseur et de l'arc. MA thesis, Department of Ethnology, University of Bordeaux, Bordeaux, France. At http://perso.wanadoo.fr/archeries/MEMOIRE.htm, accessed August 20, 2001.
2004   Un cadre chronologique pour l'utilisation du propulseur et de l'arc Durant le Paléolithique supérieur européen. *Bulletin des Chercheurs de la Wallonie* 43:29–36.

Leeth, D.
2004   *Spearthrower*. DVD, 120 min., Ice Age Arts, Inc. (privately distributed).

Lorentzen, L. H.
1993   From Atlatl to Bow: The Impact of Improved Weapons on Wildlife in the Grasshopper Region. MA thesis, Department of Anthropology, University of Arizona, Tucson.

Lutz, D. L.
2000   *The Archaic Bannerstone: Its Chronological History and Purpose from 6000 B.C. to 1000 B.C.* D. L. Lutz, Newburg, Ind.

Lyons, R. B.
2002   Atlatl Weights. *The Atlatl* 15(4):1–3.
2004   Atlatl to Bow. *The Atlatl* 17(2):12.

Mason, J. A.
1928   Some Unusual Spear Throwers of Ancient America. *Museum Journal* 19:290–324. University of Pennsylvania Museum, Philadelphia.

Mason, O. T.
1885   Throwing Sticks in the National Museum. *Smithsonian Institution Annual Report for 1884, Part 2,* 279–290, plates 1–16. Government Printing Office, Washington, D.C.

1893   Throwing Sticks [letter dated September 15]. *Science* 22(554):152–153. Reprinted in *The Cast,* Spring 2001:1.

Mau, C.
1963   Experiments with the Spear Thrower. *New York State Archaeological Association Bulletin* 29:1–13.

Moore, C. B.
1916   Some Aboriginal Sites on Green River, Kentucky. *Journal of the Academy of Natural Sciences of Philadelphia* 16:431–509. Reprinted 2006, Gustav's Library Reprints, Davenport, Iowa.

Moorehead, W. K.
1910   *The Stone Age in North America,* vol. 1. Houghton Mifflin, Boston.

Morwood, M. J.
2002   *Visions from the Past: The Archaeology of Australian Aboriginal Art.* Smithsonian Institution Press, Washington, D.C.

Murdoch, J.
1892   Ethnological Results of the Point Barrow Expedition. *Ninth Annual Report of the Bureau of American Ethnology, for 1887–88,* 19–451. Government Printing Office, Washington, D.C.

Nassaney, M. S., and K. Pyle
1999   The Adoption of the Bow and Arrow in Eastern North America: A View from Central Arkansas. *American Antiquity* 64(2):243–264.

Nelson, E. W.
1899   The Eskimo about Bering Strait. *18th Annual Report of the Bureau of American Ethnology, for 1897–98,* 19–526. Government Printing Office, Washington, D.C.

Nuttall, Z.
1891   The Atlatl or Spear-Thrower of the Ancient Mexicans. *Archaeological and Ethnographic Papers of the Peabody Museum* 1(3):171–198.

Ohtsuka, R.
1989   Hunting Activity and Aging among the Gidra Papuans: A Biobehavioral Analysis. *American Journal of Physical Anthropology* 80:31–39.

Palter, J. L.
1976   A New Approach to the Significance of the "Weighted" Spear Thrower. *American Antiquity* 41(4):500–510.

Parker, A. C.
1917   Notes on the Banner Stone, with Some Inquiries as to Its Purpose. *New York State Museum Bulletin* 196:165–176. Albany.

Peets, O.
   1959   A Butterfly Bannerstone as an Atlatl Weight. *Ohio Archaeologist* 9(3):83–87.
   1960   Experiments in the Use of Atlatl Weights. *American Antiquity* 26(1):108–110.

Pepper, G. H.
   1905   The Throwing-Stick of a Prehistoric People of the Southwest. *Proceedings of the International Congress of Americanists*, 13th session, 107–130.

Perkins, W. R.
   1993   Atlatl Weights: Function and Classification. *Bulletin of Primitive Technology* 1(5):58–61.
   1995   Effects of Stone Projectile Points as a Mass within the Atlatl and Dart Mechanical System. *Bulletin of Primitive Technology* 10:69–72.
   2000a   Archeological, Experimental, and Mathematical Evidence Supporting the Use of the Atlatl as a Primary Big Game Procurement Weapon of Prehistoric Americans. *Bulletin of Primitive Technology* 20:69–72.
   2000b   Effects of Stone Projectile Points as a Mass within the Atlatl and Dart Mechanical System and Its Relationship to the Bow and Arrow. *Indian Artifact Magazine* 19(2):8–9, 78–79.

Perkins, W. R., and P. Leininger
   1989   The Weighted Atlatl and Dart: A Deceptively Complicated Mechanical System. *The Atlatl* 2(2):1–3, 2(3):1–4, 3(1):1–3.

Precourt, P.
   1973   The Archaic Banner-Stone: A Social Category Marker. *Lambda Alpha Journal of Man* 5(1):1–26.

Ratzat, C.
   1992   Atlatls: Throwing for Distance. *Bulletin of Primitive Technology* 1(4):62–63.

Raymond, A.
   1986   Experiments in the Function and Performance of the Weighted Atlatl. *World Archaeology* 18(2):153–177.

Roth, W. E.
   1909   North Queensland ethnography, bulletin 13: Fighting weapons. *Records of the Australian Museum* 7(4):190–211, plates lviii–lxi, figure 12.

Saville, M. H.
   1925   *The Wood-Carver's Art in Ancient Mexico*. Contributions of the Museum of the American Indian, Heye Foundation, vol. 9. Museum of the American Indian, New York.

Shott, M. J.
   1993   Spears, Darts, and Arrows: Late Woodland Hunting Techniques in the Upper Ohio Valley. *American Antiquity* 58(3):425–443.
   1997   Stones and Shafts Redux: The Metric Discrimination of Chipped-Stone Dart and Arrow Points. *American Antiquity* 62(1):86–101.

Sliva, R. J.
1999   Cienega Points and Late Archaic Period Chronology in the Southern South-west. *Kiva* 64(3):339–367.

Spencer, B., and F. J. Gillen
1938   *The Native Tribes of Central Australia*. Macmillan, London.

Stodiek, U.
1992   A propos de l'emmanchement des propulseurs au Paléolithique Supérieur. In *Le Peuplement Magdalenien: Paléogeographie Physique et Humaine*, ed. J.-P. Rigaud, H. Laville, and B. Vandermeersch, 317–331. Comité des Travaux Historiques et Scientifiques, Paris.
1993   *Zur Technologie der jungpaläolithischen Speerschleuder: Eine Studie auf der Basis archäologischer, ethnologischer, und experimenteller Erkenntnisse*. Verlag Archaeologica Venatoria, Tübingen.

Tankersley, K. B.
2002   *In Search of Ice Age Americans*. Gibbs Smith, Salt Lake City.

Tate, B.
1995   Long Distance Record Shattered. *The Atlatl* 8(3):1–2.

Thomas, D. H.
1978   Arrowheads and Atlatl Darts: How the Stones Got the Shaft. *American Antiquity* 43(3):461–472.

Tindale, N. B.
1928   Natives of Groote Eylandt and of the West Coast of the Gulf of Carpentaria. *Records of the South Australian Museum* 3:61–134.

Tolley, A. R., and J. Barnes
1979   Reinventing the Atlatl. *Journal of the Steward Anthropological Society* 10(2): 161–180.

Turnbow, C., and R. Fields
2004   Ancient Spearthrowers from the Museum of Indian Arts and Culture, Laboratory of Anthropology. *The Atlatl* 17(3):14–15.

VanderHoek, R.
1998   The Atlatl and Dart. MA thesis, Department of Anthropology, University of Illinois at Urbana-Champaign, Urbana-Champaign.

Vanpool, T. L.
2006   The Survival of Archaic Technology in an Agricultural World: How the Atlatl and Dart Endured in the North American Southwest. *Kiva* 71(4):429–452.

WAA
2005   World Atlatl Association ISAC Rules Package. At http://www.worldatlatl.org/waa_2005_isac.html, accessed July 21, 2005.

Walker, R., K. Hill, H. Kaplan, and G. McMillan
2002   Age-Dependency in Hunting Ability among the Ache of Eastern Paraguay. *Journal of Human Evolution* 42:639–657.

Webb, W. S.

1946   Indian Knoll, Site Oh 2, Ohio County, Kentucky. *University of Kentucky Reports in Anthropology and Archaeology* 4(3), part 1, 115–365. Reprinted 2006 as *Atlatls and Bannerstones: Excavations at Indian Knoll*, by Gustav's Library Reprints, Davenport, Iowa.

1957   The Development of the Spearthrower. *University of Kentucky Occasional Papers in Anthropology* 2. Reprinted 1981, Program for Cultural Resource Assessment, Department of Anthropology, University of Kentucky.

Webster, G. S.

1980   Recent Data Bearing on the Question of the Origins of the Bow and Arrow in the Great Basin. *American Antiquity* 45(1):63–66.

Whittaker, J. C.

2007a   Clovis Atlatls? Hemmings' Evidence from Florida Rivers. *The Atlatl* 20(3):14.

2007b   Late Survival of Atlatls in the American Southwest? *The Atlatl* 20(1):10–12.

2008a   Annotated Atlatl Bibliography. At http://web.grinnell.edu/anthropology/Faculty/johnw.html, accessed July 10, 2008.

2008b   Atlatl Artifacts at Indian Knoll. *The Atlatl* 21(2):1–3.

Whittaker, J. C., and C. Hilton

2003   Throwing with the Atlatl: Myths, Theories, and Photographs. Paper presented at the World Atlatl Association Annual Meeting, Marshall, Michigan, May.

Whittaker, J. C., and K. A. Kamp

2005   ISAC Sport and Science. *The Atlatl* 18(2):1–4.

2006   Primitive Weapons and Modern Sport: Atlatl Capabilities, Learning, Gender, and Age. *Plains Anthropologist* 51(198):213–221.

2007   How fast does a dart go? *The Atlatl* 20(2):13–15.

Whittaker, J. C., and A. Maginniss

2006   Atlatl Flex: Irrelevant. *The Atlatl* 19(2):1–3.

Whittaker, J. C., and R. Mertz

2002   Atlatls for Teaching and Sport. *Anthropology News* 43(4):26.

Winters, H.

1968   Value Systems and Trade Cycles of the Late Archaic in the Midwest. In *New Perspectives in Archeology,* ed. S. Binford and L. Binford, 175–222. Aldine, Chicago.

CHAPTER TEN

Replicating Bone Tools and Other Fauno Technologies

Leland C. Bement

○ ○ ○
○ ○ ○
○ ○ ○

Replicative bone tool studies have coexisted with their stone counterparts for decades (Semenov 1964), although they have not received the attention given lithic studies (see Bamforth, this volume). Animal remains provide a wealth of raw material that can be manipulated into tools or other objects. The technology to make these tools can be reconstructed through the analysis of manufacture debris, residue or use-wear on stone tools, and the scars left by the manufacturing technique on the tool itself. Although this chapter is principally concerned with the manufacture and use of bone tools, similar technologies are associated with the manufacture and use of other animal products, such as shell. A brief look at replicative butchering studies covers one additional dimension of prehistoric manipulation of animal products.

The term "fauno technology" is offered here as an overarching category that includes all aspects of technologies involving animal remains. Historically, terms such as "osteodontokeratic technology" (Dart 1957) described the use of bone, teeth, and antler as tools. But the fabrication into tools is only one dimension of the use of animal remains by prehistoric peoples. Animal products were also turned into items of personal adornment, ceremonial objects, gaming pieces, and clothing.

Fauno technology, like lithic technology, is reductive or subtractive. The desired implement is shaped and fashioned by the removal of raw material. For this

226

reason, models of reduction strategies developed for studying lithic technologies (Callahan 1979; Crabtree 1972) are easily adapted to the manufacture of bone tools. As such, the reduction sequence can be described through the stages of raw material, core, blank, preform, and finished implement. Likewise, the detritus can often be described as primary, secondary, and tertiary debris. Many bone implements undergo predictable changes throughout their use-life. Often, the discarded tool form is substantially different from its original configuration. In addition, the tool may be employed in tasks other than that for which it was originally manufactured. Bone, like stone, retains traces of manufacture as well as use; thus, bone tools are suitable for replicative or actualistic studies.

Since bone is softer than stone, objects are fashioned through a number of techniques, including direct percussion, percussion on anvil, whittling, sawing, drilling, and abrasion. Each of these leaves behind diagnostic debris, telltale signs on the implement, and, as indicated by lithic use-wear studies, diagnostic polish and morphologies on the stone tools employed in their manufacture (Odell 2004; see Bamforth, this volume).

The most important concept in replicating fauno technologies is the realization that these technologies are often context-specific. This means the cultural milieu in which a particular item is made and employed must serve as the final sounding board in determining the degree to which a replicative sequence matches that particular society's temporal and spatial setting. There are many ways to make a bone awl, but only one fits the situational criteria described by the assemblage from a single site or, more specifically, a single feature within a site.

The sections that follow describe replicative studies devised to aid archaeologists in the study of fauno technologies. The steps in setting up a replicative study are presented to provide a guide for researchers. Most examples describe bone tool manufacture, use, abuse, and discard.

ACQUIRING RAW MATERIALS

Bones are a readily available raw material for tool manufacture. Unlike stone sources that are fixed on a landscape, bones are part of a living, often mobile source. Only when the animal dies does the raw material source become fixed on the landscape. As such, the acquisition of raw material is often truly embedded (sensu Binford 1979) in subsistence technology, that of procuring animals for food. Scavenging of animal carcasses for the sole purpose of mining bone, antler, or ivory, however, is also indicated in the archaeological record (Holen 2001; Soffer and Praslov 1993) and may account for the acquisition of shell in many instances. Less common is the actual hunting of animals for the sole purpose of acquiring material for tool manufacture. The taking of birds for their feathers and talons may be an exception to this situation. A final consideration is the raising of animals for the sole purpose of tool raw material production. Although animal products such as wool may be considered a prime reason for keeping domesticates, other materials that require the death of the animal for harvesting (e.g., bone) are usually secondary to the acquisition of meat.

Bone has properties that are softer than most stone materials yet more durable than wood. Although there is wide variance in the size of bones (determined by the animal species within a particular region), the characteristic of bone as a raw material does not vary from region to region within the same taxon. Bone also undergoes a predictable series of changes starting from the time an animal dies and ending with the disintegration of the bone as a result of taphonomic factors, including weathering or chemical alteration (Behrensmeyer 1978). The workability changes in step with time since death. Fresh bone can be predictably fractured. This is most apparent in the helical fracture initiated by percussion (Johnson 1985). As a bone loses its fat content, small cracks appear, and the predictable aspect of fracture planes is replaced with stepped terminations following the cracks (Lyman 1994).

Once a bone shows signs of mechanical alteration as a result of drying and weathering, little can be done to reverse its degradation. However, similar to lithic material, bone can be enhanced through hydration and heat annealing (Campana 1989). Prior to the loss of fat content and the onslaught of cracking, the workability of bone can be enhanced or changed by two principal agents: water and fire. Soaking in water can soften the cortical bone, reducing the force needed to fracture or cut the piece. Fire also has an effect on bone, rendering it easier to reduce by drilling and whittling.

REPLICATIVE STUDIES

The first step in any tool-manufacturing technique is the acquisition of raw materials. Here, a brief look at actualistic butchering studies is considered first, followed by replicative bone tool production, use, and discard studies.

The most common fauno technological replicative study is seen in reconstructions of butchering sequences, although many of these are not specifically designed to identify which bones are to be selected for tool production. An example of this type of study is presented here.

General butchering studies, including those designed to assess what a cut mark represents in terms of time and effort (such as Egeland 2003), are of limited use in a study attempting to replicate a specific butchering sequence described by the materials in an archaeological site. To be of any use, these studies must be context-specific. Setting up the replicative butchering study should begin with a site-specific butchering sequence defined through a detailed analysis of the bones. Once a sequence of events is defined from the archaeological sample, then a replicative study can be designed.

An example of the description of a butchering sequence derived from the archaeological record is provided by Joe Ben Wheat (1972) for the Olsen Chubbuck

Cutmark distribution

FIGURE 10.1 | Blackened areas identify the clustering of butchering damage on Cooper site bison skeletons.

bison kill site. Eileen Johnson (1987) provides other examples for bison kills at the Lubbock Lake site. However, to illustrate how a replicative study is employed to substantiate aspects of the reconstructed butchering sequence, the Folsom-age bison assemblage from the middle kill at the Cooper site in northwestern Oklahoma is described (Bement 1999).

The butchering sequence at the Cooper site, a Folsom bison kill site in western Oklahoma (Bement 1999), was reconstructed through a detailed skeletal analysis that identified butchering marks on the bones and related this information to the context of articulations within each of the three bone beds. General patterns emerge for all three kill episodes. Cut marks were routinely identified on the thoracic vertebrae and ribs (Figure 10.1). Occasionally, cut marks were also observed on the proximal humerus and femur. The presence at Cooper of completely articulated skeletons facilitated the reconstruction of the butchering sequence (Bement 1999). Many of the skeletons retained positional attributes, suggesting the animals

FIGURE 10.2 | Cooper site bison pelvis with legs turned under to support the positioning of the carcass.

were propped up on their stomachs with their legs and feet tucked under the carcass for stabilization (Figure 10.2). By combining the cut mark locational data with the carcass positional information, this butchering sequence was proposed (Bement 1999): (1) the animals were propped up on their bellies, with their legs either tucked underneath or splayed to steady the carcass; (2) the hide was removed, exposing the meat on the hump, shoulders, and back; and (3) meat was filleted from each side of the animal by cutting along the backbone and then down each side. Because of the positioning of the animal, meat on the legs was obscured under the animal or only the upper extremities were available.

A comparison of this butchering sequence with food utility indexes (Emerson 1993) suggests that the Folsom butchers were able to remove approximately 50 percent of the meat on each bison in what is described as a gourmet butchering style (Binford 1978). This butchering style, combined with the relatively large numbers of animals killed during each event (thirty to sixty animals) compared with the usual small kill of three to six animals, led to the postulation that the Cooper kills were the result of multi-group communal hunting activities (Bement 1999, 2003). Confirmation of parts of this conclusion rested on the verification that the reconstructed butchering process actually yielded up to 50 percent of the meat on a bison.

The replicative experiment called for a bison in a prone position. Stone flake knives comparable to those recovered in the Cooper bone bed were employed to

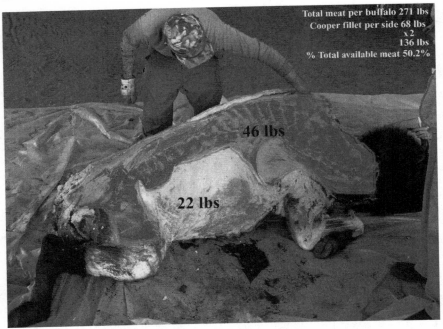

Total meat per buffalo 271 lbs
Cooper fillet per side 68 lbs
x 2
136 lbs
% Total available meat 50.2%

46 lbs

22 lbs

FIGURE 10.3 | Results of the butchering experiment replicating the Cooper site butchering sequence and yield.

butcher the animal. Once the hide was removed, butchering commenced with the placement of a cut following the dorsal spines of the thoracic vertebrae. This cut was extended caudally along the lumbar vertebrae and sacrum (Figure 10.3). Hump meat, backstrap or tenderloin, and upper rump were removed as a single piece weighing 46 lbs (20.90 kg). A second slab of meat weighing 22 lbs (9.98 kg) was removed from the rib cage. This technique yielded 68 lbs (30.84 kg) of meat per side, for a total of 136 lbs (61.68 kg) of the 271 lbs (122.92 kg) total carcass yield. This is 50.2 percent of the available muscle mass from this animal.

The large flake knife employed in this procedure contacted bone along the vertebral dorsal spines and upper rib segments, matching the pattern seen archaeologically. The folded position of the legs protected the proximal femur and humerus from inadvertent contact with the knife.

The experimental butchering of the bison supported the archaeologically reconstructed sequence. The distribution of cut marks mirrored those on the Cooper animals. In addition, the projected quantity and quality of meat produced by this gourmet butchering technique is supported by the experiment and lends credence to the postulated social context of the Cooper bison kills (Bement 1999, 2003).

This example of the experimental butchering of a bison to evaluate the reconstructed prehistoric sequence illustrates the basic steps employed in fauno technological replication:

1. Select a site-specific activity described from the archaeological material.

2. Acquire the requisite raw material and tools employed in the activity. Again, duplicate as nearly as possible the items and tools described from the archaeological context.

3. Perform the experimental activity.

4. Compare the experimental results, debris, product, and wear with those described from the specific archaeological context. If the experimental residue/products do not duplicate items in the archaeological record, then reevaluate the purported use or manufacture sequence for the prehistoric item. Also, check that the replicative material and procedures matched the archaeological items and sequence. If necessary, repeat steps 1–4 until the experimental results match the archaeological items.

The key to the usefulness of experimental archaeology of fauno technology lies in the closeness of fit between the experimental results and the observed archaeological materials. The site-specific context of a sequence of events is important because there are numerous ways to butcher an animal or to make and use a bone tool. However, the residue obtained from a particular site reflects a method of manufacture or tool use often defined by specific situational factors. Further, the sequence constructed from one site may not be applicable to another. It cannot be assumed that the steps followed to make a bone awl from a deer metapodial are the same as those employed to make the same implement from a bison metapodial. Bison metapodials do not split as easily or predictably as deer metapodials (Bement 1997).

This is not to say that there are not general technological sequences in the manufacture and use of bone tools. At a very general level, a bone hoe is a bone hoe is a bone hoe. However, variation exists in the manufacture and use of this implement that may have cultural significance.

CONDUCTING EXPERIMENTS

The remainder of this chapter deals with the experimental manufacture, use, and analysis of bone tools. Common problems experienced in bone replicative studies are also discussed, where appropriate.

Setting up the Experiment

1. Select an archaeological sample that illustrates the tool to be duplicated.

2. Describe the archaeological specimens, noting manufacture, hafting, and use marks.

3. Acquire raw materials and tools.

4. Apply tools to raw material in the sequence described by the selected archaeological sample.

5. Document break morphology, manufacture debris, and time invested in each
step of the tool-manufacture sequence.

6. Use the implement in the manner described in the literature and on the postulated material.

7. Document breakage from use, debris from use, and efficiency of implement for
prescribed task, including time span of use.

8. Compare the experimental tool, debris, wear, and use with the archaeological
sample to verify or dispute the purported manufacture, use, and discard of the
implement. An additional step to be taken following the completion of a sufficiently large sample of site-specific replications is a cross-cultural comparison
of fauno technologies to search for regularities or universals in technological
development. Such comparisons will identify evolutionary trajectories within
regions and cultures (Griffitts 2006).

Problems in Setting up an Experiment

Many published works do not describe the bone debris in detail. In these
instances, the researcher is left with the description of the implement as a guide to
its manufacture, use, and condition at discard. Other reports describe bone tool
forms and seriate them according to size and condition. Generally, a sequence of
manufacture, use, and breakage is gleaned from the sample of specimens recovered
at a site (Bell 1980). These descriptions provide the best test cases for researchers interested in experimental archaeology. While the general sequence for
the manufacture of a tool follows a logical progression, the actual steps and the
methods employed remain to be verified. Plus, it is only through the replicative
experiment that the effort expended in the manufacture of many bone tools can
be quantified.

Bison Scapula Hoe

This description utilizes bison scapula hoes from unpublished collections
housed at the Oklahoma Archeological Survey, University of Oklahoma, Norman
(Step 1). Such implements have a long history of being interpreted as hoes (e.g.,
Bell 1980). But do the implements' manufacture, wear, and use-history support
this conclusion? Scapulae are also altered into cutting and scrapping implements.
These other uses should be kept in mind, as they will display use characteristics not
found on hoes. Figure 10.4 illustrates a typical bison scapula hoe life history from
a Plains Village site. Inspection of the more complete implements provides details
of the manufacturing sequence (Step 2). Initial alteration to a scapula includes the
removal of the acromion, spine, and cartilage margin and thinning or reduction of
the posterior border. No manufacturing debris was collected from the site; thus,

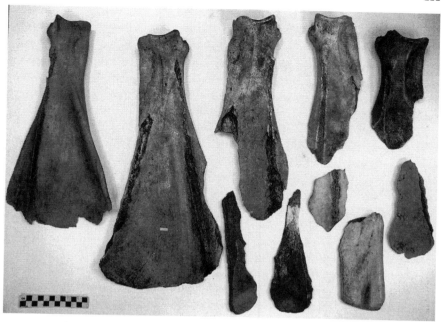

FIGURE 10.4 | Bone scapula hoes and use debris from a Plains Village site.

the reduction sequence must be inferred from the scars on the tools. The acromion and spine were removed by a series of percussive blows, leaving scars that exhibit smooth, sharp edges typical of green bone fractures. These fractures indicate that the scapula was fresh or green when the tool was manufactured. The posterior border was thinned in a similar fashion. Removal of the cartilage margin is less well-defined. However, one implement bears characteristics of the groove and snap technique. In this partial implement, the cartilage thickening was removed, as was a portion of the anterior border.

No alteration is evident on the glenoid cavity or tuberosity. Polish on the neck below the glenoid cavity suggests the implement was hafted there. Smoothing on the scars after the removal of the spine and thinning of the posterior border may indicate deliberate honing of the implement prior to use. Alternatively, the smoothing may represent use-wear from repeated insertion into soil. This is a topic to be clarified by the replicative experiment. Perhaps microwear study in these areas of the tool would clarify the situation.

Other information gleaned from the archaeological implements includes the fracture sequence of the tool bit through use. Initially, bit width is reduced at a faster rate than bit length. However, once narrowed, the bit undergoes a series of fractures that shorten its overall length. The recovery of use-fracture debris from the site illustrates the sequence. The posterior border and adjoining segments of the infraspinous fossa (blade) fail during use, leaving the spine, anterior border (supraspinous fossa), and adjoining infraspinous fossa (blade). Increased levels of smoothing on the spine and blade edges with bit reduction through use suggest that grinding of these edges was not part of the tool-manufacture sequence.

It is suggested that tool use terminated when the implement was shortened to one-third of its initial length; however, without primary contextual information, we do not know if the short hoe was discarded or stored away for later use. Smoothing of the bit edge demonstrates continued use of the tool up to this stage. There are no unmodified edges or fractures to suggest the tool was discarded because of a break.

At this point, sufficient information has been gleaned from the archaeological specimens to set up a replicative study. The basic hypothesis is: bison scapula implements and debris recovered from a Plains Village site are the result of tool manufacture and use as hoes.

This study is now at Step 3: acquire raw materials and tools. Supplies needed are scapulae, hammerstone, cutting implement, abrader, and hafting material, including a handle. This is where the "experimental" phase (Steps 4–8) kicks in. It is the experimenter's job to replicate the archaeological signature. Rather than detail the replicative part of this study (Steps 4–8), the discussion now turns to factors that are common to most fauno technology replicative studies.

Bone technology allows the question "why" to be asked. For example, in the manufacture of a bone hoe, the scapula margin is trimmed in an L-shape to remove the thick cartilage margin and one corner. Why remove the corner? Obviously, the thick margin must be removed to allow blade sharpening. In one experiment the corner was left on the hoe. Early in its use the corner split, removing a large splinter along the edge. This uncontrolled break yielded a narrower blade. Had the corner been removed during the manufacture sequence, the edge would have been strengthened and the hoe width would have remained broader. Hence, the removal of this corner serves a functional enhancement of the tool, prolonging tool life as defined by hoe width.

Not all reduction decisions are functional. However, the experimental use of the implement at various stages in its manufacture allows the archaeologist to understand many of the "why" questions in the reduction sequence.

Proficiency of the Researcher

In replicative lithic studies, the proficiency of the flintknapper is a key variable in the successful outcome of the experiment. A similar proficiency must be acquired by the experimenter in bone technology. Just because the material is softer than stone does not mean it requires any less skill to achieve the desired form. Proficiency is gained through the repetitious application of technology. As with anything else, the more times a task is performed, the higher the level of efficiency and confidence. For this reason, most replicative studies benefit from a series of experiments.

While repeated experiments improve the proficiency of the experimenter, they are not a prerequisite to acquire a sense of the benefits of replicative or actualistic studies.

Analytic Techniques

Bone tool manufacture and use studies are basically descriptive and quantitative. Bone tool analyses parallel those of lithic tools. Often, marks from manufacture are retained on the tool even after extensive use. Macro- as well as microscopic techniques are necessary to segregate manufacture marks from use-wear. Low-power and high-power magnification are common techniques (Griffitts 2006; Odell 2004). Similar to stone tool analysis, bone tools develop distinct polishes from specific uses. Bone's softness and porosity sometimes preserve the material being worked as detritus embedded in the pores. Also, directional striae are produced during manufacture and use. Finally, fracture patterns from the use and abuse of tools can be task-specific.

Labor investment (expediency versus intensive) can be measured as the amount of time required either to make a tool or to utilize the tool to complete a task. Such analyses are important when questions of craft specialization and nonutilitarian items are discussed.

Impediments to Analysis

Bones are particularly susceptible to destructive post-depositional processes and often have complex taphonomic histories (Hesse and Wapnish 1985; Lyman 1994). Surface degradation by chemical and mechanical factors (perthotaxic processes), such as weathering (Behrensmeyer 1978) and root etching (Todd 1987), remove use-wear and manufacturing marks. Soil characteristics often promote the further destruction of bone. Taphonomic factors must be considered in any bone analysis, including fauno technology.

Examples

Two recent studies serve as examples of studies that incorporate portions of the methods outlined here. The first is a study of fauno technology in the Kodiak region of Alaska by Amy Margaris (2006). The second study by Janet Griffitts (2006) addresses the effects of metal tools on bone tool technology among early historic Middle Missouri villagers on the northern Plains of North America. Both studies incorporate methods similar to those outlined here. In addition, both add to these methods by drawing on ethnographic analogy and historical sources in their respective regions.

Margaris (2006) incorporates fauno technology to understand the use-lives of various bone implements, especially bone harpoon tips. Extensive literature reviews aid in interpreting breakage patterns resulting from various stresses placed on the tips during hunting. Compilations of bone material attributes—including strengths, weaknesses, and hardness—are considered within the framework of form and function.

Griffitts's (2006) study has three goals. The first is to conduct an extensive bone use-wear study to ascertain form/function designations and to compare these designations with assumed functional categories found in the literature about the site producing the artifacts. This begins with the experimental development of a bone use-wear comparative collection similar to those developed for lithic use-wear studies (Keeley 1980; Odell 2004), including a quantitative compilation of tool use on different materials and a qualitative assessment of bone use strategies. A second goal is to study bone tool manufacture and use-life history, particularly changes associated with the introduction of metal tools. The third goal is to assess bone and antler properties and performance characteristics as they relate to issues of stability and change over time with the introduction of metal tools.

Both studies develop hypotheses to test the use-lives of bone implements—harpoons for Margaris and hoes for Griffitts. In addition, both add ethnographic analogy, historical accounts, or other researchers' experiences to embellish Step 6, outlined previously: experimental use of the objects. These additions provide a direct link between the manufacturers and practitioners of fauno technology not available to the researcher of prehistoric materials. However, ethnographic or historical accounts should not replace Step 6. If this happens, then the study forgoes the opportunity to develop firsthand knowledge about tool use and the problems, tendencies, and solutions to these problems adopted by practitioners.

Conclusions

Archaeologists turn to actualistic or replicative studies to better understand the manufacture, use, abuse, reuse, and discard of tools found on archaeological sites. Fauno technologies can be studied in this way. Key to the usefulness of these studies is the closeness of fit between the experimental procedures, debris, and tool form and the prehistoric material. The best studies are those that attempt to replicate a tool manufacture and use sequence defined from a specific spatial/temporal context. It is only through comparison with the archaeological record that replicative study results can be evaluated. If the replicative study cannot duplicate the various stages of the tool use-life from manufacture to discard, then results or subsequent deductions concerning tool use cannot be supported. More general technological studies tend to overlook situational factors that are often responsible for the range of variation within a tool type. The future of this kind of study lies in the integration of more than one technology.

INTEGRATIVE STUDIES:
BONE TECHNOLOGY INTEGRATED WITH STONE TOOL STUDIES

The next generation of faunal analysts will elevate the current state of knowledge to a new level. One area that is certain to receive attention is the integrated study of technologies. The integrated study considers, for example, lithic and bone analyses as inseparable components of a single technology. This is similar to behavioral chain analysis proposed by Michael Schiffer (1975:118–119) to correlate or link activities, thereby explaining organizational hypotheses when a best fit to the archaeological data is achieved. For example, the results of lithic use-wear analysis will be incorporated in reconstructing bone tool technologies. After all, many of the tools employed in making bone tools are made of stone. Knowing the morphology of stone tools that possess use-wear from working bone should aid in the identification of cut mark morphology on the bone. If the bone-working lithic tool edge does not match the general morphology of marks on the bone, then the reconstructed bone tool–manufacture sequence is either false or incomplete.

This integrative technological approach is kin to forensic science. While the analyst cannot be expected to be able to tie a particular tool edge to a particular mark on a bone, there should be moderate correlation between the two. Stone tool–edge morphology and directional clues in the use-wear should parallel corresponding morphology and directionality on bone specimens.

Initial questions will include, what lithic tool was used to groove this deer metapodial in the early bone awl manufacture sequence? Similarly, advances in bone tool use-wear analysis, such as that detailed by Griffitts (2006), should promote a better understanding of technologies/tasks employing bone tools. Integrated lithic and bone replicative studies will form the core of this research, but consideration of other artifact classes, such as wood and fiber, will be equally fruitful.

Additional questions will include, why are some tools made of bone while others are of stone (Knecht 1997)? Or of metal (Griffitts 2006)? What role does lithic source abundance/proximity have on the decision to make and use bone tools when a stone tool could function equally well, if not better? These questions and others move beyond the basic form/function descriptive analyses and potentially into the sociopolitical realm or gender studies, where tool material and form follow gender roles (e.g., Gero and Conkey 1991). Research into fauno technology has a promising future. Practitioners are needed to move this study forward.

ACKNOWLEDGMENTS

I thank Jeff Ferguson for organizing this volume. Had it not been for his stubborn determination, the volume would never have been completed. This chapter was greatly improved by the comments of Michael B. Schiffer and an anonymous reviewer. Many of the ideas presented here have been hammered out in discussions with my co-conspirator Kent Buehler and our many students through our years of teaching fauno technology.

REFERENCES CITED

Behrensmeyer, A. K.
    1978   Taphonomic and Ecologic Information from Bone Weathering. *Paleobiology* 4(2):150–162.

Bell, R. E.
    1980   Oklahoma Indian Artifacts. *Contributions from the Stovall Museum, University of Oklahoma* 4:1–114.

Bement, L. C.
    1997   Replicating Bone Tool Manufacture, Use, and Abuse. Graduate seminar notes on file at the Oklahoma Archeological Survey, University of Oklahoma, Norman.
    1999   *Bison Hunting at Cooper Site: Where Lightning Bolts Drew Thundering Herds.* University of Oklahoma Press, Norman.
    2003   Constructing the Cooper Model of Folsom Bison Kills on the Southern Plains. *Great Plains Research* 13:27–41.

Binford, L. R.
    1978   *Nunamuit Ethnoarchaeology.* Academic Press, New York.
    1979   Organization and Formation Processes: Looking at Curated Technologies. *Journal of Anthropological Research* 35(3):255–273.

Callahan, E.
    1979   The Basics of Biface Knapping in the Eastern Fluted Point Tradition: A Manual for Flintknappers and Lithic Analysts. *Archaeology of Eastern North America* 7(1):1–180.

Campana, D. V.
    1989   *Natufian and Protoneolithic Bone Tools: The Manufacture and Use of Bone Impliments in the Zagros and the Levant.* BAR International Series 494. Archaeopress, Oxford.

Crabtree, D. E.
    1972   *An Introduction to Flintworking.* Occasional Papers 28. Idaho State University Museum, Pocatello.

Dart, R.
    1957   The Osteodontokeratic Culture of Australopithecus Prometheus. *Memoir of the Transvaal Museum, Pretoria* 10:1–105.

Egeland, C. P.
    2003   Carcass Processing Intensity and Cutmark Creation: An Experimental Approach. *Plains Anthropologist* 48(184):39–51.

Emerson, A. M.
    1993   The Role of Body Part Utility in Small-Scale Hunting under Two Strategies of Carcass Recovery. In *From Bones to Behavior: Ethnoarchaeological and Experi-*

mental Contributions to the Interpretation of Faunal Remains, ed. J. Hudson, 138–155. Occasional Paper 21. Center for Archaeological Investigations, Southern Illinois University at Carbondale, Carbondale.

Gero, J. M., and M. W. Conkey
1991   *Engendering Archaeology: Women and Prehistory.* Blackwell, Oxford.

Griffitts, J.
2006   Bone Tools and Technological Choice: Change and Stability on the Northern Plains. PhD dissertation, Department of Anthropology, University of Arizona, Tucson.

Hesse, B., and P. Wapnish
1985   *Animal Bone Archeology from Objectives to Analysis.* Manuals on Archeology 5. Taraxacum, Washington, D.C.

Holen, S. R.
2001   Clovis Mobility and Lithic Procurement on the Central Great Plains of North America. PhD dissertation, Department of Anthropology, University of Kansas, Lawrence.

Johnson, E.
1985   Current Developments in Bone Technology. In *Advances in Archaeological Method and Theory,* vol. 8, ed. M. B. Schiffer, 157–235. Academic Press, Orlando.
1987   *Lubbock Lake: Late Quaternary Studies on the Southern High Plains.* Texas A&M Press, College Station.

Keeley, L. H.
1980   *Experimental Determination of Stone Tool Uses: A Microwear Analysis.* University of Chicago Press, Chicago.

Knecht, H.
1997   Projectile Points of Bone, Antler, and Stone: Experimental Explorations of Manufacture and Use. In *Projectile Technology,* ed. H. Knecht, 191–212. Plenum, New York.

Lyman, R. L.
1994   *Vertebrate Taphonomy.* Cambridge University Press, Cambridge.

Margaris, A.
2006   Alutiiq Engineering: The Mechanics and Design of Skeletal Technologies in Alaska's Kodiak Archipelago. PhD dissertation, Department of Anthropology, University of Arizona, Tucson.

Odell, G. H.
2004   *Lithic Analysis.* Kluwer Academic, New York.

Schiffer, M. B.
1975   Behavioral Chain Analysis: Activities, Organization, and the Use of Space. In *Chapters in the Prehistory of Eastern Arizona,* vol. 4, ed. P. S. Martin, W. A. Longacre, and J. N. Hill III, 103–119. Fieldiana Anthropology, vol. 65. Field Museum of Natural History, Chicago.

Semenov, S. A.
  1964   *Prehistoric Technology: An Experimental Study of the Oldest Tools and Artifacts from Traces of Manufacture and Wear.* Barnes and Noble, London.

Soffer, O., and N. D. Praslov
  1993   *From Kostenki to Clovis Upper Paleolithic-Paleo-Indian Adaptations.* Plenum, New York.

Todd, L. C.
  1987   Taphonomy of the Horner II Bone Bed. In *The Horner Site: The Type Site of the Cody Complex*, ed. G. C. Frison and L. C. Todd, 107–198. Academic Press, Orlando.

Wheat, J. B.
  1972   The Olsen-Chubbuck Site, a Paleo-Indian Bison Kill. *Society for American Archaeology Memoirs* 26:1–179.

CHAPTER ELEVEN

Experimental Zooarchaeology: Research Directions and Methods

Patrick M. Lubinski and Brian S. Shaffer

○ ○ ○
○ ○ ○
○ ○ ○

Zooarchaeology, put simply, is the study of animal remains from archaeological sites (Reitz and Wing 1999:1). In the United States the term is used interchangeably with terms such as faunal analysis, archaeozoology, and osteoarchaeology (Baker, Shaffer, and Steele 1997:298). The research goals of zooarchaeologists can be divided into three broad camps: those primarily biological in nature (e.g., paleoenvironmental studies, paleozoogeography), those primarily anthropological in nature (e.g., studies of human mobility, diet, butchery, hunting patterns, exchange systems), and those focused on methods (e.g., quantification, identification, field methods for recovery).

Experimental zooarchaeology can be thought of as the derivation and use of experimental data to interpret the zooarchaeological record. As an interdisciplinary field, zooarchaeology can be informed by experimental work from a variety of perspectives, such as zoology, geochemistry, paleontology, forensic anthropology, and ethnoarchaeology. Because of this breadth of goals, perspectives, and disciplinary affiliations, any discussion of experimental zooarchaeology in general requires a statement of limitations. For the purposes of this chapter, we limit ourselves primarily to the archaeological literature, with a focus on laboratory or actualistic experiments. Although they are typically considered part of zooarchaeology, we largely avoid reference to experiments on bone artifacts, which are discussed elsewhere in this volume (Bement, this volume). We also exclude reference to experimental elemental and molecular-level investigations of animal remains, such as trace element, stable isotope, and protein studies.

The chapter's principal aim is to discuss fruitful avenues for, and limitations of, experimental zooarchaeology, theoretical considerations, and experimental design for student use in developing experiments. At this general level of discussion, no attempt is made here at a critique or comprehensive review of past experimental zooarchaeology work. The reference section provides a selection of relevant example experiments. This chapter begins with a discussion of the range of experimental zooarchaeology, then provides a number of working interpretative hypotheses susceptible to experimental work, discusses applicability and experimental design, and concludes with retrospect and prospects.

Experimental zooarchaeology can be conceived to include a range of approaches, from tightly controlled laboratory experiments to more realistic field experiments, or "natural experiments." Controlled experiments are ones in which an attempt is made to hold a number of variables constant so that one or a few variables can be studied. Most are laboratory studies (e.g., Coard 1999; Egeland 2003; Lubinski 1996; McCutcheon 1992; Richter 1986; Shaffer 1992a; Shipman, Foster, and Schoeninger 1984; Smoke and Stahl 2004; Von Endt and Ortner 1984; Willis, Eren, and Rick 2008). For example, Patrick Lubinski (1996) placed various fish bones in aqueous solution and measured weight loss over time to model natural tendencies toward differential skeletal part survivorship.

Controlled experiments grade into somewhat more realistic but less controlled "natural experiments," sometimes called actualistic studies. These are commonly contemporary field experiments or observations (e.g., Behrensmeyer 1978; Bennett 1999; Binford and Bertram 1977; Brain 1981; Haynes 1988; Hockett 1995; Jones 1986; Lubinski and O'Brien 2001; Lyman 1989; Marean et al. 1992; Payne and Munson 1985; Stiner et al. 1995; Thomas 1969; Whyte 1991). For example, Sebastian Payne and Patrick Munson (1985) fed carcasses of squirrels, rabbits, and goats to dogs, then collected and examined the fecal remains to evaluate bone survival under such conditions. Taken to an even more realistic level are studies that involve direct observation of faunal remains in natural settings, with data collection similar to typical controlled experiments. For example, Lubinski and Christopher O'Brien (2001) collected the mandibles from a 1991 cliff fall of 150 pronghorn to examine the distribution of seasonality and age estimates from this known event. This study established a comparative analog against which archaeological age and seasonality distributions could be compared.

Experiments of all stripes in zooarchaeology have tended to focus on formation processes (Schiffer 1987), particularly taphonomic processes. Taphonomy is a term borrowed from paleontology (Efremov 1940) and is generally considered to focus on how faunal remains were collected and modified to form what was recovered by archaeologists and paleontologists (Shipman 2001) or, put another way, to focus "on the postmortem, pre- and post-burial histories of faunal remains" (Lyman 1994:3). The objective is typically to derive archaeological expectations for given processes that might have operated in the past. Clearly, assumptions of method-ological uniformitarianism or actualism (Gould 1965; Simpson 1970) are called for in such work. That is, natural laws and processes are assumed to be invariant in time and space, and past results may be attributed to processes currently in opera-tion (Lyman 1994:47). Processes observed in the modern experiment are assumed to be comparable to the same processes operative in the past, so modern results can be used as strong analogies for the archaeological record.

For the purposes of experimental zooarchaeology, the most broadly appli-cable work, providing the strongest analogies, revolves around the most basic and unchanging processes—such as the way a bone breaks or deteriorates given spe-cific conditional parameters (see also Domínguez-Rodrigo 2008). Works such as these can be very useful, but archaeologists are often interested in more complex and unpredictable processes involving human behavior. Experiments in these latter areas may not be as broadly applicable, but they can provide insightful potential explanations for the archaeological record. One class of work is not better than the other, but the ways in which each should be used are different. The key concern is a careful consideration of the applicability of experimental results to a particular archaeological problem (see also Domínguez-Rodrigo 2008).

Closely allied with experimental zooarchaeology are ethnoarchaeological stud-ies of faunal remains. These are normally very realistic regarding human actions on faunal remains, but they often suffer a lack of control. As such, it is unclear as to what archaeological situations the findings can be compared. Nonetheless, ethnoar-chaeological work in zooarchaeology has made significant contributions to the field, as the continual reference to Lewis Binford's (1978) *Nunamiut Ethnoarchaeology* alone attests. In that seminal work, Binford described a number of effects of human butchery, consumption, and storage on caribou bone assemblages. Other, more recent works have also produced significant findings for interpretation of archaeo-logical faunas (e.g., Bartram and Marean 1999; Bunn, Bartram, and Kroll 1988; Gifford-Gonzales 1989; Hudson 1993; Lupo and O'Connell 2002; O'Connell, Hawkes, and Blurton Jones 1990; Schmitt and Lupo 2008).

ZOOARCHAEOLOGICAL EXPERIMENTS AND INTERPRETATION

Robust interpretation of zooarchaeological data depends on a careful consideration of as many plausible explanations as feasible. The use of multiple working hypoth-eses (Chamberlin 1965 [1890]) and multiple independent lines of evidence will lead to the most reliable interpretations, and experimental zooarchaeology can pro-vide important analogs for selecting the most compelling or parsimonious hypoth-eses. The examples in this section should illustrate both a consideration of multiple working hypotheses and fruitful avenues for zooarchaeological experimentation.

Suppose deer bones are more common than rabbit bones in an archaeofaunal assemblage. How could this be explained? The typical interpretation that might follow would be that deer were not just more commonly utilized but also that the animals' larger size would have provided more resources than rabbits; so we see an economy with a focus on deer hunting. In fact, it could have been that there was an equal focus on procurement and that deer just happened to be more readily available as a result of hunting technology or habitat limitations. Or food taboos may have been at work in which most people ate deer but a few of the site occupants were not permitted to eat deer and thus focused their animal hunting on the ubiquitous rabbits in the immediate area. There are, indeed, many possible explanations—some resulting from human behavior, some from subsequent natural transformations and site formation processes, and some from current methods of archaeological recovery and analysis. Modern experiments may provide important information for the evaluation of competing hypotheses, such as differential processing, preservation, recovery, and identification of the remains. Other hypotheses, such as differential deposition of the deer and rabbit remains for ritual, labor organization, or other reasons, lend themselves less readily to experimental modeling.

One alternative explanation is differential processing. There may have been practices in which the ways the animals were processed have biased our ability to recover each equally. For example, while a variety of bones may have been processed for marrow, smaller taxa such as rabbits and rodents may have had many of their bones completely ground into pulp (along with muscle and other tissues) and been consumed in their entirety, with the exception of a few larger bones that may have been discarded during processing (e.g., Fowler 1989:29; Michelsen 1967). It could be that rabbits were the primary source of animal food, but differences in processing practices resulted in a reversed representation of remains in the archaeological record; in such cases, an interpretation could be made that was actually the opposite of what was correct. Expectations for different sorts of processing, and bone modification by humans in general, can be derived from zooarchaeology experiments, such as in butchery (e.g., Bar-Oz and Munro 2007; Braun, Pobiner, and Thompson 2008; Church and Lyman 2003; Domínguez-Rodrigo 1997; Egeland 2003; Greenfield 1999; Jones 1980; Lupo and O'Connell 2002; Outram 2002; Pickering and Egeland 2006; Pobiner and Braun 2005; Sadek-Kooros 1975; Seetah 2008; Toth and Woods 1989; West and Louys 2006), hunting technology (e.g., Frison 1989; Letourneaux and Pétillon 2008; Smith, Brickley, and Leach 2007; see also Whittaker, this volume), burning (e.g., Bennett 1999; Buikstra and Swegle 1989; Hanson and Cain 2007; McCutcheon 1992; Nicholson 1995; Shipman, Foster, and Schoeninger 1984; Stiner et al. 1995), and human consumption (e.g., Butler and Schroeder 1998; Jones 1986; Nicholson 1992).

Another possible explanation is differential preservation. In a given soil environment, it may be that the more robust deer elements stand a much greater chance of surviving in the immediate matrix than do the more fragile rabbit elements. Thus,

the greater number of deer remains may reflect more about the ongoing site formation processes than about actual cultural practices. Experimental zooarchaeology
can be a useful avenue for generating expectations for natural tendencies of preservation and bone modification under different environmental conditions, such as
ravaging by various non-human predators (e.g., Binford and Bertram 1977; Faith,
Marean, and Behrensmeyer 2007; Hockett 1996; Marean et al. 1992; Moran and
O'Connor 1991; Munson and Garniewicz 2003; Payne and Munson 1985; Schmitt
and Juell 1994; Thornton and Fee 2001) and physical or chemical decay in the soil
(e.g., Fiorello 1989; Lubinski 1996; Nicholson 1996; Olsen and Shipman 1988;
Von Endt and Ortner 1984). R. Lee Lyman (1994) and Christiane Denys (2002)
discuss these and other taphonomic factors and provide many useful references to
zooarchaeological experiments.

Recovery methods also come into consideration here. Screen size obviously
plays a potential role, and expectations for recovery of skeletal elements of deer and
rabbits (and other taxa) with different mesh sizes can be derived from experimental
data. For this example, experiments indicate that screen mesh sizes down to ¼" will
recover the vast majority of deer elements, but they miss a fairly large number of
rabbit elements (Shaffer 1992a). Screen size experiments can more broadly address
issues of bias, abundance, and diversity in taxonomic, element, and animal size distributions (e.g., Nagaoka 2005; Shaffer 1992a; Shaffer and Sanchez 1994; Vale and
Gargett 2002; Zohar and Belmaker 2005). Other potentially fruitful avenues for
experimental zooarchaeology research here include examination of the role of flota-
tion, wet versus dry screening, and the use of deflocculents.

Another possibility is differential identification. Larger taxa such as deer may
be much more readily identified than smaller taxa. While numerous osteological
guides can be found for larger taxa, some of which are comparative guides in which
similar taxa are compared and contrasted by element, such guides for smaller taxa
are largely lacking. It may be possible to distinguish a deer metapodial or sesamoid
from that of a pronghorn antelope, but a similar distinction between rock squir-
rel and prairie dog has not been described in the literature. On encountering such
small elements, assuming they were recognized as bone, there is little chance they
would have been identified to a specific taxon. There may be a role for experimental
zooarchaeology here as well, for example, in experiments with identification (e.g.,
Gobalet 2001; Sykes and Symmons 2007). More generally, experimental zooarchaeology can examine the role of zooarchaeological methods and their impact on interpretation, such as through blind tests and computer modeling (e.g., Blumenschine,
Marean, and Capaldo 1996; Rogers 2000).

APPLICABILITY OF EXPERIMENTAL DATA

One could discuss a number of concerns about experimental zooarchaeology, but one
important set relates to the applicability of the experimental data to archaeological

cases. Experimental results may be widely applicable or applicable only to a narrow range of similar cases. The applicability should be considered both in experimental design and in the use of experimental data for archaeological interpretation. As the potential issues addressed in an experiment become more uncertain (i.e., as the number of uncontrolled variables increases), the issue of equifinality is more problematic. By equifinality we mean that a given outcome can be the result of multiple causes (see also Lyman 2004; Rogers 2000). For example, determining if differential representation of recovered fauna is the result of a bias in recovery methods can be more readily tested than can ascertaining changes in animal exploitation (cultural factors) or taphonomic factors over time (site formation factors). This is the case because recovery bias is a simple problem to address compared to the countless potential reasons a people might change their food choices or the myriad factors that may influence the faunal assemblage between the initial deposition and subsequent recovery. Bias in recovery is a research-induced methodological impact on the assemblage that does not occur until the time of recovery. As such, it is a bias that can be controlled much more so than can controlling for hunting decisions a prehistoric people made or site formation influences since the time of deposition. The following example describing two different screen size experiments should illustrate this point.

A classic screening experiment was completed by David Hurst Thomas (1969), who used nested screens on an archaeological faunal sample to determine exactly what was missed by successive larger sizes of screens within three individual Great Basin sites. While this was an excellent actualistic test, it was site-specific. The amounts of recovery or loss could not be directly applied as corrections at other sites because of differing cultural and taphonomic factors. In addition, the experiment was limited to a small area of the site, and application of the results even to other areas of the site could be justified only with the assumption that the remaining site was homogeneous with the units tested.

By contrast, Brian Shaffer (1992a) and Shaffer and Julia Sanchez (1994) conducted controlled screening of various mammals (from a modern comparative research collection) using complete or nearly complete skeletons with little or no fragmentation. While it was widely known prior to these experiments that larger screen sizes recover less than smaller screen sizes do, just what would be recovered or lost by each screen size under ideal circumstances of complete and unfragmented animal skeletons was not known. For the taxa tested, the experiments showed which elements could be expected to be recovered by ¼" or ⅛" mesh screens if they were complete. This experiment was directly applied to recognizing full carcass internment (either by cultural or natural burial) versus dietary remains by Shaffer (1991, 1992b), who used the results to address whether gopher remains from a Mimbres site in southwestern New Mexico were actually noncultural interlopers into the assemblage or were food remains. The argument was that gophers naturally occurring in the area would die in their burrows and leave behind complete skeletons with little or no fragmentation. However, gopher parts expected to be recovered given the screen size used were not recovered at this site. In addition, comparison with ethnographic accounts of utilization of similarly sized animals revealed that humans would have discarded many of the bones recovered before processing or consumption. For both reasons, the gophers were interpreted as human food remains rather than as natural, died-in-hole specimens.

DESIGNING EXPERIMENTS

Probably the biggest issue in developing an experimental design is ensuring that the results will be useful for archaeological interpretation. This requires a consideration of how to make the experiment as robust as possible and of how it should be appropriately applied (see previous section). Reasonable linking arguments between the experimental results and comparable archaeological situations are clearly keys to success. Many issues of concern in designing experiments for zooarchaeology are common to all scientific experimentation, such as stating assumptions clearly, attempting to control for as many variables as possible, considering the limitations of one's instruments, using control samples, evaluating results with proper statistics, repeatability, and similar factors. A good starting point is a consideration of the overall objectives, including what variables will be examined and which will be held "constant." For example, Lubinski (1996) found a pattern of fish-head elements predominating over trunk and tail elements at an archaeological site and designed an experiment to help determine if this pattern was likely to occur "naturally" because of anatomical differences in skeletal parts. This is a good example in part because of its familiarity to the author but also because it has both strong points and weaknesses useful for illustration in the discussion that follows.

In addition to the issues discussed previously, another concern common to experimental zooarchaeology is representativeness—to what extent are the experimental data representative of the phenomena being investigated? There are ways to evaluate this directly, such as by resampling one's own experimental data (see also Mooney and Duvall 1993), but in general larger samples are more likely to be representative. Samples in zoooarchaeological experiments are often small, which can lead one to question the wider applicability of the results. In experimental design, it is probably best to limit the number of "situations" modeled and provide large samples for those few cases rather than use a wide variety of cases, each with a small sample size. For example, if the objective is to determine natural patterns of decay or survivorship in skeletal part distributions of fish subject to burial (Lubinski 1996), there are many possible situations to model, including different species, burial durations, and burial environments. Although the most widely applicable findings will result from a large array of species and modeled burial environments, each with a large number of samples or runs, it is generally impractical to carry out such work. Instead, one may choose to experiment with one species of fish and only two model burial environments in order to have larger samples. Although this may limit applicability to similar fish species and burial settings, at least there will be robust samples from which to derive basic insight into the patterns.

Use of control samples is another consideration. While not always practical, their use can measurably strengthen an experiment. For example, such controls would have been helpful in Lubinski's (1996) fish bone experiment. Bones had been soaked in aqueous solutions (one acidic and one alkaline), dried and weighed at regular intervals, and the weight loss curves used to model bone decay over time. The data showed a significant difference between bone loss in acidic compared with alkaline solution, but use of a control set in pH-neutral solution would have allowed the researcher to note whether the alkaline solution produced results any different than those obtained with neutral water.

Some experiments require thought about the relationship between rates and magnitudes of the phenomena modeled. This is most obvious where an experiment is meant to inform us about trends that might take hundreds or thousands of years to develop in the archaeological record. Clearly, some linking argument will have to be made to relate findings of a short-term experiment with long-term archaeological phenomena. For example, Lubinski's (1996) experiment placing bones in aqueous solution used somewhat extreme pH values to argue that the trends observed with "very" acidic (large-magnitude) short-term (fast-rate) experiments were likely in the same directions as those obtained with "moderately" acidic (small-magnitude) long-term (slow-rate) archaeological situations. This was an obvious concession to the problem of time, as it would have been impractical to wait several hundred years for experimental results. An alternative approach is to model time by use of heating or perhaps boiling to speed up weathering (Roberts et al. 2002).

One use sometimes made of experimental zooarchaeology data, particularly in taphonomic studies, is the "correction factor." For example, if an experiment showed that salmon bones were destroyed at twice the rate of deer bones, an analyst might wish to "correct" a site's bone count by multiplying the salmon bone count by a factor of two. Although it sounds reasonable and could provide interesting comparative information, this is dangerous for several reasons. First, it is unknown how similar the taphonomic history of the experimental case is to the archaeological case and thus how similar the mathematical relationship might be. Second, the sample in the experiment is unlikely to be sufficiently robust to have a high degree of confidence in a particular numerical relationship. That is, the trends and directions might be robust (e.g., deer bones survive better than salmon bones), but one should be conservative with the experimental numbers. Finally, if used beyond a simple comparison and actually used to "correct" the data for further interpretations, the corrected numbers to which other samples would be compared would not be actual data but instead an extrapolation of the data with no known level of accuracy. In the case of the application of screen size correction factors (e.g., James 1997), this extrapolation precludes the possibility that recovered fauna might differ between recovery contexts (Cannon 1999).

An additional consideration in zooarchaeological experimentation is not so much design as reporting. In reporting an experiment, it is important to be thorough and unambiguous in describing the materials and methods used so that others can replicate the experiment for verification. Objectives, assumptions, and limitations should be clearly and honestly enumerated, as should any mishaps in execution of the experiment. The more comprehensive the reporting, the more broadly useful the experiment will be.

RETROSPECT AND PROSPECT

We believe experimental zooarchaeology has and will continue to supply important analogs for archaeological interpretation, but only when well conceived and cautiously used. All of experimental archaeology—including experimental zooarchaeology—has made progress, in part as a result of numerous carefully designed and executed experiments. While significant progress has been made, it still pays to consider Ruth Tringham's comments on experimental archaeology published in 1977, if only to ensure careful design and application: "I shall argue that experiments in archaeology have for the most part been justifiably ignored because of (1) their lack of [a] strong theoretical base and a resulting lack of general applicability in testing archaeological hypotheses (this is also true of many ethnoarchaeological observations), and (2) their lack of rigor and attention to scientific experimental procedure in design, execution, recording, and analysis" (Tringham 1977:171).

Much progress has been made with regard to Tringham's second point, but there is room for improvement. Recent comments by Denys regarding experiments in taphonomy highlight some of these areas: "The experimental work remains timely and is generally not replicated. The samples used for the experiments are in most cases too small to be statistically significant, and the protocols are not always detailed in the published papers" (Denys 2002:480).

We believe all of these problems can be resolved. In addition to clearer statements on experimental protocols, there needs to be continual testing of prior results as well as expansion of variables and processes considered. These are necessary to better use these data for interpreting archaeological assemblages that result from multi-agent, complex processes that operated either simultaneously or in unknown combinations and sequences in the past. Although the best samples and experimental replication might most easily be generated by large research programs with several collaborators working intensively on an issue over time, small experiments can still contribute a great deal. Indeed, both authors have published results of small experiments undertaken as students for class projects (Lubinski 1996; Shaffer 1992a). With a concerted effort toward well-conceived and reported experiments at all scales, experimental zooarchaeology can move beyond providing "cautionary tales" to providing more robust analogs for interpreting the past.

ACKNOWLEDGMENTS

Suggestions were provided by B. Baker, L. Bement, J. Driver, J. Ferguson, B. Hockett, P. McCutcheon, M. Partlow, and two anonymous reviewers. Any flaws are ours alone.

REFERENCES CITED

Baker, B. W., B. S. Shaffer, and D. G. Steele
  1997   Basic Approaches in Archaeological Faunal Analysis. In *Field Methods in Archaeology*, 7th ed., by T. R. Hester, H. J. Shafer, and K. L. Feder. Mayfield, Mountain View, Calif.

Bar-Oz, G., and N. D. Munro
  2007   Gazelle Bone Marrow Yields and Epipalaeolithic Carcass Exploitation Strategies in the Southern Levant. *Journal of Archaeological Science* 34:946–956.

Bartram, L. E., Jr., and C. W. Marean
  1999   Explaining the "Klasies Pattern": Kua Ethnoarchaeology, the Die Kelders Middle Stone Age Archaeofauna, Long Bone Fragmentation and Carnivore Ravaging. *Journal of Archaeological Science* 26:9–29.

Behrensmeyer, A. K
  1978   Taphonomic and Ecological Information from Bone Weathering. *Paleobiology* 4(2):150–162.

Bennett, J. L.
  1999   Thermal Alteration of Buried Bone. *Journal of Archaeological Science* 26:1–8.

Binford, L. R.
  1978   *Nunamiut Ethnoarchaeology*. Academic Press, New York.

Binford, L. R., and J. B. Bertram
  1977   Bone Frequencies and Attritional Processes. In *For Theory Building in Archaeology*, ed. L.R. Binford, 77–153. Academic Press, New York.

Blumenschine, R., C. Marean, and S. Capaldo
  1996   Blind Tests of Inter-Analyst Correspondence and Accuracy in the Identification of Cut Marks, Percussion Marks, and Carnivore Tooth Marks on Bone Surfaces. *Journal of Archaeological Science* 23:493–507.

Brain, C. K.
  1981   *The Hunters or the Hunted? An Introduction to African Cave Taphonomy*. University of Chicago Press, Chicago.

Braun, D. R., B. L. Pobiner, and J. C. Thompson
  2008   An Experimental Investigation of Cut Mark Production and Stone Tool Attrition. *Journal of Archaeological Science* 35:1216–1223.

Buikstra, J. E., and M. Swegle
  1989   Bone Modification Due to Burning: Experimental Evidence. In *Bone Modification*, ed. R. Bonnichsen and M. H. Sorg, 247–258. Center for the Study of the First Americans, University of Maine, Orono.

Bunn, H. T., L. E. Bartram, and E. M. Kroll
   1988   Variability in Bone Assemblage Formation from Hadza Hunting, Scavenging, and Carcass Processing. *Journal of Anthropological Archaeology* 7:412–457.

Butler, V. L., and R. A. Schroeder
   1998   Do Digestive Processes Leave Diagnostic Traces on Fish Bones? *Journal of Archaeological Science* 25:957–971.

Cannon, M. D.
   1999   A Mathematical Model of the Effects of Screen Size on Zooarchaeological Relative Abundance Measures. *Journal of Archaeological Science* 26:205–214.

Chamberlin, T. C.
   1965   The Method of Multiple Working Hypotheses. *Science* 148:754–759. Originally published 1890, *Science* (Old Series) 15.

Church, R. R., and R. L. Lyman
   2003   Small Fragments Make Small Differences in Efficiency When Rendering Grease from Fractured Artiodactyl Bones by Boiling. *Journal of Archaeological Science* 30:1077–1084.

Coard, R.
   1999   One Bone, Two Bones, Wet Bones, Dry Bones: Transport Potentials under Experimental Conditions. *Journal of Archaeological Science* 26:1369–1375.

Denys, C.
   2002   Taphonomy and Experimentation. *Archaeometry* 44:469–484.

Domínguez-Rodrigo, M.
   1997   Meat-Eating by Early Humans at the FLK 22 Zinjanthropus Site, Olduvai Gorge (Tanzania): An Experimental Approach Using Cut Mark Data. *Journal of Human Evolution* 33:669–690.
   2008   Conceptual Premises in Experimental Design and Their Bearing on the Use of Analogy: An Example from Experiments on Cut Marks. *World Archaeology* 40:67–82.

Efremov, I. A.
   1940   Taphonomy: New Branch of Paleontology. *Pan-American Geologist* 74:81–93.

Egeland, C. P.
   2003   Carcass Processing Intensity and Cutmark Creation: An Experimental Approach. *Plains Anthropologist* 48(184):39–51.

Faith, J. T., C. W. Marean, and A. K. Behrensmeyer
   2007   Carnivore Competition, Bone Destruction, and Bone Density. *Journal of Archaeological Science* 34:2025–2034.

Fiorello, A. R.
   1989   An Experimental Study of Trampling: Implications for the Fossil Record. In *Bone Modification*, ed. R. Bonnichsen and M. H. Sorg, 61–71. Center for the Study of the First Americans, University of Maine, Orono.

Fowler, C. S.
    1989   *Willard Z. Park's Ethnographic Notes on the Northern Paiute of Western Nevada,*
            1933–1944. University of Utah Anthropological Papers 114. Salt Lake City,
            University of Utah Press.

Frison, G. C.
    1989   Experimental Use of Clovis Weaponry and Tools on African Elephants. *American Antiquity* 54:766–784.

Gifford-Gonzalez, D.
    1989   Ethnographic Analogues for Interpreting Modified Bones: Some Cases from
            East Africa. In *Bone Modification,* ed. R. Bonnichsen and M. H. Sorg, 179–246.
            Center for the Study of the First Americans, University of Maine, Orono.

Gobalet, K. W.
    2001   A Critique of Faunal Analysis: Inconsistency among Experts in Blind Tests.
            Journal of Archaeological Science 28:377–386.

Gould, S. J.
    1965   Is Uniformitarianism Necessary? *American Journal of Science* 263:223–228.

Greenfield, H. J.
    1999   The Origins of Metallurgy: Distinguishing Stone from Metal Cut-Marks on
            Bones from Archaeological Sites. *Journal of Archaeological Science* 26:797–
            808.

Hanson, M., and C. R. Cain
    2007   Examining Histology to Identify Burned Bone. *Journal of Archaeological Science* 34:1902–1913.

Haynes, G.
    1988   Mass Deaths and Serial Predation: Comparative Taphonomic Studies of Modern Large Mammal Death Sites. *Journal of Archaeological Science* 15:219–235.

Hockett, B. S.
    1995   Comparison of Leporid Bones in Raptor Pellets, Raptor Nests, and Archaeological Sites in the Great Basin. *North American Archaeologist* 16(3):223–238.
    1996   Corroded, Thinned and Polished Bones Created by Golden Eagles (*Aquila
            chrysaetos*): Taphonomic Implications for Archaeological Interpretations. *Journal of Archaeological Science* 23:587–591.

Hudson, J. (editor)
    1993   *From Bones to Behavior: Ethnoarchaeological and Experimental Contributions to
            the Interpretation of Faunal Remains.* Center for Archaeological Investigations
            Occasional Paper 21. Southern Illinois University, Carbondale.

James, S. R.
    1997   Methodological Issues Concerning Screen Size Recovery Rates and Their Effects
            on Archaeofaunal Interpretation. *Journal of Archaeological Science* 24:385–
            397.

Jones, A. K. G.

1986   Fish Bone Survival in the Digestive Systems of the Pig, Dog and Man: Some Experiments. In *Fish and Archaeology: Studies in Osteometry, Taphonomy, Seasonality, and Fishing Methods*, ed. D. C. Brinkhuizen and A. T. Clason, 53–61. BAR International Series 294. Archaeopress, Oxford.

Jones, P. R.

1980   Experimental Butchery with Modern Stone Tools and Its Relevance for Palaeolithic Archaeology. *World Archaeology* 12:153–165.

Letourneaux, C., and J.-M. Pétillon

2008   Hunting Lesions Caused by Osseous Projectile Points: Experimental Results and Archaeological Implications. *Journal of Archaeological Science* 35:2849–2862.

Lubinski, P. M.

1996   Fish Heads, Fish Heads: An Experiment on Differential Bone Preservation in a Salmonid Fish. *Journal of Archaeological Science* 23:175–181.

Lubinski, P. M., and C. J. O'Brien

2001   Observations on Seasonality and Mortality from a Recent Catastrophic Death Assemblage. *Journal of Archaeological Science* 28:833–842.

Lupo, K. D., and J. F. O'Connell

2002   Cut and Tooth Mark Distributions on Large Animal Bones: Ethnoarchaeological Data from the Hadza and Their Implications for Current Ideas about Early Human Carnivory. *Journal of Archaeological Science* 29:85–109.

Lyman, R. L.

1989   Taphonomy of Cervids Killed by the 18 May 1980 Volcanic Eruption of Mount St. Helens, Washington. In *Bone Modification*, ed. R. Bonnichsen and M. H. Sorg, 149–167. Center for the Study of the First Americans, University of Maine, Orono.

1994   *Vertebrate Taphonomy*. Cambridge Manuals in Archaeology. Cambridge University Press, Cambridge.

2004   The Concept of Equifinality in Taphonomy. *Journal of Taphonomy* 2:15–26.

Marean, C., L. M. Spencer, R. J. Blumenshine, and S. D. Capaldo

1992   Captive Hyena Bone Choice and Destruction, the Schlepp Effect and Olduvai Archaeofaunas. *Journal of Archaeological Science* 19:101–121.

McCutcheon, P. T.

1992   Burned Archaeological Bone. In *Deciphering a Shell Midden*, ed. J. K. Stein, 347–370. Academic Press, San Diego.

Michelsen, R. C.

1967   Pecked Metates of Baja California. *The Masterkey* 41(2):73–77. Southwest Museum, Los Angeles.

Mooney, C. Z., and R. C. Duvall

1993   *Bootstrapping: A Nonparametric Approach to Statistical Inference*. Sage, Newberry Park, Calif.

Moran, N. C., and T. P. O'Connor
  1991   Bones That Cats Gnawed Upon: A Case Study in Bone Modification. *Circaea, the Journal of the Association for Environmental Archaeology* 9(1):27–34.

Munson, P. J., and R. C. Garniewicz
  2003   Age-Mediated Survivorship of Ungulate Mandibles and Teeth in Canid-Ravaged Faunal Assemblages. *Journal of Archaeological Science* 30:405–416.

Nagaoka, L.
  2005   Differential Recovery of Pacific Island Fish Remains. *Journal of Archaeological Science* 32:941–955.

Nicholson, R. A.
  1992   An Investigation into the Effects on Fish Bone of Passage through the Human Gut: Some Experiments and Comparisons with Archaeological Material. *Circaea, the Journal of the Association for Environmental Archaeology* 10(1):38–51.
  1995   Out of the Frying Pan into the Fire: What Value Are Burnt Fish Bones to Archaeology? *Archaeofauna* 4:47–64.
  1996   Bone Degradation, Burial Medium and Species Representation: Debunking the Myths, an Experiment-Based Approach. *Journal of Archaeological Science* 23:513–533.

O'Connell, J. F., K. Hawkes, and N. G. Blurton Jones
  1990   Reanalysis of Large Mammal Body Part Transport among the Hadza. *Journal of Archaeological Science* 17:301–316.

Olsen, S. L., and P. Shipman
  1988   Surface Modification on Bone: Trampling Versus Butchery. *Journal of Archaeological Science* 15:535–553.

Outram, A. K.
  2002   Bone Fracture and Within-Bone Nutrients: An Experimentally Based Method for Investigating Levels of Marrow Extraction. In *Consuming Passions and Patterns of Consumption*, ed. P. Miracle and N. Milner, 51–63. McDonald Institute for Archaeological Research, Cambridge.

Payne, S., and P. J. Munson
  1985   Ruby and How Many Squirrels? The Destruction of Bones by Dogs. In *Paleobiological Investigations: Research Design, Methods, and Data Analysis*, ed. N.R.J. Fieller, D. D. Gilbertson, and N.G.A. Ralph, 31–39. BAR International Series 266. Archaeopress, Oxford.

Pickering, T. R., and C. P. Egeland
  2006   Experimental Patterns of Hammerstone Percussion Damage on Bones: Implications for Inferences of Carcass Processing by Humans. *Journal of Archaeological Science* 33:459–469.

Pobiner, B. L., and D. R. Braun
  2005   Strengthening the Inferential Link between Cutmark Frequency Data and Oldowan Hominid Behavior: Results from Modern Butchery Experiments. *Journal of Taphonomy* 3:107–119.

Reitz, E. J., and E. S. Wing
  1999   *Zooarchaeology.* Cambridge Manuals in Archaeology, Cambridge.

Richter, J.
  1986   Experimental Study of Heat Induced Morphological Changes in Fish Bone Collagen. *Journal of Archaeological Science* 13:477–481.

Roberts, S. J., C. I. Smith, A. Millard, and M. J. Collins
  2002   The Taphonomy of Cooked Bone: Characterizing Boiling and Its Physico-Chemical Effects. *Archaeometry* 44:485–494.

Rogers, A. R.
  2000   On Equifinality in Faunal Assemblages. *American Antiquity* 65:709–723.

Sadek-Kooros, H.
  1975   Intentional Fracturing of Bone: Description of Criteria. In *Archaeozoological Studies*, ed. A. T. Clason, 139–150. American Elsevier, New York.

Schiffer, M. B.
  1987   *Formation Processes of the Archaeological Record.* University of New Mexico Press, Albuquerque.

Schmitt, D. N., and K. E. Juell
  1994   Towards the Identification of Carnivore Scatological Faunal Accumulations in Archaeological Contexts. *Journal of Archaeological Science* 21:249–262.

Schmitt, D. N., and K. D. Lupo
  2008   Do Faunal Remains Reflect Socioeconomic Status? An Ethnoarchaeological Study among Central African Farmers in the Northern Congo Basin. *Journal of Anthropological Archaeology* 27:315–325.

Seetah, K.
  2008   Modern Analogy, Cultural Theory and Experimental Archaeology. *World Archaeology* 40:135–150.

Shaffer, B. S.
  1991   The Economic Importance of the Vertebrate Faunal Remains from the NAN Ruin (LA 15049), a Classic Mimbres Site, Grant County, New Mexico. MA thesis, Department of Anthropology, Texas A&M University, College Station.
  1992a   Quarter-Inch Screening: Understanding Biases in Recovery of Vertebrate Faunal Remains. *American Antiquity* 57(1):129–136.
  1992b   The Interpretation of Gopher Remains in Southwestern Archaeological Assemblages. *American Antiquity* 57(4):683–691.

Shaffer, B. S., and J.L.J. Sanchez
  1994   Comparison of ⅛" and ¼" Mesh Recovery of Controlled Samples of Small-to-Medium-Sized Mammals. *American Antiquity* 59(3):525–530.

Shipman, P.
  2001   What Can You Do with a Bone Fragment? *Proceedings of the National Academy of Sciences of the United States of America* 98:1335–1337.

Shipman, P., G. Foster, and M. Schoeninger
    1984   Burnt Bones and Teeth: An Experimental Study of Color, Morphology, Crystal Structure and Shrinkage. *Journal of Archaeological Science* 11:307–325.

Simpson, G. G.
    1970   Uniformitarianism: An Inquiry into Principle, Theory, and Method in Geohistory and Biohistory. In *Essays in Evolution and Genetics in Honor of Theodosius Dobzhansky*, ed. M. K. Hecht and W. C. Steere, 43–96. Appleton, New York.

Smith, M. J., M. B. Brickley, and S. L. Leach
    2007   Experimental Evidence for Lithic Projectile Injuries: Improving Identification of an Under-Recognised Phenomenon. *Journal of Archaeological Science* 34:540–553.

Smoke, N. D., and P. W. Stahl
    2004   Post-Burial Fragmentation of Microvertebrate Skeletons. *Journal of Archaeological Science* 31:1093–1100.

Stiner, M. C., S. L. Kuhn, S. Weiner, and O. Bar-Yosef
    1995   Differential Burning, Recrystallization, and Fragmentation of Archaeological Bone. *Journal of Archaeological Science* 22:223–237.

Sykes, N., and R. Symmons
    2007   Sexing Cattle Horn-Cores: Problems and Progress. *International Journal of Osteoarchaeology* 17:514–523.

Thomas, D. H.
    1969   Great Basin Hunting Patterns: A Quantitative Method for Treating Faunal Remains. *American Antiquity* 34(4):392–401.

Thornton, M., and J. Fee
    2001   Rodent Gnawing as a Taphonomic Agent: Implications for Archaeology. In *People and Wildlife in Northern North America: Essays in Honor of R. Dale Guthrie*, ed. S. G. Gerlach and M. S. Murray, 300–306. BAR International Series 944. Archaeopress, Oxford.

Toth, N., and N. Woods
    1989   Molluscan Shell Knives and Experimental Cut-Marks on Bones. *Journal of Field Archaeology* 16:250–255.

Tringham, R.
    1977   Experimentation, Ethnoarchaeology, and the Leapfrogs in Archaeological Methodology. In *Explorations in Ethnoarchaeology*, ed. R. Gould, 169–199. University of New Mexico Press, Albuquerque.

Vale, D., and R. H. Gargett
    2002   Size Matters: 3-mm Sieves Do Not Increase Richness in a Fishbone Assemblage from Arrawarra I, an Aboriginal Australian Shell Midden on the Mid-North Coast of New South Wales, Australia. *Journal of Archaeological Science* 29:57–63.

Von Endt, D. W., and D. J. Ortner
    1984   Experimental Effects of Bone Size and Temperature on Bone Diagenesis. *Journal of Archaeological Science* 11:247–253.

West, J. A., and J. Louys
  2006   Differentiating Bamboo from Stone Tool Cut Marks in the Zooarchaeological Record, with a Discussion on the Use of Bamboo Knives. *Journal of Archaeological Science* 34:512–518.

Whyte, T. R.
  1991   Small-Animal Remains in Archaeological Pit Features. In *Beamers, Bobwhites, and Blue-Points: Tributes to the Career of Paul W. Parmalee*, ed. J. R. Purdue, W. E. Klippel, and B. W. Styles, 163–176. Scientific Papers 23. Illinois State Museum, Springfield.

Willis, L. M., M. I. Eren, and T. C. Rick
  2008   Does Butchering Fish Leave Cut Marks? *Journal of Archaeological Science* 35: 1438–1444.

Zohar, I., and M. Belmaker
  2005   Size Does Matter: Methodological Comments on Sieve Size and Species Richness in Fishbone Assemblages. *Journal of Archaeological Science* 32:635–641.

Index

259